TWO POLITICAL WORLDS

TWO POLITICAL WORLDS
Parties and Voting in British Columbia

Donald E. Blake
with the collaboration of
David J. Elkins and Richard Johnston

THE UNIVERSITY OF BRITISH COLUMBIA PRESS
VANCOUVER
1985

TWO POLITICAL WORLDS: Parties and Voting in British Columbia
©The University of British Columbia Press 1985
Reprinted 1986
All rights reserved

The authors wish to acknowledge the generous support of the Social Sciences and Humanities Research Council of Canada for the research on which this book is based. The book has been published with the help of a grant from the Social Science Federation of Canada, using funds provided by the Social Sciences and Humanities Research Council of Canada.

Canadian Cataloguing in Publication Data.

Blake, Donald E., 1944-
  Two political worlds

Includes index.
ISBN 0-7748-0223-5

1. Political parties — British Columbia.
2. Political parties — Canada.
3. Party affiliation — British Columbia.
4. British Columbia — Politics and government — 1975-*
5. Canada — Politics and government — 1963-*
I. Elkins, David J. II. Johnston, Richard. III. Title.
UL428.B592 1985   320.9711   C85-091252-0

International Standard Book Number 0-7748-0223-5

Printed in Canada

Contents

For my family.

Preface

This book grew out of a research project begun by David Elkins, Richard Johnston and myself in 1979 which yielded the first comprehensive survey of the political attitudes and behaviour of British Columbia voters. While it focuses on my own special interests in B.C. and Canadian politics, it would have been impossible to complete without their help. Each of them read my draft chapters several times and wrote or co-authored others. Their names appear beside the chapters to which they made the most direct contributions. This scarcely acknowledges my debt to them for this book and for their friendship and scholarly companionship over many years. In truth every chapter reflects their help through their comments on it or through the use made of the B.C. Election Study which the three of us designed and executed.

I have found my colleagues at UBC, no matter what their own fields of interest might be, always willing to read and criticize my work. Lynda Erickson, Ken Carty, Paul Tennant, Keith Banting, Alan Cairns, and Phil Resnick fall into that category. The last three in particular must be thanked for the detailed suggestions they provided me. Alan Cairns got me interested in B.C. politics in the first place, and his own work guided the approach to the separation of federal and provincial party systems in B.C. used here.

Election surveys are mammoth undertakings. Since the field work for the B.C. Election Study began many people have been involved in coding, data entry, and analysis which contributed directly or indirectly to this book. Jim Bruton and Stephen Tomblin served as research assistants throughout the entire period while pursuing their doctorates. They were joined at various times by Kathy Teghtsoonian, Pam Frost, Karen Layng, Tom Kinneavy, Miriam Maisonville, and Dave Fenn. Joan Prentice typed and retyped the draft questionnaire, most of the codebook, and the book manuscript too. All were indispensable.

Scholarship in the humanities and social sciences in Canada and especially in the province of British Columbia faces many obstacles. In this context we must be increasingly aware of how much we owe the agencies and institutions on which our research depends. I have been privileged to share the scarce resources made available to the Social Sciences and Humanities

Research Council through their funding of the B.C. Election Study from 1979 to 1985 and a leave fellowship during 1981-1982 when much of the book was drafted. In addition to providing sabbatical leave, the University of British Columbia subsidized extensive use of its computer facilities. Publication of the bulk of Chapter 3 in *B.C. Studies* and parts of Chapter 9 in the *Canadian Journal of Political Science* helped to create an audience for the book. Their permission to reprint should also be acknowledged.

Finally I must thank my publisher. Jim Anderson welcomed my approach to UBC Press. Jane Fredeman took the manuscript under her wing, kept after the reviewers, and supervised the submission to the Social Science Federation of Canada. Jane Fredeman and Jean Wilson also proved to be excellent spotters of unnecessary jargon and convoluted prose.

There are many others whose contribution to my research has been less direct but just as crucial. At the top of the list are Lorna, Erin and Arlette.

1

Introduction

British Columbia has long been a source of fascination to political observers. Canadian socialism sank its earliest and deepest roots there, and it is one of only three provinces where the New Democratic Party has formed the government. It is one of only two provinces where Social Credit has governed, and the only one in which that party still commands significant support. Provincial idiosyncracies have affected federal politics too. While all provinces exhibit some differences between the patterns of provincial and federal politics, British Columbia has come closest to effecting a complete separation of federal and provincial party systems.

This book presents a detailed look at the inhabitants of these two political worlds. It traces the evolution of the two party systems, seeks to identify the dimensions of conflict which structure them, and analyses the behaviour of voters who participate in them.

The book is partly a case study. It outlines and explores the insights about British Columbia politics provided by the first comprehensive survey of attitudes and voting undertaken in the province. This unique source of information about British Columbians allows us to re-examine the portrayal of the province and its cleavage patterns presented in the scholarly literature. However, the research site and analytical approach are also used to address questions which have preoccupied students of Canadian politics for a long time. What role does class position play in determining choice among parties? Why does class voting appear in some provinces and not in others? Do voters see ideological differences among the parties? How do voters cope with the complexities of divided partisanship associated with the federal system?

The principal political actors in this book are voters. But, while the individual is the primary unit for purposes of analysis, in developing propositions about individual behaviour, strong efforts have been made to consider the contexts within which individuals live and work and the characteristics they share with others. In this way, we hope to capture social reality as it exists for individuals making political choices. To do this we provide empirical measurements of key environmental characteristics featured in accounts of B.C. politics: the class composition of neighbourhoods; position in the work-force, distinguishing especially between those whose economic fortunes are tied to the boom and bust cycles and unstable labour relations climate of the resource industries and those associated with services and public sector employment; and the division between metropolis and hinterland.

While centred on voters, the analysis is also anchored to the history of federal and provincial politics in the province. The actions of political élites, past and present, were largely responsible for the separation of party systems and the polarization of provincial politics. During World War II, Liberal and Conservative leaders developed a marriage of convenience into a firm coalition to keep the left out of power. Their successor, the Social Credit government under W.A.C. Bennett, pursued the same objective during the 1950s and 1960s and, in the process, destroyed the provincial Conservative party and seriously weakened the Liberals. Their federal counterparts carried on, periodically sending messages of hope and receiving refugees from the provincial legislature into their federal ranks, but apparently content with the federal-provincial division of labour. The provincial alliance broke down in 1972—the NDP formed the government—but a new appeal to the "free enterprise majority" soon rebuilt the alliance and wrested control of the provincial government from the hands of the left. These actions were and are based on assumptions about the motivations of voters which we can test. Are voters polarized between left and right? Do they respond to appeals to unite against the left? Does the growth of the NDP, even in defeat, signify increased support for socialism?

Explanations of partisanship in British Columbia almost invariably stress the impact of the economy on politics, and this one is no exception. The broad outlines of this relationship are well known: British Columbia has a resource-based economy characterized by large-scale enterprises and large, industry-wide trade unions in an atmosphere conducive to labour militancy and class conflict. However, the assumptions about individual behaviour used in developing explanations from this base have rarely been critically examined.[1] Nor has the partisan impact of changes in the province's economic structure been explored. This book examines both phenomena.

During the past two decades, resource extraction and processing activity have spread throughout the province, reducing industrial concentration on the coast and on Vancouver Island. Geographical diffusion of this industrial base has changed the balance of power between the principal contenders for power in Victoria, and, as elsewhere in Canada, has coincided with massive expansion of the public and service sectors of the economy. Alternative views of the role of the state, the major basis for competition between the philosophies represented in the provincial party system, have accordingly increased in significance.

Economic development has become increasingly state-directed and has helped to generate new classes of workers in state bureaucracies, in the public sector generally, and in service occupations which do not fit conventional categories. W.A.C. Bennett, Social Credit premier from 1952 to 1972, was arguably the first modern "province-builder," directing the pace and type of economic development via Crown corporations such as B.C. Hydro and the provincially-owned railway to incorporate the interior and the north into the resource economy.

The internal effects of these policies, aside from their impact on local communities and the environment, and their implications for dependence on foreign investment capital, have rarely been examined.[2] Economists, in fact, stress stability. They note that the structure of the province's economy has remained tied to resources and that the province has not evolved from its staple base to develop industrial processes other than those directly related to resource processing.[3] But the changes associated with the Bennett era, expansion of resource industries and the infrastructure associated with them across the provincial landscape, coincided with major alterations in the party system: the collapse of the provincial Liberal and Conservative parties, transformation of Social Credit, and the phenomenal growth of the NDP to a position where it now offers serious competition to Social Credit across the province.

The clash of economic development strategies has come to a head in B.C. As such strategies consume a greater share of provincial revenues, they have heightened the significance of the tradeoff with social services while creating increased demand for them. New classes of workers employed by or dependent upon the public sector provide a new constituency for both parties and especially new opportunities for expansion of NDP support beyond its working class and geographical strongholds. These arguments are elaborated on and tested in the following chapters through an examination of the determinants of partisanship in the provincial party system.

Despite the cross-class appeal of both major provincial parties, social class differences in party choice are sharper than anywhere else in Canada and play an important part in the calculations of political strategists. The most recent treatment of class voting in Canada attributes the weakness of class divisions in federal elections to a failure of parties based on the working class to change the "definition of the political," in part because of the reformist and even apolitical stance of Canada's trade unions, the natural organizational allies of the working class party.[4] An analysis focused on British Columbia provides an excellent opportunity to test the limits of this explanation. The clash between individualism and collective responsibility is trumpeted rather than avoided in provincial political debate. The ideologies these differences represent are themselves powerful symbols used to justify alternative views of the role of the state in the market economy and in ensuring the well-being of individuals. Rather than avoiding this basis for political division, the major non-left party, Social Credit, made it the foundation for an electoral strategy which kept the CCF/NDP at bay until 1972 and helped drive it from office three years later. After its re-election in 1983, Social Credit launched a series of bold initiatives to reduce the size and scope of government, while waving the banners of free enterprise and neo-conservatism.

Yet, as we will demonstrate, support for each point of view is not a simple function of the middle class/working class division even in a setting where the two perspectives virtually monopolize the definition of the political, and where trade unions are closely tied to the NDP. The concept of class must be suitably refined to take new occupational groupings into account. Moreover, the link between class and ideology at the individual level is mediated by the environment in which people live and work, by the experience of public or private sector employment, by characteristics of the work-place or industrial setting, and the degree to which individuals share similar positions on the class ladder with their neighbours. Trade union membership is a powerful influence on the relationship between class and party, but according to the evidence presented in this study, trade unions are more effective mobilizers than educators. Indeed, working class supporters of the NDP are somewhat *less* likely to endorse interventionist policy proposals than the party's middle class backers.

In exploring the dynamics of the provincial political world, this book does not reject the traditional emphasis on the economic basis for partisanship in British Columbia or the emphasis on social class. It does, however, offer a detailed explanation of the structure of provincial politics which incorporates changes in the geography of the resource economy and the growth of the "new middle class."[5] It also explores the ways in which links between social class position, political ideology, and partisanship have undermined our traditional conception of class voting.

That explanation does not account for the pattern of federal partisanship in British Columbia. Federal politics in B.C. takes place in a different world. Two parties, Social Credit and the NDP, dominate the provincial system, but the federal stage is shared by three parties, and only the NDP performs on both. Provincial partisan enemies become federal allies as British Columbians grapple with a federal agenda on which issues of left and right must compete for a place with the politics of culture, national unity, and government responsiveness. In accounting for the differences between federal and provincial party systems, the book provides an alternative explanation for the weakness of class politics at the national level and a different perspective on British Columbia's place in the national political community.

British Columbia's resource economy and its position on the Canadian periphery link it to the other western provinces. It shares a dependence on the export of natural resources and the unsettling boom and bust experiences it generates. Because of its small population relative to that of Ontario and Quebec, its voters share the frustration of having only a limited impact on federal politics. It shares with Alberta and Saskatchewan a history and ethnic composition which create suspicion and even hostility towards bicultural visions of the national political community.

In part because of these similarities British Columbia has usually been viewed as "western" in its outlook on national political and economic issues. Yet B.C.'s resource sector has been more diversified than that in the prairie West, and it has created a different pattern of employment, settlement, and wealth generation. The agrarian sector was too small to supply the workforce needed by the resource industries, necessitating recruitment of workers from outside the province. The labour requirements associated with the processing of forest products, the province's major natural resource, were also greater than, for example, the requirements of Alberta's oil and natural gas processing industries.[6] Immigration patterns have also made it more British than its western neighbours. The economic and political significance of forestry, mining, and hydro-electricity link its economic interests to Ontario's. As in Ontario, provincial control over natural resources came with entry into Confederation rather than after a prolonged struggle with the federal government, thus limiting the credibility of appeals to a "quasi-colonial" past in mobilizing opposition to federal parties and policies. Studies of regional political culture have also shown that B.C. voters share the optimism of Ontario voters regarding the ability of individuals to affect the political process.[7] These similarities and differences are borne in mind when federal partisanship and the feelings British Columbians have about their province's place in Confederation are analysed in detail.

However, there is an institutional component to the differences between federal and provincial political worlds, not just economic and psychological ones. British Columbia shares with all the provinces a public policy agenda shaped by its constitutional responsibilities. The provinces have been assigned a primary role in establishing the pace and direction of economic development, in the regulation of business and labour, and in the provision of social services. Whatever differences remain, we should expect these similarities to be reflected in political debate at the provincial level.

Existing attempts to compare provincial political systems have placed heavy reliance on stage theories of economic development. John Wilson's attempt to link level of economic development, party system structure, and political culture is a notable example.[8] Simply put, these theories suggest that the emergence of social class as a basis for partisan division depends on the existence of an appropriate value pattern in the electorate. This in turn depends on the level of industrialization and urbanization since these processes break down traditional bases for political loyalties such as religious attachments or ethnic group membership.

This book utilizes economic explanations as well, but without adopting the complete explanatory framework presented in stage theories. Whatever its attractions, attempts to understand provincial variation from this perspective have been handicapped by imprecision about timing, problems in classifying the level of development reached by some provinces,[9] and the lack of a satisfying explanation for the fact that British Columbia operates a two-party system in provincial politics and a three-party system in federal politics.[10] British Columbia also does not seem to have experienced a stage in its history when traditional cleavages based on religion or ethnic origin dominated partisan alignments. Socialism has been a visible alternative in provincial politics almost since the first miners from Great Britain reached the Vancouver Island coalfields over one hundred years ago, and since the late nineteenth century all British Columbia governments have been preoccupied with so-called "modern" questions of economic development and industrial conflict.

The perspective developed in this book can be extended to help explain why some provinces have developed very different party systems in federal and provincial politics, and why class voting seems to have limited significance in federal elections. Institutional incentives for class politics are stronger at the provincial level given the primary importance of provincial governments in the provision of social services, determination of the conditions of work and the structure of labour-management relations for most workers, and the centrality of economic development questions on provincial agendas.[11] Crucial development/distribution questions can be debated in left-right terms in many provinces, especially in the West, without the complications introduced by considerations of interregional equity or complaints that federal social policies constitute cultural interference. Given these institutional and structural conditions, the weakness of the class cleavage in federal politics is understandable. It may not simply be testimony to the success of a smokescreen by the traditional parties, the widespread acceptance of individualist ideology, or uneven levels of economic development across the regions.[12]

The explanation is also used to account for a pattern of attachments to party which, on the surface, appears bewildering. As we shall see, provincial Social Credit supporters abandon the alliance designed to thwart the NDP in provincial politics. They divide federally between the Liberals and Progressive Conservatives joining large numbers of voters who support the NDP only in provincial politics. Without denying the importance of economic issues in national politics, it seems clear that the alternatives offered by federal parties with a realistic chance of success, the Liberals and Progressive Conservatives, are not as fundamental as Social Credit/NDP differences provincially. Moreover, Liberal/Conservative differences seem to have become linked to perceptions of regional economic self-interest, providing the basis for a Conservative appeal to British Columbians as westerners.[13] Insofar as national conflicts revolve around cultural and language issues, as they surely have done during the 1970s, they engage regional, ethnic and religious loyalties which are largely irrelevant in provincial politics.

A detailed analysis of the mental journeys taken by British Columbians as they move between party systems provides important insights for the explanation of the separation of federal and provincial party systems more generally. It also provides the basis for testing the impact of divided loyalties on electoral volatility. Some have identified this phenomenon as a source of unstable voting habits,[14] but given the basis for the development of separate but overlapping federal and provincial party systems in British Columbia, the existence of divided loyalties should come as no surprise. Moreover, as we shall show in Chapter 9, there is little evidence to suggest that those with divided loyalties — the largest group of voters in B.C. — are any less faithful to party than voters who maintain the same loyalties in both party systems.

SUMMARY

There is no question that British Columbia politics have been preoccupied with economic questions. The province was enticed into Confederation by the prospect of greater riches than might be had outside of it, and subsequent governments have usually been judged by the degree to which they have contributed to economic prosperity. The salience of economic questions and the structure of the economy have also contributed to the importance of divisions between left and right in the provincial legislature and in the electorate.

The perennial importance of conflict between management and labour and the position of government as a potential ally for either side reduces the appeal of explanations which relate changes in provincial cleavage patterns simply to changes in the level of economic development. Provincial prosperity was and continues to be dependent on the health of the resource industries, but the significance of polarization between left and right has been conditioned by élite political strategies, experiences such as coalition government during the 1940s, and the complications of populism. Nevertheless, despite the degree of continuity in the province's economy, provincial voting patterns are more polarized now than in the past. We believe that these changes are linked to changes in the geographical distribution of the resource economy, growth of the public sector, and the development of new kinds of occupations rather than industrialization per se.

The common threads running through the province's history should also not blind us to fundamental changes which have occurred in the relationship between government and society. The terms "left" and "right" have lost their traditional meanings both in terms of the policy positions they are intended to describe and the class interests to which they once appealed. Governments of the right, no matter how ideologically pure and non-interventionist they claim to be, must administer the welfare state. They preside over a state sector with unparalleled power to shape the investment decisions of private enterprise whether it be through the provision of energy and transportation infrastructure, loans, subsidies, or financial guarantees. Governments of the left must cope with the power of private capital and are equally dependent on revenues generated by the resource industries. The support base of the left has become much more diversified and contains increasing numbers of state sector and white collar employees, whose demands and interests do not always coincide with those voiced by the NDP's traditional blue collar supporters. Both parties must cope with populist elements in their electorates who oppose concentration of political power and bureaucratization and are suspicious of the "tyranny" of the expert. Our exploration of the provincial political world will document these changes and assess their impact on provincial partisanship.

Our analysis of federal politics will reveal a different pattern of conflict. Voters moving from the provincial world to the federal one enter a setting with different party histories, different coalitions and different strategic considerations. Class and left-right issues understandably recede in importance and religious cleavages, alienation and cultural issues emerge linking British Columbians to other Canadians in their choices among the federal parties.

These perspectives on the two worlds of the B.C. voter will be supported and expanded in the following pages. Chapter 2 contains a brief account of the political history of the province. This will provide necessary background for those unfamiliar with the province as well as identify crucial developments in B.C. politics, especially the growth of the CCF/NDP and Social Credit and the separation of federal and provincial party systems. Chapter 3 explores the structural basis for the realignment of provincial politics which occurred during the 1970s and analyses the composition of the modern Social Credit and NDP electorates. The focus in Chapter 4 shifts to the attitudinal realm for an assessment of orientations towards the political process and the ideological alternatives presented in the contemporary party system. Chapter 5 takes these orientations and uses them together with an analysis of the links between social class position and party support to develop a sophisticated explanation of provincial partisanship. The results in this chapter provide the key to understanding the crucial part played by mass attitudes regarding the role of the state in interpreting the relationship between class and provincial party support. Chapter 6 develops and tests several propositions linking the development of attitudes on issues of individual versus collective responsibility, the central ideological dimension in provincial politics, to characteristics of the work-place, union membership, employment in the public or private sectors, and neighbourhood class composition.

The focus in the next two chapters shifts to the world of federal politics. Chapter 7 provides an assessment of the psychological ties between British Columbians and the national political community, focusing especially on the phenomenon of alienation from the federal government. Feelings of alienation, while perhaps not as intense as those in other parts of western Canada, divide the province's voters along different lines than do the issues of provincial politics. Chapter 8 provides a detailed analysis of the fracturing of provincial electoral coalitions and their re-formation in the three-party federal system based on levels of alienation and the degree of support for or opposition to attempts to forge a bicultural national community.

By this point we hope to have convinced the reader that the two worlds of the B.C. voter each have firm institutional, ideological, and social bases. In Chapter 9 we attempt to generalize beyond the British Columbia context, limited by the data available, by engaging in a parallel analysis using other provinces. The chapter shows that British Columbians, despite a reputation for eccentric political behaviour, participate in the same federal issue space as other Canadians, and provides evidence that a similar basis for the separation of federal and provincial party systems exists in other provinces. Moreover, contrary to prevailing notions regarding Canadian partisanship, the dual loyalties associated with the separation of party systems are not clearly associated with unstable voting habits.

Most of the raw material for the analysis in chapters 3 through 9 comes from a comprehensive survey of the British Columbia population conducted following the provincial and federal elections of 1979, supplemented by national survey data[15] and statistics supplied by government. Over 1000 residents of the province were interviewed in the B.C. survey for an average of two hours each. The sample mirrors almost exactly the age, religious, ethnic, and partisan characteristics of the province as a whole. It included residents of party strongholds as well as competitive ridings; metropolitan areas as well as the hinterland.[16] Our respondents shared their views on public policy questions, discussed their party loyalties and their positive and negative feelings about parties. The information they provided allowed us to differentiate between supporters and opponents of an activist state, the primary division in provincial politics; and between supporters and opponents of the vision of the national political community articulated by the party which has formed the federal government for most of this century. The study was deliberately designed to allow us to measure the social, economic and political characteristics of the areas in which our respondents lived, using census and electoral data gathered at low levels of aggregation.

Much of what we have to say will challenge previous interpreters of partisanship in British Columbia who, by and large, have been unable to test their assumptions about the pattern of mass responses to the province's party systems, or have assumed that politics in B.C. have little to do with politics in the rest of Canada. Some of our explanations and arguments must themselves remain tentative until further evidence can be gathered.

2

Politics on the Pacific

History has bequeathed to British Columbia a provincial party system based on the class divisions of the modern industrial state. Contemporary politics are suffused with the rhetoric of fundamental conflict between left and right. Politicians display and manipulate the powerful symbols of free enterprise and socialism, although a significant populist residue remains affecting the style of politics as well as its substance. Labour leaders have described cabinet ministers as thugs, and ministers of the Crown have sneered at the alien influence implied by the British accents among labour leaders. In the most unionized province in Canada, the party of the right advertises right-to-work legislation as a gesture on behalf of workers, while the party of the left supports the entrenchment of property rights in the Constitution. The federal party system continues as a miniature replica of that found in most other provinces. The actors differ in strength, but the issues they address cross provincial boundaries and, for the bulk of the electorate, rarely involve fundamental choices between economic philosophies.

The genesis of this pattern of politics is a complex story. It is linked to an economy which attracted workers and entrepreneurs eager to compete for shares of resource wealth, each jealous of the claims of the other; to settlement patterns which produced higher rates of population growth than in any other province and to geography which isolated developing provincial communities from each other; and to the conflict management styles of politicians forced to choose between the financial power of capital and the numerical superiority of labour or keeping the choice from the political agenda. It is also linked to the strains of competition between provincial and federal political élites for the resources needed to pursue their visions and for the allegiance of the population they hoped to attract with them.

In part the British Columbia story is little different from that which unfolded in other, especially western, provinces as economic development proceeded, population grew, and government assumed a larger role in the economy and society.[1] But somewhere along the way competition between left and right developed into the principal axis of conflict in the provincial party system leaving federal politics to revolve around the traditional themes of alienation, regional economic competition, and the struggle for national unity.

Most of this book examines the outcome of this political and economic story. However, so much of the analysis depends on identifying the sources of division in British Columbia's two political worlds that an exploration of the past is essential. The purpose of this chapter is not to provide a comprehensive history but rather to trace the evolution of conflict between left and right, to identify the sources of separation between provincial and federal party systems, to analyse the rise of the Co-operative Commonwealth Federation and Social Credit, and to describe the social and economic transformations which underly the present party system. In the process the reader unfamiliar with British Columbia should become much better acquainted with the vagaries of the province's politics.

Despite British Columbia's reputation as a battleground between free enterprise and socialism, it was not always this way. The first thirty years after Confederation were dominated by issues such as the terms of union with Canada, and politicians focused on harnessing and directing the development boom produced by completion of the Canadian Pacific Railway. Legislative politics revolved around individual and local self-interest, a context in which political principles or even party attachments had little place. The next thirty years witnessed the establishment of a two-party system in provincial politics, the building of formidable party machines to replace shifting personal alliances on the right, and continuing organizational weakness of the left. The foundations of the present system, seemingly anchored in responses to the threat represented by the CCF/NDP, did not emerge until World War II, despite an economic structure conducive to working class militancy and a higher level of support for socialism than found anywhere else in Canada.

The period from 1871, when British Columbia joined Confederation, to 1903 was characterized by official non-partisanship in the provincial legislature. In a very real sense the business of provincial politics was business. The first cabinets contained only the portfolios of attorney-general, provincial secretary, and public lands.[2] Most members of the assembly had business interests and pursued them unabashedly. Such divisions as appeared in the assembly tended to parallel divisions of interest within the business class: Island versus mainland and (on the question of the routing of the CPR) interior and Island versus the lower mainland. Early legislatures were preoccupied with public works, land grants, and subsidies for the construction of roads and railways.

Provincial self-interest dictated strong support in federal elections for the

Conservative party. The party was committed to fulfilling the terms of union it had negotiated, terms denounced as extravagant by the Liberals. The political wisdom of that position was confirmed when Liberal Prime Minister Alexander Mackenzie proceeded to delay construction of the railway to British Columbia soon after taking office in 1874. Secession resolutions were passed in the provincial legislature in 1876 and 1878, and it was not until Macdonald's return to power in 1878 that the province was mollified.[3] Competition for federal elective office, when it occurred, invariably pitted several candidates all bearing the Conservative label against each other or against independents pledged to support the ministry of Sir John A. Macdonald. The strong provincial rights and anti-imperial stance which sustained the Liberal party at the centre had limited appeal in the province given its dependence on a beneficent federal government and the use of the former colonial power as an ally in battles for better terms.

The overwhelmingly British and Protestant character of the white population virtually eliminated religion and ethnic origin as a source of partisan division. Unlike the case in central Canada, "there was no feud of ruling faces to allay, no Clergy Reserve to divide, no complicated fiscal policy to arrange."[4] In other words, when Liberal and Conservative party labels were finally imported from the east, they came without the social and historical baggage which governed their adoption elsewhere.

The success of the Laurier Liberals in the federal election of 1896 broke the spell cast by Confederation. The development of a successful federal Liberal party organization led naturally to an interest in provincial politics, since the national Liberal party's success was based on strong provincial organizations in Ontario and Quebec. A non-partisan legislature consisting of individuals with competing ties in federal politics undoubtedly contributed to the difficulties of creating and maintaining governing coalitions.

Non-partisanship in the provincial legislature was ultimately abandoned in the face of chronic government instability, scandal, and, according to most authorities, an emerging threat from the left. In 1903, the lieutenant-governor dismissed the ministry of Colonel Edward Prior after an inquiry revealed his assistance in awarding a government contract to a firm in which he was involved.[5] His was the fifth ministry to fall in five years, and when Richard McBride was asked to form a new cabinet he did so by inviting only avowed Conservatives to join. Shortly afterwards he went "to the country with the cry that 'the day of individualism has gone by.' "[6]

It is more difficult to demonstrate the effect of growing support for the left on this decision. A handful of socialist and labour members had appeared in the assembly after each election since 1890, but their small numbers did not prevent them from exacting concessions on labour and racial issues from shaky ministries. McBride himself was forced to seek periodic help from this group, since the election of 1903 gave him only twenty-two of the forty-two seats in the legislature.

Despite continuation of this practice from non-partisan days, the period from 1895 to 1905 has been described as a "watershed in the development of the British Columbia labour movement," marked by the emergence of syndicalist and socialist ideologies, and the transformation of labour disorder into a "fundamentally political question."[7] Major strikes complicated by battles for union recognition occurred in the salmon fishery in 1900 and 1901, and in the mines of the Kootenay region in 1902. The latter may have seemed particularly ominous since it marked the arrival of the radical Western Federation of Miners[8] whose socialist ideology included support for the idea of a party based on organized labour.

If the "threat from the left" was really responsible for encouraging the establishment to organize itself into Liberals and Conservatives, the strategy must be judged a success. Combined labour and socialist support peaked at 15.2 per cent in 1903, and from then until 1928 the left received, on average, the votes of just over 12 per cent of the electorate.[9]

However, explanations for the limited impact of the left are as likely to be found in the struggle between different champions of the working class as in a conspiracy of the free enterprise parties. Workers were treated to a panoply of solutions to varying definitions of their plight. Marxists implored them to ignore the legislative game lest minor concessions delay the arrival of the revolution. Radical trade unionists counselled rejection of political activity or even co-operation with socialist and labour parties, preferring instead to hone the strike weapon to bring about fundamental change. The job of waging the legislative battle fell mainly to moderate socialists and trade union leaders who saw nothing wrong with ameliorating the plight of workers while waiting for the socialist utopia to arrive.

Several attempts to form labour parties with the support of trade union leaders were frustrated by the influence wielded in the union movement by prominent socialists.[10] Finally, in 1918, with the support of the B.C. Federation of Labour, moderate socialists and labour leaders combined to form the Federated Labour Party. The Marxist-dominated Socialist Party of Canada, which had been the main left-wing party since 1900, was severely weakened by defections to the new party and ultimately disintegrated in 1925 over the issue of affiliation with the Communist International.[11] The appearance of the FLP, however, did nothing to enhance the political power or electoral support of the left.

The anti-union campaigns waged by many employers, often in league with the provincial government, added to the organizational difficulties associated with seasonality, labour mobility, remoteness, and "decentralized patterns of ownership and production"[12] to restrict trade union membership to a minority of the labour force. Even more significant given the focus of this book, the possibility exists that "high labour mobility sustained a climate of opinion in many ways uncongenial to the growth of class awareness."[13] The resource frontier held out the prospect of significant material gain through exercise of the same kind of initiative and risk-taking attributed to capitalist entrepreneurs. Whatever their frequency prior to World War II, attitudinal patterns like these were clearly recognized by W.A.C. Bennett and his successors, who extolled the benefits to workers to be expected from massive development projects and castigated the small-mindedness of trade union leaders and the CCF/NDP.

While slow to adopt party as an organizational vehicle, B.C. Tories proved remarkably adept at using the instruments available to government to build an impressive party machine. A full public treasury allowed the vigorous pursuit of public works projects using government patronage thus generated in the classic style of machine politicians. The hundreds of road superintendents, foremen, fire wardens, and constables beholden to the government party which appointed them could themselves offer employment, licences or other government services in return for political support.[14] Government advertising contracts helped to create a friendly press.[15] In the elections of 1909 amd 1912, opposition was nearly eliminated from the legislature.

Differences between Liberals and Conservatives proved to be based on little more than the distinction between being in or out of office.[16] The Liberals denounced the familiar evils of machine politics, patronage, dishonesty, and inefficiency, only to face the same charges soon after winning office in 1916. In 1922, five years after creating a Civil Service Commission to administer examinations and recommend candidates for government jobs (but retaining Cabinet authority to hire and fire), Liberal premier John Oliver apologized to his supporters for his "innocence" in giving "over to a commission patronage rights that should have been exercised by the members of the government and the representatives elected by the people" and promised to rectify the "error."[17] Both parties continued to make appeals to the working man, although when the crunch came, as it frequently did, particularly in the mining areas of the province, both displayed a willingness to intervene on behalf of employers faced with rebellious workers.

The onset of the Great Depression brought an end to the two-party period and to this pattern of party alignment. Simon Fraser Tolmie, a federal Conservative Member of Parliament, had returned to the province to keep the peace between factions of his own party and led them to a resounding victory (thirty-five of forty-seven seats) over the Liberals in 1928. However, he proved unable to keep the party together or to cope with economic collapse. In desperation he turned to leaders of the business community for ideas. They repaid his trust with an indictment of the government's political machine and of the party system itself, while offering traditional conservative remedies for the province's economic ills. Tolmie's attempts to form a coalition with the Liberals were rebuffed and further weakened his position in his own party. The provincial Conservative Association took no official part in the 1933 election, leaving its adherents to campaign on their own while advertising themselves as part of whichever faction they favoured, virtually assuring the Liberal victory which ensued.[18]

Economic collapse rekindled interest and enthusiasm on the left. In the year following the stock market crash, membership in the Independent Labour Party (the name adopted by the FLP in 1926) increased fivefold,[19] and preliminary negotiations began with other western labour and socialist parties to lay the groundwork for the Co-operative Commonwealth Federation. The CCF entered the 1933 provincial campaign promising a "radical transformation of society including the socialization of the financial machinery of the country...the socialization of the basic resource industries, the socialization of health services, free education from public school through university, the rapid expansion of social services," and reallocation of the tax burden.[20] When the results were in the CCF had doubled the best previous showing of the left and replaced the Conservatives as the official opposition.

The reaction of the major newspapers and business opinion to the arrival of the CCF was uniformly hostile. They described the party as the captive of ultra-radicals and communists aiming to pillage successful industry. They saw recruitment of candidates on the basis of their knowledge of socialism and the demand for strict adherence to the party line as threats to the principles of representative and constitutional government.[21] Yet despite what we might have expected given the vitriolic campaign against the CCF, and from reading the present into the past, the incorporation of the CCF into what became effectively a three-party system was relatively peaceful. "No special strategies were employed to contain the left."[22] The strong CCF showing in 1933, 31.5 per cent of the vote, could have been viewed as a fluke given Conservative disarray and the previous level of support for the left, and tactical disagreements complicated by personality conflicts soon returned to plague the party caucus.[23] The Liberals obtained a majority of seats in 1933 and did so again in 1937 despite a modest Conservative revival, which was itself sufficient to relegate the CCF to third place in the legislature.

The Liberal premier, Dufferin Pattullo, also moved his party leftward, reducing the notoriety of CCF proposals, by advocating massive public works expenditures to provide jobs for the unemployed, state health insurance, a permanent advisory council on the economy, and increased government regulation of utilities. Pattullo's moves were more than tactical. They reflected a conviction that government had a moral responsibility for the welfare of the individual and must be prepared to intervene and regulate the economy to that end.[24] Specific Liberal reform proposals, even if inspired by a different economic philosophy, looked similar enough to CCF policies that it was the Conservatives who seemed out of step when they campaigned in 1937 on the familiar themes of economy, efficiency, and the restoration of free enterprise.

The foundations of the present provincial party system and its separation from the federal one can be traced to the impact of coalition following the provincial election of 1941. A substantial decline in Liberal support produced nearly a dead heat in the race for the popular vote.[25] The CCF actually finished first with 33.4 per cent compared to the Liberals' 32.9 and the Conservatives' 30.9, but the Liberals remained the largest party in the legislature with twenty-one seats (the CCF held fourteen and the Conservatives twelve). The exigencies of war combined with the normal requirement for reliable legislative allies in a minority government situation led to the formation of a coalition between the Liberals and Conservatives. This lasted through two elections before being terminated prior to the 1952 election.

Appearances to the contrary, the coalition was not designed as an instrument to contain the left by preventing the fragmentation of the free enterprise vote. The CCF was initially invited to participate in an all-party coalition and even offered to guarantee support for a Liberal minority government should the Tories drive too hard a bargain. However, the success of the coalition experience (the press frequently referred to it as "the best government B.C. ever had") combined with the incentives of the parliamentary system to transform "the non-left into the anti-left"[26] and ultimately to redefine the basis of provincial politics. Co-operation within coalition reduced Liberal and Conservative differences in their own eyes as well as in the eyes of the electorate, and the very existence of the CCF as the official, and only, opposition raised the salience of the division between free enterprise and socialism, especially given the doctrinaire stance of the CCF leader, Harold Winch.

The coalition won resounding victories in 1945 and 1949, reducing CCF representation in the legislature to ten and then to seven seats, despite modest CCF vote gains in 1945 and a level of support in 1949 still above their 1941 showing. However, strains were produced by an arrangement in which the coalition partners retained their separate identities, legislative caucuses, and party organizations, and by a system of rewards which seemed to the Conservatives to perpetuate their minority status. These strains, and clashes of ambition and personality between the successors to the architects of coalition, combined with pressure from the federal wings of the parties to lead inexorably to dissolution.[27] Even the need to contain the left temporarily lost its urgency as the perennial battle between moderates and radicals resurfaced in the CCF following defeat in 1949, and the Liberal party became convinced that it could win on its own.

As insurance against a victory by the CCF based on only a plurality of the popular vote, the coalition partners introduced the alternative vote system prior to the 1952 election. The ballot required voters to rank candidates in order of preference. If a candidate received a majority of first choices in a given riding, he or she was declared elected. Failing that, the candidate with the lowest number of first choices would be eliminated from the count, and the second choices on his or her ballots would be allocated among the other candidates. The procedure would be repeated until one candidate received a majority of the combined ballots. Proponents of the ballot change reasoned, apparently, that the Liberal and Conservative voters would divide their first two choices between those parties, that the CCF would win only those ridings in which it had a majority on the first count, and that a coalition could be arranged, if necessary, should neither the Liberals nor the Conservatives win a legislative majority.[28]

None of these assumptions proved correct. The Liberals and Conservatives finished third and fourth rather than first and second, both in terms of seats and votes, as the leaderless Social Credit party eked out a single-seat victory over the CCF.[29] Not even the assumption that the CCF would be effectively isolated on the left proved well founded, since many Liberal and Conservative voters behaved as if Social Credit and CCF votes were alternative ways of protesting against their former coalition partners. Many vote transfers took place between the CCF and Social Credit, further testimony to the degree to which they shared the protest image.[30] However, by the time of the next election less than a year later, with former Conservative MLA W.A.C. Bennett as leader, there could be no mistaking Social Credit's stance vis-à-vis the CCF. Bennett had long been an advocate of a permanent coalition to confront the left, and by harnessing Social Credit, he achieved his goal of developing a free enterprise party free from the entanglements of federal politics.

Bennett's success in the 1952 and 1953 elections is testimony to his political skills and the accident of timing. In its previous forays in British Columbia elections (1937, 1945, and 1949), Social Credit had never received more than 2 per cent of the vote. However, in 1950 with the organizational and financial support of the powerful Alberta Social Credit party, British Columbia's Social Credit League launched a major membership drive. They met with phenomenal success in the interior, where expatriate Albertans formed the nucleus of local organizations to which hundreds of local politicians and businessmen flocked. With the Liberal/Conservative alliance crumbling, Social Credit offered an alternative, sanctified by its reputation as the party governing Alberta, to those starved of political opportunities.[31]

Bennett, who had toyed with the idea of forming his own fusionist party, instead moved to Social Credit. He thus became the party's first MLA, and given that position and his vastly greater political experience compared to other activists, he was able to secure the leadership of the party despite the initial opposition of those in the Social Credit League who viewed his conversion with scepticism.[32]

The current separation of federal and provincial party systems also had its roots in the coalition experience and the severe strains it placed on relations between the federal and provincial wings of the Liberal and Conservative parties. The federal parties lost the organizational support normally offered by provincial activists in federal campaigns, a factor which the Conservatives in particular blamed for their poor showing in the 1949 federal election.

The Conservative party seems to have been most affected, partly because many provincial constituency associations defected to Social Credit. Relations between federal and provincial leaders, never very good after 1945, were strained further by charges that the federal party was unwilling to assist in the provincial rebuilding effort and, indeed, had cultivated Social Credit support in the federal campaign of 1953.[33] Provincial activists were so outraged by what they perceived as attempts to undermine the provincial party that they passed a motion of non-confidence in the federal leader at their convention in 1954.[34]

After 1953, the fortunes of the Liberal and Conservative parties in federal politics fluctuated independently of the level of support achieved by their provincial counterparts. The effects of the 1958 Diefenbaker landslide (49 per cent of the vote and eighteen of twenty-two seats in B.C.) were barely discernible in the results of the next provincial election. Conservatives contested all fifty-two seats (up from twenty-two in the previous election), but raised their share of the vote from 2.8 per cent to only 6.7 per cent. The provincial Liberals duplicated this experience in the 1969 provincial election, when their share of the vote increased by less than one percentage point despite the federal Liberals garnering sixteen of the province's twenty-two seats with nearly 42 per cent of the vote in 1968.

Only the CCF/NDP seemed to enjoy comparable levels of success in the two arenas, although the provincial party consistently finished slightly ahead of its federal counterpart until the gap increased with provincial victory in 1972.[35] Social Credit obtained approximately 25 per cent of the federal vote in 1953 and 1957, but since that time its federal showing has been only a pale reflection of the party's provincial dominance, despite W.A.C. Bennett's reputation as a "fed-basher." Since 1968 only a token number of Social Credit candidates have even appeared in federal campaigns.

Despite Social Credit's antecedents and Bennett's previous life as a Conservative, the party was not simply the inheritor of the free enterprise mantle. An anti-establishment sentiment was reflected in its support base in the interior and among small businessmen. The absence of members of traditional élite groups in its legislative contingent forced Bennett to reach outside the legislature for an attorney-general and minister of finance. The victory of the party represented in part a victory of the hinterland over the metropolis, and a victory for small "c" conservative values in social policy, for the importance of religion, and for a version of free enterprise emphasizing the virtues of small business and competition. The CCF now had to face a competitor which also had credentials as a challenger to entrenched economic and social power. Even when the economic élites of the province shifted their political and financial support to Social Credit as the best guarantee against a CCF victory, they could never prevent its leader from making successful appeals to these populist symbols when his development schemes clashed with their own.

Under Bennett, the "free enterprise versus socialism" slogan became part of every election campaign as a device to discredit the CCF and discourage support for the Liberal and Conservative parties. From 1956 until its defeat in 1972, his party never held fewer than 60 per cent of the seats in the legislature. The Social Credit vote dropped below 40 per cent only once, to 38.8 per cent in 1960, when a major push was made by the provincial Conservative party hoping to capitalize on the showing made by John Diefenbaker in 1958. That year also saw a surge in support for the CCF, reflecting unprecedented unity in the labour movement and official support from the B.C. Federation of Labour.

The Liberal party struggled bravely on, continuing to compete in nearly every riding during the first twenty years of Social Credit rule, but it gradually slipped from 23.3 per cent of the vote in 1952 to less than 20 per cent during the sixties. However, they maintained a presence in the legislature (varying from two to six members), whereas the Conservatives disappeared altogether between 1956 and 1972. After 1952 the Conservatives nominated a full slate only once, in 1960. In the two elections before the Social Credit defeat in 1972, they were barely visible with three candidates in 1966 and one, the party leader, in 1969. Their effort in 1972, which is analysed in the next chapter, produced a modest revival and a return to the legislature, but the party's hopes were dashed in the struggle to re-establish a bulwark against the NDP.

The Bennett strategy which grew out of the coalition experience proved very successful. But it contained inherent weaknesses. Alan Cairns has pointed out that Social Credit could not guarantee victory forever given the occasional scandal, "organizational malaise, and electorate disenchantment" which inevitably undermine any government. Its strategy of "polarizing the electorate between itself and the CCF/NDP...ensured that its eventual defeat would be at the hands of the NDP" and could be irrelevant if the left refused to play the polarization game, by downplaying its socialism.[36]

Nor could Social Credit control developments within the CCF/NDP, whose brand of socialism gradually moderated, especially after the retirement of Harold Winch as party leader in 1953. During the 1960s the party developed a new appeal along with a new name, the New Democratic Party, with a stress on the need for innovative social policy, the perils of foreign ownership, and opposition to the alienation of the province's natural resources. Ties with organized labour became stronger, culminating in the election of a labour lawyer, Thomas Berger, as party leader in 1969. While Berger was unable to increase the party's share of the vote in the one election he contested (in fact the party lost four seats and failed to elect Berger), his presence and the type of campaign he fought arguably prepared the way for the victory which followed in 1972.

Bennett also presided over major transformations in the economy and social structure of the province which created new political forces and thrust new issues onto the public agenda. The labour force doubled during his twenty years as premier, and changed in character. Employment in the public sector expanded along with new demands in the health, education, and social welfare fields brought about, in part, by Bennett's development policies. The service, finance, and real estate sectors rather than primary industry experienced the highest growth rates. Phenomenal population growth occurred in the interior. Kamloops and Prince George, which ranked eleventh and seventeenth, respectively, among B.C. cities in 1952 became important regional centres, and by 1972 they were the fourth and third largest cities in the province.[37] In part because of the growth of employment in tertiary industries, membership in the trade union movement peaked at 55.4 per cent of the paid labour force in 1958,[38] although British Columbia remained the most unionized province in Canada.

Bennett may not have fully comprehended the changes he had helped to bring about and which form the basis for the analysis of realignment in the next chapter. While we can never be certain about the reasons for his government's defeat in 1972, some part was undoubtedly played by dissatisfaction among occupational groups he had helped to create and nourish. His defeat was preceded by major battles with hospital and government employees and with doctors and schoolteachers. As Martin Robin put it, "British Columbia's classic confrontation between labour and capital was complemented...by a second struggle; between the old and the new middle classes, between Sunday politicians administering a welfare state and Monday morning professionals eager to ensure its efficiency and humanity," yet Bennett recognized only the first.[39]

Despite Bennett's warning during the campaign that "the socialist hordes [were] at the gates," and an initial whirlwind of legislative activity, the New Democratic Party government under Premier David Barrett did not attempt a wholesale restructuring of the provincial economy and society.[40] Barrett retained the traditional cabinet structure developed by his predecessor which emphasized the authority of individual ministers and made policy initiatives dependent on the personal strengths of individuals and their ability to insulate their departments from other members of the cabinet and the prying eyes of the Treasury Board. It was not until his last few months in office, when spending initiatives greatly outran the resources available to pay for them, that Barrett began to establish bureaucratic co-ordinating and planning mechanisms.[41] By then, with the economy in recession, the government had established a reputation for management failures which has plagued the NDP ever since.

Despite the absence of an overall plan, the NDP took a number of important initiatives. In the area of economic policy it created the B.C. Petroleum Corporation, giving the Crown a monopoly in the production and marketing of natural gas, established a government monopoly over automobile insurance, and created a comprehensive set of controls administered by the B.C. Land Commission over the use of land suitable for agriculture. It granted full collective bargaining rights to public servants, established a human rights code barring discrimination in employment, accommodation, and the provision of services, and drafted a new labour code. Social policy initiatives included a Landlord and Tenant Act, rent controls on certain classes of accommodation, the creation of a Department of Consumer Services, and the establishment of elected Community Resource Boards to assist in the planning and administration of social services at the local level. It ignored the strong nationalization stance approved by previous party conventions, but it did establish a public presence in the forest industry through the purchase of a number of sawmills and pulp mills, most of which prospered under public ownership.[42]

Some of these developments, especially the creation of the government automobile insurance scheme and the establishment of the B.C. Land Commission, sparked strong opposition from the groups most affected by them.[43] Perhaps the most vehement opposition developed over government plans to change the basis of taxation for the mining industry from a tax on income to a royalty on production. The mining industry launched a vigorous campaign against the proposal and eventually forced the government to back down.[44] However, by then suspicion of the government by the business community had already contributed to the revival of the Social Credit party which was to defeat it in 1975.

The revival of Social Credit under William R. Bennett, W.A.C. Bennett's second son, has been attributed largely to the organizational skills of the party's new leader and the then party president, Grace McCarthy, and the trauma induced by the short-lived NDP government. While these were important factors, they operated against the backdrop described in this chapter. The middle way offered by the Liberal and Conservative parties could not be presented as a credible alternative since *both* of them were in the field between 1972 and 1975 and each refused to surrender it to the other. Neither could utilize the ties to their stronger federal partners since they had atrophied long ago. Polarization between Social Credit and the CCF/NDP had been the norm since 1953, and the first time Social Credit support dropped below one-third, the NDP was elected. Even sincere supporters of the Liberals and Conservatives had to face the fact that the revival of both their parties was unlikely, and, in the short run, neither of them was strong enough to defeat the NDP by itself.

There was still another, deeper, meaning to the NDP victory and the Social Credit revival signified, in part, by the fact that the NDP retained and even increased its share of the vote while failing to retain control of government. Polarization remained the principal characteristic of the provincial party system, but the province's political geography was reshaped. A substantial realignment of political loyalties had taken place in the mass electorate, nearly eliminating the Liberals and Conservatives completely. These changes are analysed further in the next chapter.

The historical sketch provided here is designed to set the stage for the analysis of provincial and federal partisanship which follows. It has traced the evolution of the provincial party system from a two-party system based on Liberal and Conservative alternation in office to a two-party system structured largely in response to a strong left party, the CCF and then the NDP, which virtually excludes the province's first parties. It began the task of describing changes in the provincial economy and social structure which helped produce a realignment of political loyalties in the 1970s and to separate further the federal and provincial party systems. The next four chapters provide a detailed account of that realignment, the provincial political culture which is tied to it, and the attitudes and behaviour of voters in the provincial political world. Exploration of the world of federal politics resumes in Chapter 7.

3

The Modern Provincial Party System

Donald E. Blake, Richard Johnston, and David J. Elkins

The seventies began and ended with Social Credit firmly established as the governing party.[1] Just three years after the defeat of W.A.C. Bennett in 1972, his son William R. Bennett led a revitalized Social Credit party back into office. His success astonished most political observers in the province, who did not believe that the party could survive the defeat and the retirement of the man who dominated the party for most of its existence in B.C., especially when the leadership fell to a man with no previous political experience.

The apparent continuity of party and premiership is deceptive. The younger Bennett's victory came after a scramble for leadership of the anti-NDP forces in which he not only maintained his own position in the party but also convinced most Liberal and Conservative members of the legislature to join it, a feat never achieved by his father. While his competitors intrigued in the legislature and with the province's élites, his allies created the largest mass membership party in the province.[2]

The NDP also continued to grow despite its defeat. Social Credit coalition-building in the legislature could not automatically convert Liberal and Conservative electoral support into votes for Social Credit. Indeed, as we shall show in this chapter, the NDP was much more successful than Social Credit in attracting former supporters of the Liberal party. Moreover, the NDP continued to benefit from developments in the economy and society which increased the size of its constituency and distributed it more evenly across the province.

Changes during the seventies have simplified electoral choices in the province to an unprecedented degree. Social Credit and the NDP now divide between them the support of 95 per cent of the provincial electorate. Neither Liberals nor Conservatives have been able to affect significantly the character of political debate in which variations of the clash between "free enterprise" and "socialism" continually reappear, no matter how misleading they may be as descriptions of party policy.

Social Credit and the NDP both entered the eighties as new parties with new followings, created by the realignments of the seventies, realignments which reflected short-term strategic considerations and long-term policy or ideological ones. In exploring these changes in this chapter we shall show that the development of the two coalitions has been asymmetric in two senses. Voters attaching themselves to one or the other of the two coalitions have done so for quite different reasons and with different degrees of enthusiasm. Second, the growth of the NDP popular vote over the last fifteen years has not been matched by complementary changes in the Social Credit vote. The two parties have converged on the political centre, but by building coalitions with very different strengths and weaknesses, and with different histories. We shall also show that this realignment can be traced to structural changes in the economy of the province, especially growth of the unionized work-force and geographical diffusion of large-scale industry. The analysis is conducted at the level of the electorate as a whole and within regions. In the next three chapters we will focus more closely on the individuals who compose these electorates, their political attitudes, and the characteristics and settings to which they are linked.

VOTE SHIFTS FROM 1972 TO 1983

Figure 1 presents a summary of the official election results from 1952 to 1983. The figure shows the substantial gap between Social Credit and the CCF/NDP which began to erode in about 1966. The aggregate pattern associated with the NDP victory in 1972 seems simple—a temporary dip in Social Credit support matched by gains in NDP strength with the Conservative party playing a spoiler role and assuring an NDP victory. An analysis of riding level results does not support this view. In fact, only nine NDP seats could plausibly be attributed to a split in the free enterprise vote. Social Credit victories in these cases would not have been sufficient to eliminate the NDP majority, but, taken together with continued support for the Liberals, the result helped to convince many that the NDP could be defeated (and would not have won) were it not for the fractionalization of non-NDP support.

A "coalition of the right" did materialize in 1975 and seems to have been crucial to the defeat of the NDP government—it lost the election while receiving almost exactly the same share of the vote which brought it to office in 1972. In 1979 the "right" received another scare. The final collapse of the Liberals and a poor Conservative performance did not add significantly to the anti-NDP vote. NDP support increased sufficiently to bring them within five seats of the government. The 1983 election results suggest that the NDP has reached a new plateau. Despite what seemed to be a basis for defeating the government — high unemployment and a large drop in resource revenues — their vote dropped slightly costing them four seats.

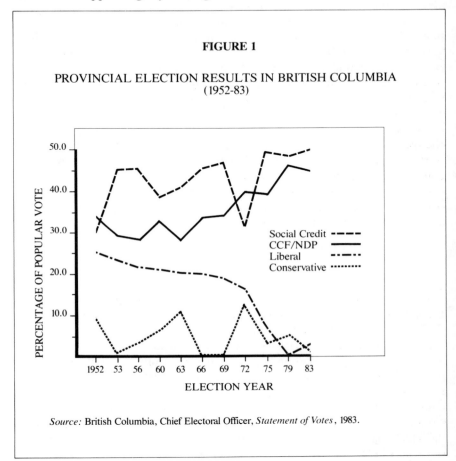

FIGURE 1

PROVINCIAL ELECTION RESULTS IN BRITISH COLUMBIA
(1952-83)

Source: British Columbia, Chief Electoral Officer, *Statement of Votes*, 1983.

While the aggregate pattern seems clear, survey data show that, in fact, it masked a great deal of movement at the individual level.[3] Insofar as we can reconstruct the past using data gathered in 1979, it appears that the 1975 NDP vote did not represent a complete repeat of its 1972 support. Without compensating defections from other parties, its defeat would have been very convincing. The 1979 election seemed to complete the electoral collapse of the provincial Liberal and Conservative parties begun in 1975, but Social Credit was not the only beneficiary.

The first stage in the realignment pattern saw the collapse of the Liberal and Conservative vote. Only about half the respondents who voted Liberal in 1972 repeated that choice in 1975 although candidates were available in most areas, with most of the switchers moving to Social Credit (Table 1). Many of them undoubtedly followed the sitting Liberal MLAs who joined Social Credit prior to the 1975 election. Two of the best known, Garde Gardom and Pat McGeer (a former leader of the provincial Liberal party), raised their level of support in the double-member riding of Point Grey from 43 per cent as Liberals to 58 per cent as Social Credit candidates. Both entered the cabinet following the election. One of our sample ridings, North Vancouver-Seymour, was wrested from the NDP's Colin Gabelmann by Jack Davis, a former federal Liberal cabinet minister turned Social Credit, despite the fact that Gabelmann increased his vote slightly. The combined Liberal and Conservative support in the riding was 48 per cent in 1972. In 1975 it dropped to 11 per cent.

TABLE 1

PROVINCIAL VOTE SHIFTS, 1972-1975[1]
(vertical percentages)

		1972 Vote					
		Liberal	PC	NDP	Social Credit	Did not vote	Total
	Liberal	53.1	0.0	1.2	0.0	6.7	4.5
1975	Conservative	0.0	82.9	5.2	2.9	8.6	9.4
vote	NDP	15.6	2.9	76.0	4.6	47.6	42.5
	Social Credit	31.3	14.3	17.6	92.6	37.1	43.6
		(32)	(35)	(250)	(175)	(105)	

1. Table entries report the distribution of the vote in 1975 within the group identified by the column label. For example, of the respondents who reported that they had voted Liberal in 1972, 53.1 per cent said they voted the same way in 1975, 15.6 per cent said they switched to NDP, and 31.3 per cent reported switching to Social Credit.

The Conservatives managed to hold on to their vote in another sample riding, Oak Bay, largely because of the popularity of the then party leader, Scott Wallace. Much of his support was undoubtedly personal. When he left the Social Credit party to run as a Conservative in 1972, he received almost exactly the same share of the riding's vote. Conversely, after he retired as leader, his riding was won by Social Credit in 1979 by a 2 to 1 margin over the new Conservative leader who had won the riding in a 1978 by-election.

Table 2 completes the story. Only a quarter of those who voted Conservative in 1975 repeated that choice in 1979, while a third of the 1975 Liberals did so. All but three of our sample ridings were contested by the Conservatives, but only one had a Liberal candidate. While these proportions mirror the proportion of seats the parties contested in the province as a whole, the numbers of respondents are sufficiently small to make precise estimation of patterns of change difficult. However, an analysis of changes in party identification[4] presented later helps to confirm these patterns with the major caveat that focusing on the elections of 1975 and 1979 underestimates the support picked up by the NDP from the provincial Liberal party—support it gained before 1972.

TABLE 2

PROVINCIAL VOTE SHIFTS, 1975-79
(vertical percentages)

| | | 1975 Vote | | | | | |
		Liberal	PC	NDP	Social Credit	Did not vote	Total
	Liberal	34.8	2.0	0.4	1.6	1.5	2.3
1979	Conservative	13.0	24.0	2.2	4.0	5.2	5.4
vote	NDP	26.1	22.0	90.0	5.2	50.0	44.4
	Social Credit	26.1	52.0	7.3	89.2	43.3	47.8
		(23)	(50)	(232)	(250)	(134)	

While disintegration of the Liberal and Conservative electorate has been the most prominent feature of the 1970s, Table 1 makes it clear that the Barrett NDP government was the victim of defections to Social Credit from the NDP's own coalition. Social Credit, on the other hand, retained over 90 per cent of its 1972 support and added to it the bulk of defections from the Liberal and Conservative parties. The survey data reveal a rather more complex picture of change than implied by the negligible net shift in the aggregate level of NDP support. Most commentators, pointing out that the NDP lost the 1975 election while maintaining its share of the vote, have assumed that they were defeated by a non-left coalition. While it is impossible to reconstruct the 1975 electorate exactly with our sample, there is clear-cut evidence that defections of their own supporters were a factor as well. The aggregate results masked this loss, the compensating defections from other parties, and the NDP support gained from those who did not vote in 1972.

The short-lived NDP administration made a number of enemies among voters—just over 20 per cent of those who changed their vote in 1975 cited "poor performance" of the NDP government as a major reason. Almost the same number cited dislike of the party in general or of particular policies as reasons for joining the coalition of forces to oust the government.

The 1975 Social Credit coalition emerged more from antipathy to the NDP than from positive attachment to Social Credit itself, its policies, or its leader. These allegiances, discussed in more detail below, were sufficient to sustain Social Credit in 1979, despite a slight vote loss, as roughly 90 per cent of 1975 New Democrats and Socreds stayed with their party. The Social Credit party maintained its lead among former Liberals and Conservatives but, again, the NDP won the support of most new voters.

These developments may shed light on the apparent volatility of the B.C. electorate. As recently as the 1972 election the provincial Liberal and Conservative parties commanded the support of nearly 30 per cent of the province's voters. By 1975 that share had dropped to 11 per cent, by 1979 to less than 6 per cent, and in 1983 to 4 per cent. The 1979 electorate undoubtedly contained many voters whose normal loyalties would lie with the two older parties but who were unable to vote for them in nearly half the ridings in the case of the Conservatives and all but four ridings in the case of the Liberals. In 1983, the Liberals exerted more effort than the Conservatives, nominating in forty-seven ridings compared to the Conservatives' twelve, but they were no more successful.

Table 3 provides a profile of the 1979 Social Credit and NDP electorates constructed with these factors in mind. Roughly 12 per cent of the Social Credit and 5 per cent of the NDP electorate consisted of those who reported attachment to the provincial Liberal and Conservative parties in response to the standard question on party identification.[5] A further 17 per cent of the Social Credit electorate and 20 per cent of the NDP electorate was made up of former Liberals and Conservatives who have apparently come to identify with the party for which they vote. If we add to these figures the percentages who came to the NDP and Social Credit from each other (called "former opponents" in the table), both voting blocs contained approximately 27 per

TABLE 3

COMPOSITION OF SOCIAL CREDIT AND NDP ELECTORATES
BY PARTISAN HISTORY, 1979[1]
(vertical percentages)

	Social Credit	*NDP*
Independents	15.3	11.8
PC identifiers	4.9	2.3
Liberal identifiers	7.6	2.6
Own identifiers	43.7	55.1
Former PC	9.2	5.6
Former Liberal	7.6	14.4
Former opponent	10.4	6.6
Current opponent	0.9	1.0
Returned defectors	0.3	0.7
	(327)	(305)

1. "Former opponents" are former Social Credit identifiers in the case of the NDP, former New Democrats in the case of Social Credit. "Current opponents" are those who claim to have never changed partisan allegiance, but in 1979 voted for the NDP in the case of Social Credit identifiers and for Social Credit in the case of NDP identifiers. "Returned defectors" are those who claim to have switched allegiance from the NDP to Social Credit or vice versa, but in 1979 voted for the party they switched from.

cent who at some time were attached to a party other than the one to which they now claim allegiance.

The strength of these new commitments as well as the relatively greater significance of newly arrived or non-identifiers in the Social Credit electorate have important implications for the stability of the Social Credit coalition and for the success of attempts to revive the provincial Liberal and Conservative parties. The NDP electorate also exhibits some vulnerability. While a larger proportion is made up of those who have never identified with another party, rather more NDP supporters than Social Credit supporters have had ties to the Liberals or Tories.

FORMATION OF THE NDP AND SOCIAL CREDIT COALITIONS

Table 4 provides a profile of the destination of all those who have at some time changed their provincial party identification. Liberals have tended to become New Democrats and Conservatives to join Social Credit. The two major provincial parties have exchanged roughly equal proportions of their own "defectors" although, since the absolute number of NDP defectors has been higher, Social Credit has come out slightly ahead. The magnitude of exchanges between these two supposedly bitter enemies is startling despite the fact, noted in Table 3, that these defections make up only 10 per cent and 7 per cent, respectively, of the Social Credit and NDP electorates. Nevertheless, in an election which saw the two parties separated by roughly two percentage points, these components were crucial.[6]

TABLE 4

DESTINATION OF ALL THOSE CHANGING PROVINCIAL PARTY IDENTIFICATION
(vertical percentages)

	Changed from			
	Liberal	PC	NDP	Social Credit
Changed to				
Independent, other	6.0	8.0	13.2	6.5
Liberal	-	12.0	11.8	14.5
PC	10.0	-	14.5	19.4
NDP	53.0	26.7	-	59.7
Social Credit	31.0	53.3	60.5	-
	(100)	(75)	(76)	(62)

Despite the disintegration of Liberal and Conservative voting support, 15 per cent of all provincial identifiers remain attached to those parties.[7] Retention of ties to parties with such bleak electoral futures in the short term may reflect a relative lack of interest in provincial politics. Our survey indicates that those who retained ties to the provincial Liberal and Conservative parties are much less likely than NDP or Social Credit partisans to give "provincial" as an answer to questions probing level of government respondents felt closer to, perceived as more important, paid more attention to, or felt provided an election with "higher stakes" in May 1979.[8]

We argued earlier that 1972 to 1975 marked a period of realignment in B.C. politics, although the weakness of the Liberal and Conservative parties goes back to 1952, the first election after the breakup of Coalition, and the penetration of the NDP and Social Credit parties into previously unrewarding areas of the province can be traced back to the mid-sixties. Table 5 provides some evidence of when major changes took place. The table is organized by decade until 1970, when periods immediately preceding and including the elections of 1972, 1975, and 1979 are demarcated. This division acknowledges the difficulty many voters have of recalling specific dates in the past and helps to focus attention on those elections most responsible for the current partisan division. The fourth column for each party provides a rough indication of the "normal" growth of each party's core—the time

TABLE 5

WHEN CURRENT PROVINCIAL PARTY ATTACHMENT FORMED,
BY PARTY OF ORIGIN
(vertical percentages)

Current New Democrats

	Former Liberal	Former PC	Former Socred	Always NDP	Total
Long time ago[1]	7.7	0.0	10.8	13.6	11.8
pre-1950	7.7	0.0	0.0	12.3	9.6
1950-59	9.6	11.8	5.4	6.0	6.8
1960-69	23.1	35.3	10.8	17.0	17.5
1970-72	26.9	29.4	29.7	18.7	21.4
1973-75	7.7	17.6	13.5	15.7	14.6
1976-79	17.3	11.8	27.0	16.6	18.0
	(52)	(20)	(37)	(236)	

Current Social Credit

	Former Liberal	Former PC	Former NDP	Always Socred	Total
Long time ago[1]	3.2	7.5	7.1	14.7	11.5
pre-1950	0.0	0.0	0.0	4.4	2.6
1950-59	16.1	20.0	19.0	21.3	20.0
1960-69	19.4	20.0	19.0	19.6	19.3
1970-72	12.9	7.5	11.9	13.1	11.8
1973-75	29.0	17.5	26.2	10.9	16.1
1976-79	16.1	27.5	16.7	15.3	18.0
	(23)	(40)	(44)	(182)	

1. This category includes those who cannot name a specified date or era, but state that the tie was formed early in life or existed most of their lives.

when those claiming never to have changed their partisan ties became attached to the party.

A plurality (21.3 per cent) of 1979 Social Credit identifiers became associated with that party in its infancy in B.C., although some undoubtedly carried support for Alberta's Social Credit party with them when they moved to B.C. If we add to the 1950s figure most of the 14.7 per cent who cannot recall an exact date but report they have been Social Credit most of their lives, the significance of the 1950s in the party's history becomes even more apparent. From one-sixth to one-fifth of defections to Social Credit from the other three parties also occurred in that decade, suggesting that roughly one-third of all Social Credit identifiers have been attached to that party for at least twenty years.

The realignment of the 1970s is also reflected in the table. The period following the election of 1972 accounts for 26 per cent of those who have always been Social Credit but for nearly half the defections from the Liberal, Conservative, *and* NDP parties. These data reinforce the observation made earlier about the misleading impression of stability in NDP support conveyed by the official results of the 1975 election.

The relative youthfulness of the NDP coalition (mean age of forty compared to forty-five for Social Credit)[9] is apparent from these data. As must almost inevitably have been the case given the growth of the party from its traditional "threshold" of roughly one-third of the vote, over one-half of the current NDP identifiers formed their attachments during the 1970s. Moreover, well over half the defections from other parties among 1979 identifiers took place at this time, although the decade of the 1960s accounts for many of the Liberal and Conservative shifts to the NDP. Lest we overstress the novelty of an attachment to the NDP, we should point out that our sample of NDP identifiers includes over one-quarter whose attachments have been for twenty years or longer. One respondent was even present at the signing of the Regina Manifesto in 1933.

The magnitude of change in the 1970s and the fact that in 1979 nearly 40 per cent and over 30 per cent, respectively, of Social Credit and NDP identifiers came from other partisan backgrounds make it essential to our future expectations about provincial politics to try to assess the likelihood of these new patterns persisting. The partisan battles of 1975 and 1979 were exceedingly bitter. The stakes were perceived to be sufficiently high that the B.C. Liberal leader was abandoned by his colleagues in the legislature prior to the 1975 election. Three Liberal MLAs, including a former party leader, Pat McGeer, together with one of the two Conservatives elected in 1972 crossed over to Social Credit following the failure of efforts to form a "Unity Party" which would replace Social Credit as an alternative to the NDP.[10] In 1979, the provincial Conservative leader became so frustrated in his attempts to revive the party that he accused the federal leader of conspiring with Social Credit to undermine his campaign. Both parties experienced recruiting difficulties as pressures were brought to bear on potential candidates by those fearful of splitting the anti-NDP vote. Given long-term developments, detailed below, the roughly even division of the electorate produced in 1979 and 1983 probably signals the inauguration of a new two-party era in the province.

The election of 1975 witnessed a good deal of "negative voting," and that seems to characterize many of the attachments formed to the Social Credit party itself. Table 6 summarizes a variety of reasons our respondents gave for their current ties to Social Credit, Table 7, the same information for NDP partisans.

In coding responses (up to three for each individual) we distinguished between reasons which stressed qualities of parties, leaders, or candidates being *avoided* and those which stressed qualities of *current* partisanship. The former sentiments, which involve explicit rejection of parties and personnel, we have labelled "negative," to distinguish them from direct "positive" statements. The tables make it quite clear that negative reactions

TABLE 6

REASONS FOR BECOMING ATTACHED TO SOCIAL CREDIT BY PARTY OF ORIGIN[1]
(vertical percentages)

| | Previous Partisanship | | | |
	Former Liberal	Former PC	Former NDP	Always Socred
Specific issues	3.6	5.0	0.0	13.1
Free enterprise/socialism	14.3	5.0	0.0	12.6
Other ideological	3.6	0.0	6.8	0.0
Gov't management	3.6	2.5	9.1	3.3
Gov't mismanagement	3.6	0.0	2.3	2.2
Leader positive	17.9	22.5	6.8	11.5
Leader negative	0.0	5.0	9.1	3.3
Candidate positive	0.0	2.5	2.3	0.0
Candidate negative	0.0	2.5	0.0	0.5
Social Credit party positive[2]	21.4	25.0	38.6	29.7
Other party negative	35.7	35.0	13.6	14.8
Social influences positive[3]	7.1	5.0	18.2	16.3
Social influences negative	0.0	0.0	2.3	0.5
Other reasons[4]	3.6	5.0	2.3	9.7
	(28)	(40)	(44)	(182)

1. Percentages may not add to 100 per cent because of multiple responses.
2. This category contains generalized positive references to a party or its policies which did not mention specific issues or policies.
3. Including influence from friends, family, and co-workers.
4. Including positive and negative references to politics in other provinces or other countries, absence or weakness of a preferred party, credibility, or honesty of parties.

TABLE 7

REASONS FOR BECOMING ATTACHED TO NDP BY PARTY OF ORIGIN[1]
(vertical percentages)

	Previous Partisanship			
	Former Liberal	Former PC	Former Socred	Always NDP
Specific issues	32.7	10.0	35.1	16.5
Free enterprise/socialism	7.7	0.0	0.0	5.9
Other ideological	11.5	0.0	8.1	6.8
Gov't management	0.0	0.0	0.0	1.3
Gov't mismanagement	0.0	0.0	0.0	0.8
Leader positive	5.8	15.0	5.4	7.6
Leader negative	1.9	5.0	8.1	1.3
Candidate positive	5.8	5.0	0.0	0.8
Candidate negative	0.0	2.5	0.0	0.5
NDP positive	42.3	40.0	43.2	40.7
Other party negative	17.3	15.0	2.7	8.5
Social influences positive	5.8	5.0	8.1	20.3
Social influences negative	1.9	0.0	0.0	0.4
Other reasons	3.8	5.0	2.7	8.9
	(52)	(20)	(37)	(236)

1. See notes to Table 6.

are particularly characteristic of former Liberals and Conservatives who now consider themselves Social Credit. Over one-third of each group make critical comments about other parties—especially the NDP—in justifying their current allegiance. Conversely, over 40 per cent of those former Conservatives and Liberals who switched to the NDP cite attractive features of the party as reasons for doing so. Moreover, nearly one-third of the Liberals who switched to the NDP cite specific issues—welfare policy, environmental and resource issues figure prominently—as reasons for doing so. If we combine the first three categories of reasons as signifying attachment to party as a policy vehicle, each category of New Democrat (except former Tories) exhibits this characteristic at a higher level than the Social Credit counterpart.

Lest we overdraw the contrast between the two coalitions, we should point out that between one-fifth and one-quarter of the former Liberals and Conservatives among the Socreds do make positive statements about the party leadership and do have positive things to say about the party, despite the greater prominence of "negative" reasons for switching. If Social Credit can continue to provide the best insurance against an NDP victory, there is no reason to expect relative lack of affect for the party to hurt it electorally. In addition, stronger ties to party might develop with longer association. Nevertheless, there are tensions within the party on policy questions between those who endorse policies which characterized the party under W.A.C.

Bennett and those who see it as a revival of the coalition of the 1940s. Most of those former Liberals and Conservatives who directly mentioned positive qualities of Social Credit leadership in fact switched to Social Credit prior to 1973 and must have had W.A.C. Bennett in mind. Moreover, those citing negative features of other parties as reasons for joining Social Credit are more likely to have adopted that attachment after the 1972 election.

The NDP also enjoys roughly a ten-point edge over Social Credit in the percentage of its partisans who report very strong ties, a lead which is even slightly larger among those who have never identified with any other party and among former Liberals. Slightly more former Conservatives claim very strong Social Credit ties than do their counterparts in the NDP, but that lead may be illusory given that nearly half the former PC identifiers in the Social Credit party report ties which are not very strong. This may be a reflection of the fact that roughly 28 per cent of them formed their attachment just prior to or during the 1979 campaign.

The very fact that steady growth in support for the NDP led to the transformation of the Social Credit party may, of course, be sufficient to maintain the party despite weaknesses in the loyalties it has fostered. We expect, however, that debate will continue over whether Social Credit is the appropriate vehicle given an NDP "threat" which is unlikely to weaken significantly. The party is an alliance in the electorate *and* in the legislature. Future close calls such as that in 1979 could lead former Liberals and Conservatives in the party to demand leadership changes to assist the party in reaching their former co-partisans who have remained aloof from provincial politics or who are reluctant to endorse Social Credit until it sheds more features of the W.A.C. Bennett era. However, the solid Social Credit victory in 1983 seems to have reinforced W.R. Bennett's hold on the party organization and on the party's support base.

Still, at the mass level, loyalty to Social Credit, at least among former Liberals and Conservatives, may reflect the type of party attachment discussed by W. Phillips Shively in analysing party systems with salient class or ideological divisions. According to Shively:

> Such association differs from party identification . . . in that there is no direct tie to the party. The party itself is not a guide to voting choice, but is rather an expression of that choice. Expressed partisanship, then, will be synonymous with the vote and parties as such will not serve as guides to organize behavior. Under the proper organizational circumstances, support for such parties may be quite volatile, if various parties compete to represent the same class.[11]

The applicability of this model of partisanship to B.C. is supported by several pieces of evidence. While 65 per cent of the electorate agree with the statement that B.C. elections are contests between free enterprise and socialism, over 80 per cent of former Liberals and Conservatives in the Social Credit camp feel this way. They have higher incomes than those who remained loyal to those parties or who switched to the NDP, and are more likely to feel that more was at stake in the 1975 provincial election, the election which ousted the NDP, than in 1979. The contingent quality of their support for Social Credit is further indicated by the fact that over 50 per cent would switch to another party in order to prevent victory by a party they strongly disliked. In this they are joined by an equal proportion of those who have never had any party loyalty other than Social Credit. This proportion is twenty points higher than among those who have always been New Democrats or who switched to the NDP from the Liberals.

The NDP is not immune to the possible effects of strategic voting—half the former Tories and Socreds now loyal to the party would consider second-choice voting, but given the policy focus of many of its adherents and its history as a programmatic mass party we suspect it could be vulnerable to policy disagreements. The party's rise to a competitive position was rapid and unexpected, leaving it, many believe, unprepared to govern in 1972 and then torn between the objectives of implementing democratic socialism and seeking re-election. Further movement towards the centre might cost it the campaign effort or lead to abstention of those who have never supported any other party.[12] Indeed, two of the six candidates in the race to succeed Dave Barrett as party leader in 1984 stressed the need for more, not less, attention to the party's socialist ideals and grass roots activists. One of them, Robert Skelly, defeated the first-ballot leader, David Vickers, who was widely perceived as someone who would extend the appeal to the centre. Movement towards the left further cements the Social Credit alliance and makes the NDP vulnerable to policy appeals from Social Credit, whose credibility is enhanced by the presence of so many prominent former Liberals and Conservatives in government. In short, while Social Credit may appear more vulnerable to defections based on strategic considerations, it may also have more freedom to manoeuvre on policy questions. That freedom was clearly demonstrated by the rightward movement which followed the 1983 election.

REGIONAL TRENDS IN PARTY SUPPORT, 1966-1979

The Social Credit party under W.A.C. Bennett was widely perceived to be a party of the interior. Bennett himself served as the MLA for the Okanagan from 1941 until his retirement in 1972. His rise to power coincided with the rapid growth of Social Credit organization in the interior and the retreat of the Liberals and Conservatives to upper status bastions in the Vancouver area and Victoria. He cemented his party's electoral grip on the area with massive highway construction and resource development schemes. Nevertheless, an analysis of election results suggests that the 1972-79 realignment evident from survey data was prefigured by changes in the regional basis of party support at least as early as 1966.

As an aid to the discussion which follows, the major regions of the province used in our analysis are represented in Figure 2. The province's population is heavily skewed to the southwest, with approximately 60 per cent concentrated in metropolitan Vancouver and Victoria. Vancouver and its closest suburbs (Burnaby, New Westminster, Richmond, and the north shore cities of North and West Vancouver) contain approximately 55 per cent of the provincial electorate. But these communities return only 33 per cent of the members of the provincial legislature. Non-metropolitan ridings thus have an exaggerated electoral importance and with the dependence of the province on the resources sector and the spread of economic development, they have increased in political significance.

Although Figure 1 indicates no interesting net province-wide shift before 1972, the province-wide figures mask important changes in particular regions. The raw material for a regional analysis appears in Table 8, which gives party shares of each region's popular vote from 1966 to 1979.[13] The figures in Table 9 are derived from tests of the trends over time in support for each party.

The trends were measured using a statistical technique (regression) which tests the fit between the observed elections results—vote shares in each region from 1966 to 1979—and a straight line drawn through those observations. The slope of that line, b_1 in the table, measures the strength and direction of the trend over time. A large, positive value indicates a substantial election-to-election increase for a given party in the specified region. For example, the +6.9 figure for the NDP in Greater Victoria suggests that, on average, NDP support increased by 6.9 percentage points between each election from an estimated base (b_0 in the table) of 8.6 per cent in 1966. The third statistic in the table, R^2, varies between 0 and 1, and may be interpreted as a measure of how close the actual election results are to the line drawn through them. The closer R^2 is to 1, the closer the observed points cluster along the line.

Whatever the variation in a region, the character of 1966-79 changes differs profoundly between Social Credit and the NDP. For Social Credit, one can hardly speak of a trend. The trend lines (b_1s) calculated for Social Credit typically have small slopes. In most regions, the departure of each election from trend is greater than the average inter-election increment in the Social Credit base. The statistical measure of the consistency of the trend, R^2, is weak except in the Upper Status Vancouver region. Social Credit flux has been governed apparently by election-specific factors, among

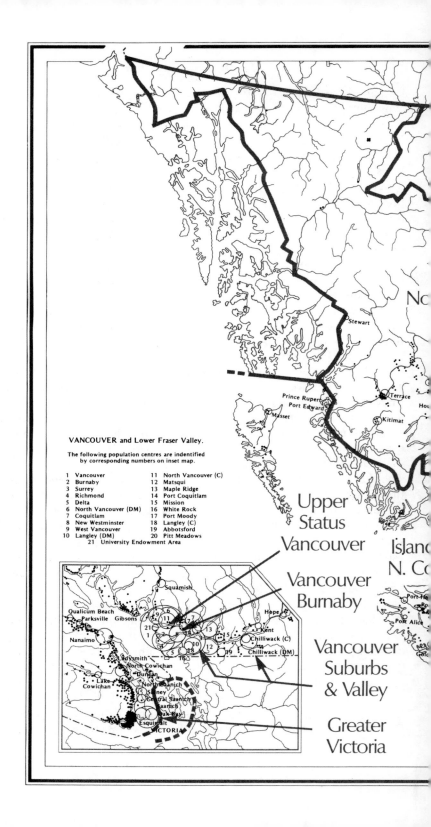

VANCOUVER and Lower Fraser Valley.

The following population centres are indentified
by corresponding numbers on inset map.

1	Vancouver	11	North Vancouver (C)
2	Burnaby	12	Matsqui
3	Surrey	13	Maple Ridge
4	Richmond	14	Port Coquitlam
5	Delta	15	Mission
6	North Vancouver (DM)	16	White Rock
7	Coquitlam	17	Port Moody
8	New Westminster	18	Langley (C)
9	West Vancouver	19	Abbotsford
10	Langley (DM)	20	Pitt Meadows
	21	University Endowment Area	

No

Stewart

Prince Rupert
Port Edward

Terrace

Hou

Masset

Kitimat

Upper
Status
Vancouver

Island
N. C

Vancouver
Burnaby

Vancouver
Suburbs
& Valley

Greater
Victoria

Squamish

Qualicum Beach
Parksville Gibsons

Nanaimo

Hope

Kent

Chilliwack (C)

Chilliwack (DM)

Ladysmith
North Cowichan
Duncan
Lake
Cowichan

North Saanich
Sidney
Central Saanich
Saanich
Oak Bay
Esquimalt
VICTORIA

Port Ha

Por

Port Alice

Gol

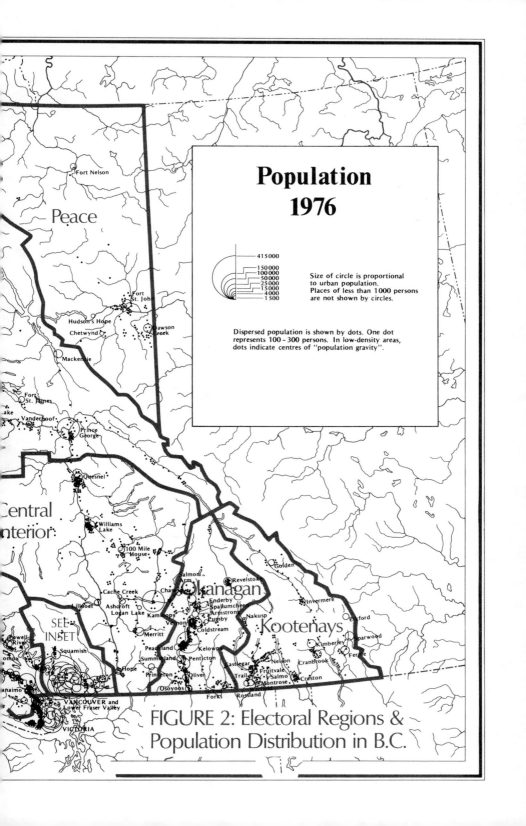

**Population
1976**

415000
150000
100000
50000
25000
15000
4000
1500

Size of circle is proportional
to urban population.
Places of less than 1000 persons
are not shown by circles.

Dispersed population is shown by dots. One dot
represents 100–300 persons. In low-density areas,
dots indicate centres of "population gravity".

FIGURE 2: Electoral Regions &
Population Distribution in B.C.

TABLE 8

B.C. PROVINCIAL PARTY SUPPORT BY REGION, 1966-79
(percentages)

	Greater Victoria	Island N. Coast	Upper Status Vanc.	Vanc. Burnaby	Vanc. Suburbs & Valley	Central Interior	Okan- agan	Koot- enays	North	Peace
Social Credit										
1966	51.5	49.4	35.3	41.5	47.9	50.7	59.2	49.5	59.1	54.5
1969	52.6	46.6	30.5	42.8	48.4	45.9	60.2	48.1	58.3	71.7
1972	29.3	29.8	23.6	30.8	31.6	34.4	42.3	35.1	35.4	44.1
1975	42.0	41.0	57.1	50.0	55.5	55.2	51.6	46.5	55.3	65.4
1979	43.0	40.7	55.2	45.5	50.3	55.9	52.2	43.7	54.2	70.9
NDP										
1966	15.6	43.0	11.2	41.1	40.1	38.5	24.9	32.2	30.4	16.9
1969	27.8	44.0	14.1	39.2	37.5	30.4	25.1	38.1	32.8	18.9
1972	21.7	54.5	15.7	46.3	44.3	39.7	31.5	49.4	41.9	20.0
1975	34.9	47.6	21.5	45.1	36.7	34.8	37.9	50.9	35.3	29.8
1979	46.7	55.4	34.7	49.6	44.2	38.6	38.8	53.0	45.3	29.1
P.C. and Liberal										
1966	20.9	7.6	53.5	16.9	11.9	10.8	15.5	18.0	10.6	18.1
1969	19.3	9.6	47.7	17.9	14.1	23.7	14.8	13.1	8.9	9.5
1972	48.8	15.4	60.6	22.6	24.0	25.8	26.1	15.5	21.9	36.3
1975	22.7	10.9	21.3	7.9	7.4	10.0	10.4	2.6	9.3	4.8
1979	8.8	3.6	6.6	3.6	5.3	4.8	9.0	3.3	0.0	0.0

TABLE 9

ASPECTS OF 1966-79 TRENDS IN THE SOCIAL CREDIT AND NDP
POPULAR VOTE BY REGION

	Social Credit			NDP		
Region	b_0	b_1	R^2	b_0	b_1	R^2
Greater Victoria	51.6	− 2.6	0.19	8.6	+6.9	0.83
Island-Coast	48.4	− 2.4	0.25	40.4	+2.8	0.60
Upper Status Vancouver	20.4	+ 6.6	0.49	5.4	+5.4	0.85
Vancouver - Burnaby	37.6	+ 1.5	0.11	37.4	+2.3	0.76
Vancouver Suburbs & Valley	43.2	+ 1.2	0.04	38.3	+0.7	0.11
Central Interior	42.5	+ 2.0	0.13	35.0	+0.5	0.04
Okanagan	59.9	− 2.3	0.25	19.5	+4.1	0.92
Kootenays	48.5	− 1.3	0.13	28.4	+5.4	0.90
North	56.3	− 1.3	0.04	27.5	+3.2	0.66
Peace	53.4	+ 2.7	0.13	12.4	+3.5	0.85
Mean	46.2	+ 0.4	0.18	25.3	+3.5	0.65

which may be strategic calculations entertained by voters seeking to avert NDP victories.

Recent years have produced some net long-term gains for Social Credit. Such a shift was especially apparent in the Upper Status Vancouver region, where several Liberal MLAs carried their mass support with them into Social Credit. Social Credit gains elsewhere did not really affect the party's competitive position. Modest Social Credit gains in the Vancouver-Burnaby region were matched almost exactly by NDP gains. Gains in the Vancouver Suburbs-Valley, Central Interior, and Peace regions only reinforced Social Credit's earlier dominance of those areas.

A very different pattern holds for the NDP. In contrast to the election-specific flux for Social Credit, the pattern for the NDP has been one of steady, secular growth. The rate of 1966-79 gain was also strongly related to the party's weakness in 1966. Even so, only in the Central Interior and the Vancouver Suburbs-Valley regions did the NDP not really grow. The greatest NDP gains of all came in the Kootenays and Greater Victoria. The party's shares grew modestly in the Vancouver-Burnaby and Island-North Coast regions, already areas of strength. More marked was the change in the North and Peace areas. In the Peace, NDP growth was matched by that of Social Credit. In the North, however, the NDP has closed the gap, making the region now very competitive. NDP growth has been even greater in two areas in which one might little expect it, the Okanagan and Upper Status Vancouver. Each region used to be one-sided, but it is now on the verge of becoming competitive. In fact, by 1984 the NDP base was sufficient to produce an upset by-election victory in North Okanagan.

The NDP trends in Table 9 pre-date 1972 and have continued through the 1970s, almost regardless of shifts to and from other parties. The typical slope for a trend line is impressive; across the ten regions, the NDP vote grew an average of 3.5 points between each election. The measure of the accuracy of the estimated trend, R^2, for an NDP 1966-79 trend line is typically four times as high as for Social Credit. In some regions (in particular, Island-North Coast, Vancouver-Burnaby, Central Interior, Okanagan, North, and Peace), one could do very well predicting the 1979 vote from a trend line calculated on the four elections from 1966 to 1975. However, 1979 also represented a peak for the NDP. In 1983 their support remained at or slightly below the 1979 level in each region except Greater Victoria. There it leaped to 51.1 per cent, perhaps the only manifestation of opposition to the public sector wage control program implemented by Social Credit.[14]

Table 10 transposes the information just described to bring out its implications for British Columbia's electoral map, using a simple measure of geographical variation in party support.[15] Smaller values of this measure, called the coefficient of variation, correspond to smaller differences between regions in the level of support for a given party.

It is clear from the table that the province has become geographically much more homogeneous than before—differences between regions in party vote shares are now quite similar. A small part of this homogenization has come from shifts in the Social Credit coalition, particularly in the Vancouver metropolitan area. Much more impressive, however, has been the geographic homogenization of the NDP vote. As the NDP province-wide share has grown from 34 to 46 per cent, the standard deviation of that vote distribution across the ten regions has shrunk.[16] Table 10 suggests that, as the Liberal and Conservative coalitions withered, the NDP and Social Credit came to mirror each other and that the NDP is now no more heterogeneous geographically than Social Credit.

TABLE 10

GEOGRAPHIC CONCENTRATION OF THE SOCIAL CREDIT AND NDP VOTE, 1966-83

| | Social Credit | | NDP | |
	Standard deviation	Coefficient of variation	Standard deviation	Coefficient of variation
1966	7.3	0.15	11.7	0.40
1969	11.1	0.22	9.5	0.31
1972	6.1	0.18	13.5	0.37
1975	7.4	0.14	8.7	0.23
1979	8.8	0.17	8.3	0.19
1983	8.6	0.16	8.1	0.19

NOTE: Standard deviations and coefficients of variation calculated over the ten regions in Table 8. A small value for the coefficient of variation indicates less regional variation in party support.

The geographic stereotypes of both Social Credit and the NDP no longer hold. The image of Social Credit as a party of the province's interior and farming regions is no longer warranted. While it is true that Social Credit still has vote surpluses in the Peace and the Fraser Valley, it no longer dominates other non-metropolitan regions. At the same time, Upper Status Vancouver has become one of the party's very bastions, while in other parts of metropolitan Vancouver the party is certainly competitive. The NDP, meanwhile, has become at least as much a party of the interior and the northern parts of the province as it is a party of Vancouver. Even Victoria is now an NDP stronghold. The stereotypical image of each party is not really warranted even for seats. The NDP holds eight, or 35 per cent of the twenty-three seats in metropolitan Vancouver and fifteen, or 44 per cent, of the seats in the rest of the province.[17]

In short, the last fifteen years have produced a sea change in British Columbia's party system. No longer is the opposition NDP too far behind the governing Social Credit party to be a serious threat. Each major party now enters competition with roughly equally sized bases, at least so far as the official returns allow us to infer underlying party loyalties. This competitive system has come about through the steady secular growth of the NDP vote. Social Credit, in contrast, has recorded marked net gains only in Upper Status Vancouver, and there only through the co-optation of Liberal MLAs and their respective mass followings. The growth in the NDP vote has been inversely related to earlier strength, such that the party now is geographically as homogeneous as Social Credit.

SOURCES OF PARTY SYSTEM TRANSFORMATION

Both survey and aggregate data point to the same conclusion—a nearly even division of the electorate between parties perceived to offer very different political agendas, and a division which has developed steadily over time and across space. The pattern seems straightforward, but what is one to make of it? We think the political change reflects underlying changes in the province's economy.

In both private and public employment, increasing numbers of British Columbians find themselves in work settings which encourage NDP support. Geographically, such work settings are now fairly common throughout the province. In the Interior and the North, as in the older industrial areas, many British Columbians work in large-scale, capital intensive firms. Work relations throughout the province are often impersonal and mediated by unions. Union membership tends to insulate individuals against relatively conservative political influences at the same time as it connects those individuals to a province-wide social influence network favouring the NDP. The argument takes on special force for public employees. The latter may have a direct stake in public sector growth, as advocated by the NDP, and are better protected against partisan reprisal than they were before full collective bargaining rights were granted.[18] Legislative proposals presented by Social Credit following the 1983 election threatened to curtail those rights very dramatically. They even included a provision allowing the dismissal of public employees "without cause." The offending clause has been eliminated but public sector unions remain fearful that their position has been seriously eroded. This episode undoubtedly strengthened the ties between public sector employees and the NDP.

At the core of the changes has been a deepening and a spatial dispersion of the province's capital stock. Table 11 indicates two facets of the change. The number of employees per manufacturing firm has increased markedly and increases have tended to be sharpest in regions with the lowest average

TABLE 11

FIRM SIZE AND PRODUCTIVITY BY CENSUS REGIONS, 1967-77

	Employees per firm			Value added per employee ($000)		
Region	1967	1977	1967-77 % Change	1967	1977	1967-77 % Change
East Kootenay	25.5	36.1	+ 42%	14.4	43.0	+199%
West Kootenay	65.4	50.2	− 23%	11.1	35.5	+220%
Okanagan	16.2	44.7	+ 176%	9.1	29.7	+226%
Lower Mainland	32.8	39.3	+ 20%	11.8	30.8	+161%
Vancouver Island	45.4	54.5	+ 20%	13.8	37.6	+172%
Thompson-Lillooet	21.0	56.2	+ 168%	11.3	39.6	+250%
Central B.C.	26.9	84.2	+ 213%	10.5	40.4	+285%
Skeena-Stikine	114.2	139.4	+ 22%	16.2	44.0	+172%
Peace-Liard	13.0	35.6	+ 179%	10.2	38.8	+280%
Mean	40.1	60.0		12.0	37.7	
Standard deviation	32.1	33.3		2.3	5.0	
Coefficient of variation	0.80	0.55		0.19	0.13	

Source: Canada, Dominion Bureau of Statistics, *Manufacturing Industries of Canada: Geographical Distribution, 1967* (Ottawa: Information Canada, 1971), Catalogue 31-209; Canada, Statistics Canada, *Manufacturing Industries of Canada: Sub-Provincial Areas, 1977* (Ottawa: Supply and Services, 1980), Catalogue 31-209.

number per firm in 1967. There is now rather less variation across regions than before in firm size. Similarly, value added per employee has grown more quickly in regions in which the 1967 values were low. In each region, of course, much of the 1967-77 increase in value added is simply inflation.[19] Specific industries bear out the general pattern. In 1961, eighteen of the twenty-nine sawmills with a daily capacity over 100,000 board feet were located in the Lower Mainland or on Vancouver Island. In 1971, fifty-seven mills exceeded 100,000 board feet daily capacity; of these, forty were outside the Lower Mainland-Vancouver Island areas. Over the same period, the number of mills with less than 100,000 board feet capacity dropped drastically, while the smaller mills that remained were generally of greater than 50,000 board feet capacity.[20] An even sharper pattern holds for pulp and paper capacity. In 1961, pulp and paper mills in the Vancouver Island-Lower Mainland areas numbered eleven; outside that area only three mills existed. In 1975, the Island-Lower Mainland total had increased by only two mills, to thirteen. Outside that area the number had increased to twelve.[21] The story for mining is more complicated, but does correspond to that for manufacturing. From 1949 to 1953, over half the total provincial production originated in the Fort Steele mining division, which includes both Kimberley and the Crowsnest Pass (located in the Kootenay region in Figure 2). From 1969 to 1973, the production pattern was more dispersed. Production values from the Liard district (in the Peace region) rivalled those from Fort Steele, while a number of divisions on the Interior Plateau gained importance. In the 1970s, the Fort Steele division regained some of its prominence, with increased coal activity, but the Interior Plateau and Liard divisions remained important.[22] In sum, economic activity spread as it deepened.

It is our sense that as economic activity has become geographically more homogeneous, so has union membership. One is now as likely to encounter a union member in an Interior locale as in a Coastal one. This is not to say, of course, that everyone has become a union member. Indeed, part of the convergence of regions may have come about as union membership declined in some regions. The shift to non-union service occupations, common throughout the province, may have been especially pronounced in the metropolitan area. This is only an impression, however. It is not possible to calculate the percentage unionized of a region's labour force. Employment data and union membership data are collected in different units and union data are especially fragmentary.

TABLE 12

UNION/NON-UNION COMPONENTS OF AGE DIFFERENCES IN NDP SUPPORT

| First Election Eligible to vote | Non-union households | | | Union households | | | | (3)+(6) |
	(1) % of House-holds	(2) % x NDP=	(3) Non-union contri-bution	(4) % of House-holds	(5) % x NDP=	(6) Union contri-bution	% NDP	Total (N)
1949 or before	70	34	24	30	51	15	39	(299)
1952-60	60	28	17	40	44	18	34	(126)
1963-69	54	28	15	46	60	28	43	(166)
1972-79	46	49	22	54	60	32	55	(177)
1949-79 difference	− 24	+15	− 2	+24	+ 9	+17	+16	

NOTES: (a) A respondent is classed as living in a union household if any member of the household, the respondent or otherwise, is reported to be a union member. (b) Only respondents eligible to vote in 1979 provincial election are included.

We do have information about the effect of union membership from our survey. Age differences in the survey should reflect the historical patterns in union membership and party growth. The reflection will not be precise, of course, as individuals may move into or out of unions at any point in their careers just as they may switch parties; immigration clouds the picture as well. Table 12 gives the components of age differences in NDP support. From older to younger groups, union membership increases, from 30 per cent to 54 per cent of households. Some of this may reflect the presence of retired persons in the oldest group. But the pattern holds across the three remaining groups, none of which will contain persons retired for reasons of age. In each age group, the union/non-union difference in NDP identification is substantial. Thus, the simple growth in union membership must have been a factor in NDP growth. In the 1963-69 group, the difference made by union membership is especially great. So far, then, the data seem to confirm the interpretation above. But the 1972-79 group indicates a diversification of the NDP coalition. Union growth was clearly a factor for the relatively young voters, as it was for older groups. But in the youngest group, the NDP percentage among non-members is impressively large, and the union/non-union difference is smaller than in the immediately older group. This may represent the addition of middle class voters, interested in environment and natural resource issues and the like, to the NDP coalition,[23] a possibility which is explored further in chapters 5 and 6.

Public employees deserve special mention. Provincial public employment, broadly defined, grew more quickly from the mid-1960s to the mid-1970s in British Columbia than elsewhere. From 1965 to 1975, the number of tax returns from direct employees of the province (but not of provincial Crown corporations) increased by 88 per cent. The national average increase was 73 per cent. Even more telling, the number of educational employees increased by 62 per cent in British Columbia, but by only 35 per cent in the country as a whole. "Institutional" employment (mostly in health care) grew by 107 per cent in British Columbia, and by only 73 per cent in the country as a whole. In each of these categories, more than two-thirds of the 1965-75 employment growth took place between 1972 and 1975.[24] Not only did the NDP government sponsor the greatest growth in the sector, but the NDP also furthered its unionization. The impact of these changes may have been especially large in Greater Victoria, the region with the most NDP growth, but public sector growth should have been a factor elsewhere in the province. Further consideration of the electoral significance of these developments is postponed to chapters 5 and 6, to allow a fuller comparison with other sources of party support. The apparent public sector/private sector division revealed here is, in fact, a major factor in the choice between provincial parties.

CONCLUSION

This chapter has documented the main feature of provincial electoral politics in the 1970s: the growth of the NDP, its capture of a substantial share of the political centre, and the transformation of the Social Credit party to meet this challenge. Both parties expanded the coalitions with which they entered the decade.

Additions to the Social Credit coalition reflect strategic decisions among the political élites who abandoned the Liberals and Conservatives and helped resurrect Social Credit between 1972 and 1975 and among members of the electorate who became convinced that the only way to defeat the NDP was to unite behind the strongest alternative. Disenchantment with the NDP was a factor too—many voters believed it had failed to live up to its responsibilities for financial management.

NDP growth came largely through the expansion of its traditional constituency into the interior of the province as well as its success in securing support among state employees and other groups linked to the expansion of state activity, especially in social policy areas, during the 1960s and 1970s. Attachment to the NDP more often reflects policy or ideological beliefs, frequently associated with concern for the externalities of rapid economic development and resource exploitation. These factors certainly help account for the share of the Liberal and Conservative electorates the party obtained.

Economic development and resource policy play an even deeper role, we believe, than our survey data indicate. But the role is ironic: the real father of the new NDP is W.A.C. Bennett. Development of the resource economy was absolutely central to the Social Credit program in the 1950s. The development strategy, involving inducements to large-scale private investment and massive infrastructure investments by the government itself, not only added greatly to the province's capital stock but also dispersed it much more evenly over the landscape than had earlier development episodes. As a result, resource sector employment outside Vancouver and a few coastal mill towns is now much more likely than before to be in large-scale, unionized firms. Paralleling these developments was a transformation of employment in the public sector. Numbers in public and para-public employment grew, jobs became less seasonal and came to include many white collar skills, and the sector became unionized. We believe, then, that just as change in the Social Credit coalition was a response to NDP growth, the growth of the NDP was an outcome of Social Credit policy.

We will return to the patterns revealed in this chapter as we analyse the attitudes and behaviour of the province's voters in more detail. The clash of ideologies represented by Social Credit and the NDP meets little competition thanks to realignment, but the economic transformation which underlay it has complicated the relationship between class and party so prominent in accounts of B.C. politics. Public sector or private sector employment, employment in traditional or modern sectors of the economy, and class composition of neighbourhoods all turn out to be crucial determinants of individual support for competing views of the proper economic and policy role for government. Moreover, despite modernization, exemplified by development of the interior and the growth of the public sector, populism has not lost its power to rally voters.

In the next chapter we will explore this and other characteristics of the B.C. political community, including the perceptions its members have of their role in the political system. We also begin detailed consideration of the ideological currents which flow through contemporary politics to shape the relationship between parties and voters. This chapter has identified the major structural changes in the British Columbia economy, social structure, and party system which provide the backdrop for that analysis.

4

British Columbia as a State of Mind

by David J. Elkins

The Greeks believed that the politics of a group could be understood in terms of character, chance, and circumstance.[1] Modern social scientists use a different terminology to say the same thing: politics is a function of political culture, history, and social and physical context. Space does not allow a chronicle of British Columbia history, although parts of this are recounted in other chapters; but this chapter will endeavour to outline several important aspects of the political culture (or character) of British Columbians and the circumstances in which they find themselves today. These circumstances or contexts include, in this chapter, the physical setting, many features of the social and demographic environment, and some contrasts between B.C. and the rest of Canada. Other chapters continue the story in other contexts (such as the work-place) and analyse the many ways in which British Columbians relate to Canada and its national institutions.

A theme which has already emerged and is developed further in this chapter concerns the contradictory images of B.C. and the apparent ambiguities and contradictions within most British Columbians. British Columbia operates two distinct party systems. It is isolated from Canada—and many people are proud of that—but steadfastly attached to Canada—and they are proud of that too. It is a very British place, but with the highest proportion of Asian-born Canadians of any province. It is a place which has welcomed immigrants from scores of countries and migrants from other provinces, but it has a history—like Canada itself—of racism, intolerance, and smugness.[2] It has British parliamentary institutions and a free press; but its legislature is an arena for bitter and vicious acrimony as much as debate, and journalism (with a few exceptions) is as yellow as anywhere in Canada. It is famous for an affluent, "laid-back" life-style, but it manifests Canada's highest rates of alcoholism and suicide. If ambiguity and contradiction are hallmarks of Canadian identity, as many argue, then B.C. is the most Canadian of provinces.

SOME FACTS AND MYTHS, BUT WHICH IS WHICH?

The images and interpretations begin with the land itself: what would be there even without people? As we bring people, history, and institutions into the picture, the land changes, but it is always present as "ground" to our "figure," as friend and antagonist, as wealth and as cost. Distance is real when measured physically, but distance in its richest sense is a human invention. A sub-theme of the ambiguity and contradiction theme will be the ways in which the physical setting—and the economic and social activities it makes possible or necessary—give meaning to the old cliché that Ottawa is 3,000 miles from B.C., but B.C. is 30,000 miles from Ottawa.

British Columbia is usually portrayed as standing apart from the rest of Canada, walled off by the imposing barrier of the Rocky Mountains. But nearly one-fifth of B.C. lies east of the Rockies in the Peace River area, which is closely tied to the economy of Alberta. As demonstrated in the previous chapter, this region still resists being incorporated into the competitive two-party battle in provincial politics. The Rockies are probably most people's predominant image of B.C. They figure prominently in travel brochures; they symbolize the wildness of which B.C. partakes; and they perhaps make concrete the image of leisure and the "west coast life-style." Yet the picture postcard resorts are in Alberta (Banff, Jasper, Waterton Lakes); and the majority of the resorts and recreational areas of B.C. are not in the Rockies but in the Coast Mountains (which are far wilder and more "remote" though closer in miles than the Rockies), in the dry interior, and in the lush islands just off the coast.

The other major image of B.C., no doubt, is the sun shining on bright new buildings in Vancouver with snow-covered mountains in the background. Atypical as that image is for anyone who lives in Vancouver, it captures another set of complexities or contradictions about B.C., those involving weather. Although changeable, the weather is, everyone knows, mild and comforting, unlike the humidity of Ottawa or the savage winter storms of Atlantic Canada. It is true that the range of variation of seasonal temperatures is relatively small in Vancouver, Victoria, and nearby places. But eighty miles north of Vancouver, the ski season at Whistler is two to three months longer than any in eastern Canada. A hundred miles further inland there is desert and rattlesnakes. The range of heat and cold in the interior (let alone the north) is as great as can be found in any of the settled areas of Canada.

When I tell you about an eagle riding the thermals for twenty minutes without moving, you may assume that this is what one expects in the many wilderness parks of rural B.C. But the one I saw was visible from my office window. It lives in the University Endowment Lands near the University of

British Columbia. Likewise, bears are just as common in the back yards of North Vancouver and West Vancouver as they are in Quesnel, Seton Portage, or Sooke. All of which confirms outsiders' view that B.C. is still frontier, the wild west, gold rush country.

Daniel Elazar, in describing the political cultures of the United States, writes of the importance of "the continuing frontier." By this he means "the constant effort of Americans to extend their control over their environment for human benefit and the consequent periodic reorganization of American social and settlement patterns as a result of the impact of that effort."[3] Canada and B.C. have their continuing frontiers too. And like the United States, that means they are old and young at the same time, another ambiguity or contradiction. Old in the sense that most of the economic activities—forestry, mining, fisheries—were begun long before Canada existed. Young in the sense that the explosion of population, investment, growth, and development occurred very recently, indeed mainly since World War II. And the new growth areas like northeast coal keep alive the feeling of a frontier, even if that frontier consists of expensive and sophisticated equipment and the building of containerized port facilities at Prince Rupert. What kind of frontier is it in which fishermen own boats costing hundreds of thousands of dollars, catch their limit in six weeks of the year, and complain about the paperwork involved in collecting unemployment insurance in the off season?[4]

If it is myth that B.C. is "cut off" by the Rockies, it is nevertheless true that B.C. was isolated from the rest of Canada for a long time.[5] As late as 1903, there was no road from Alberta to the coast. Only in the 1950s were the highways paved from Calgary and Edmonton to Vancouver. It is not the case that British Columbians want to be cut off—they participate actively in the federal political system; and, after all, the great lure of joining Confederation was the transcontinental railway. Important as that link was—for Canada as well as B.C.—the distances were so immense and the route within B.C. so twisting and slow that few bothered or could afford to travel across the continent. Now, of course, there are jet airplanes to whisk travellers in a matter of hours to any part of Canada. Distance has thus been redefined. Despite these feats of technology, it still takes longer to get from Vancouver to Newfoundland than to Tokyo. And from Nanaimo or Kimberley, it takes a lot longer.

Of equal significance, B.C. is cut off from itself.[6] The dry plateau of the Cariboo-Chilcotin is hemmed in on all sides by one or another range of mountains. Small towns deemed next door to each other by eagles might as well be in different provinces as far as road connections are concerned. Vancouver Island resisted strongly its amalgamation with the mainland in one province because of the historical differences in development, the barrier of water travel, and the "threat" of New Westminster and later Vancouver as a rival. There are still intermittent murmurings of secession from B.C. by the people of the Peace River country and of the southeastern corner (the Kootenay area). There are many communities which can even today be reached only by float plane or boat, weather permitting. It is not hard, therefore, to understand why B.C. has the largest fleet of ferries in the world, why it has one of the largest fleets of float planes, why it has so many railroad tunnels, why its highways department has such a large budget, why it has pioneered the use of satellite and other technology in the delivery of educational services, and why it feels the need for its own railroad to compensate for what is viewed as neglect by Canadian Pacific and Canadian National.

For all of the problems of internal communication and transport, there is a perception that B.C. is still fairly homogeneous. It is believed to be a very British place. If this means that B.C. is not French, one can hardly disagree, even though there is a French community which pre-dates Confederation, and French immersion schools are flourishing. Likewise, B.C. is very British in being a former British colony, many of whose institutions and traditions were imported and took root—as they did in eastern Canada—before Confederation. Unlike Alberta and Saskatchewan, which were established by the federal government, B.C. was a settled British outpost in the mid-nineteenth century, and the street names in Vancouver, Victoria, and elsewhere stand tribute to that history. This, together with its early resource-based industrialization, give it more in common with Ontario than with the agrarian West.

Despite that side of its history, B.C. has been peopled by an extraordinary variety of races, cultural groups, and mixes of all sorts. The figures from any census will reveal the proportions who spoke other languages than English or French, who came from other countries, or who moved from elsewhere in Canada. As late as 1881, a majority of the population of B.C. was Indian,[7] and even today, according to the 1981 census, B.C. has a higher proportion of Native peoples (more than 3 per cent) than any other province and nearly double the proportion for Canada as a whole.[8] Although more than 16 per cent of the residents of Canada were born in some other country, according to the 1981 census, the figure for B.C. is 23.3 per cent. Furthermore, B.C. has twice the proportion of Asian-born citizens (4.9 per cent) as does Canada (2.3 per cent). One-quarter of all Asian-born Canadians reside in B.C.

The population of B.C., of course, partakes of the same cleavages and social backgrounds as Canadians generally—predominantly European, with the British groups constituting the largest bloc. The mixture, however, is quite different in important respects. Take religion. Whereas (in 1981) 47 per cent of Canadians were Catholics, 41 per cent Protestants, and 7 per cent claimed no religion, the comparable figures for B.C. were 20 per cent Catholic, 55 per cent Protestant, and 21 per cent no religion. Nearly one-third of all Canadians who claim to have no religious affiliation live in B.C.

More vivid than raw figures, however, are a few striking facts and impressions. Vancouver has the second largest Chinese community of any city outside of Asia (second only to San Francisco). Half the children in the Vancouver public school system have English as their second language.[9] (Those with English as their first language seem to prefer the French immersion schools!) If transported blindfolded to Vancouver International Airport on a Sunday morning, when the Japan Air Lines, Cathay Pacific, and Canadian Pacific 747s arrive full of immigrants and travellers, one might wonder if this were Bombay, Manila, Hong Kong, or Tokyo.

This diaspora is not confined to Vancouver. Every small town has its old and new families of Chinese, Japanese, east Indians, Germans, Finns, Dutch, and others. Every town has at least one restaurant serving "Chinese and Canadian" food, and probably crepes, tacos, and pizza as well.

The population is ever renewed by in-migrants, and the long-term residents always appear to be on the move to other parts of the province. The 1981 census reveals that only 46 per cent of British Columbians were born there; 31 per cent were born in other parts of Canada; and 23 per cent in other countries. More and more, of course, the people who have moved to B.C. and stayed have raised their children there; and thus new generations may appear more settled. One wonders, though, if that is any more significant than 1,000 new arrivals per week. Even if the proportions of in-migrants and internal migrants drops, the absolute numbers are high. Like the ambiguous facts about distances, terrain, weather, and communication, the complex facts about the population set limits, pose problems, and offer opportunities to parties, movements, and governments. These are circumstances worth attention in their own right; but they have played their roles as well in shaping the character—or political culture—of British Columbians. Indeed, complexity and diversity make the consensus which does exist even more remarkable.

POLITICAL CULTURE, POLITICAL STYLE, AND POLITICAL CONFLICT

In our usage, political culture refers to a framework for action rather than a set of specific actions or beliefs.[10] It consists of largely unspoken assumptions about the world, so "taken for granted" most of the time that they have become "second nature."[11] Political cultures differ, among other ways, in the range of actions deemed appropriate, possible, plausible, or decent. Some things are done; others are so far beyond the pale that one never seriously considers them. To participate in a culture, one must instinctively think only about choices within the range of the acceptable.

Conflict can occur, and even be quite virulent, within this range; thus, political culture does not determine political choices and policies so much as rule out those never considered. To take a recurrent situation as an example, when a candidate loses an election in Canada, he considers certain options: ask for a recount, give a grudging concession speech, concede that the best person won, think about running again or not, and so on. No defeated candidate in Canada contemplates assassinating his opponent; nor do defeated governments call out the army, police, or RCMP to retain power illicitly. These are nevertheless logical possibilities and ones which occur frequently in some cultures. The fact that the former possibilities occur and the latter are not even considered reflects the nature of Canadian and British Columbian political culture. Within the range of conceivable actions, political culture plays no part in determining which one an individual will undertake. That choice derives from contingent circumstances, such as the closeness of the vote, the candidate's personality, the advice of friends, and the like, for the example just given.

In what follows, I propose to examine several features of political culture in B.C. which help to define the range of the possible. In most instances, we will find that, for all their differences and for all the commotion attendant on elections and legislative activities, the major political parties in B.C. partake of a common political culture.[12] Only in one major way do they appear to constitute separate sub-cultures. This area of difference, of course, will loom large in later chapters about partisan politics. To argue, however, that the parties share and are rooted in a common culture does not rule out profound policy disagreements or bitter personal rivalries. Quite the contrary. The nature of B.C.'s political culture — active, participative, populist, moralistic, and striving — ensures that *within the range of the acceptable*, the choice among alternatives is seen by the actors as momentous and consequential, in short, worth fighting over.[13]

Before turning to the "framework," the salient features of B.C. political culture, it may be helpful to see concretely what have been some of the deeper agreements underlying partisan conflict. Selective and incomplete as these examples must be, they reveal something of the style of B.C. politics, as well as something of the usefulness of this way of conceptualizing political culture. They also reveal that B.C. political culture is a variant of a broader Canadian political culture, albeit with its own peculiarities.

Suppose a visitor from Europe learned that the governments of British Columbia:
1. bought a railroad from its private sector owners and ran it at a deficit for more than six decades,

2. nationalized (or provincialized) the world's largest ferry system,
3. expropriated B.C. Electric and turned it into a provincial Crown corporation,
4. pioneered the granting of subsidies for second mortgages on residential property,
5. owned and operated a coal mine, a smelter, several towns, and the largest bus and transit system in the province,
6. founded a university world-famous for radical political activity and innovative programs, and
7. created one of the largest holding companies in Canada out of Crown-owned assets and *gave* the shares to its citizens.

Such a European visitor would be forgiven for concluding that B.C. had been governed for a very long time by a militant socialist or social democratic party. Yet all of these actions were taken by outspokenly anti-socialist parties claiming to bear the banner of free enterprise. All were accomplished by Social Credit except for B.C. Rail, which was acquired by a Liberal government in 1918. Furthermore, Social Credit, while doing most of these things, ran against a party—first the CCF and later the NDP—which advocated most of them itself; but they convinced the voters that the battle lines were "free enterprise" versus "socialism."

In presenting the case for Social Credit as an activist, interventionist government, examples more in keeping with its image as conservative or "right-wing" have been left aside. The end of the chapter returns to some recent events which might be seen in that light, but they too are understandable in terms of B.C. political culture.

Likewise, during its three years in power, the NDP undertook some actions which were opposed by Social Credit and other parties and which might be judged even more "socialist" or "leftist" than the seven listed above. These included setting up the Insurance Corporation of B.C. (and prohibiting private insurers from entering into competition with it), revising the Labour Code to give unions and workers a greater voice, expanding the civil service, trying to raise mining royalties (and failing to do so), raising forest stumpage fees over the outcry of the companies (and, ironically, watching the profit margins of the companies increase for a time), and greatly toughening pollution control standards (and then later weakening the standards).[14]

Nevertheless, rancorous legislative debates, extravagant campaign rhetoric, and partisan acrimony have often masked the underlying consensus about what is good for B.C. As Edwin R. Black has phrased it, B.C. politics revolves around "exploitation": how to harness a bountiful nature, achieve economic progress, and spread the benefits around.[15] The means to these ends are debatable, although not always contested; and that sort of dispute or even disagreement over some goals should not blind us to the apparent consensus on many political goals.

Equally important, one must recall how Canadian the above examples are. The first great nation-building enterprise, supposedly, was the use of public monies to finance a private railroad. How are Social Credit policies more ambiguous or more socialist than that? The public power-generating capabilities of the Ontario government were only the beginning of a trend in all provinces. Herschel Hardin has written about "public enterprise culture" as the quintessential Canadian way.[16] Medical and hospital care, publicly supported universities, "incentives" to businesses to locate in peripheral regions, federal ownership of Air Canada, and Alberta's ownership of Pacific Western might also be offered as contexts within which to reflect on B.C. political choices.

The fact that a party or government has many arrows for its bow—and not all of a type—should occasion no surprise. Call it inconsistency or compromise or pragmatism; parties and governments do try to satisfy diverse needs, to placate disparate interests, and to pursue a broad range of policies. In a competitive political system, that is how to get elected and re-elected. That is also why the study of political culture can reveal important aspects of provincial politics, since parties, leaders, and candidates operate within limits set by political culture and reflect to some degree the contours of the society they seek to lead and shape.

In the following discussion, parties will mean "parties in the electorate" rather than the elected members of the Legislative Assembly, the leaders, or the active workers in their organizations. Whether looking at élites or at their "followers" or supporters, one can always find individual cases which do not fit the general patterns outlined below. Interesting as those deviant cases are, the concern here is with the general thrust of party sub-cultures: all things considered, is the average Social Credit supporter different from an average NDP supporter? Are the ranges of variation within each party so great that inter-party differences pale by comparison?

On many matters of style and some matters of belief or ideology, there is little difference between the NDP and Social Credit supporters. This will be demonstrated in the next two sections, which treat political efficacy and trust and aspects of populism. On one major aspect of ideology, however, the parties stand opposed. That aspect of ideology, called "individual versus collective responsibility," partakes of elements of liberalism and conservatism but is not equivalent to these standard slogans. It appears superficially similar to "free enterprise versus socialism"—and may help to explain the continuing appeal of that slogan—but it is a fundamentally different orientation. The fact that these major political forces diverge on this dimension might be taken as evidence that it is not a "cultural" factor; but their agreement on the nature of the dimension to be contested reflects a profound consensus within the political culture.

EFFICACY, TRUST, AND CITIZEN TYPES

Political *efficacy* refers to a person's belief that he can, if he tries, have a say about political matters of concern to him. It does not, of course, reference a megalomania, a belief that one can single-handedly dictate political solutions. It may be usefully contrasted to beliefs in divine intervention beyond human control, to beliefs about the essential randomness or irrationality of politics, and to beliefs about the operation of conspiracies beyond one's ability to comprehend. In a province characterized, as we will see, by populist ideas about the goodness and wisdom of ordinary people, it is reasonable to find that many people share the belief that "people like me" can get things done, that trying to have a say will often result in one's view being taken seriously even if more popular views may finally win out in any given instance.

Based on comparable efficacy scales in national surveys in the 1960s and 1970s, British Columbians consistently have the highest mean score of any provincial population, somewhat higher even than Ontario or the prairie provinces and considerably higher than Quebec or the Atlantic provinces.[17] Furthermore, these contrasts are not just a function of the higher income or educational levels in B.C. When one compares groups in different provinces equated in particular ways (blue collar workers, for example, or people with a specific level of schooling or income), the differences between B.C. and elsewhere are not eliminated.

Political *trust* does not refer simply to satisfaction with a particular policy, leader, or party, but to a general orientation towards the political process as a whole. It concerns the extent to which people feel that government and politicians are competent, considerate of citizens' views, and interested in the public welfare rather than their own private fortunes. It is obviously part of what one means by the legitimacy of a regime. Its obverse can take several forms—cynicism, disrespect for authority, malaise, feelings that government is hopelessly misguided or evil, or a belief that however well intentioned, politicians are simply incompetent.

Many governments retain power without a trusting populace to support them, but analysts generally call such regimes "police states" because of their reliance on military power to retain office or their use of intimidation and police surveillance. No regime is completely trusted, and none relies exclusively on terror or force and lasts for long periods. Instead, political trust is a matter of degree—to what extent are a government's view of its citizens and the citizens' views of government relatively benign and trustful?

Surveys and attitude questionnaires alone cannot answer such a question fully. One also needs to know about the degree of force or threat of force against citizens, the extent to which genuine competition occurs between political parties allowed to operate publicly, and the responsiveness of political authorities to the problems which their constituents believe are important. Since these conditions are met to a large extent in B.C.—and in Canada generally—it is meaningful to ask about the proportions of citizens who have relatively trusting views and those who are especially cynical or suspicious of governments.

Once again, British Columbians come out somewhat more trusting than do the populations of several other provinces and much more so than the citizens in Atlantic Canada or French Canadians. There is a wide variation in outlooks, to be sure; not every British Columbian expresses trust. But the highly trustful outnumber the cynical by a wider margin than in other parts of Canada. As with efficacy, so with trust, these regional variations are not eliminated or significantly reduced by controlling for social and demographic differences between areas or by focusing on particular groups to compare.[18]

Both efficacy and trust, then, constitute deep-seated orientations which are characteristic of provincial populations. As such, they reflect and indicate provincial political cultures. In the case of B.C., they suggest a culture which is supportive of active political involvement but without widespread cynicism or mistrust. The fact that these orientations are so pervasive in a polarized political setting, where many political decisions are portrayed as zero-sum—gains by one side require losses by the other—is even more remarkable.

An important question about trust concerns its coherence. If people trusted their friends or just the members of their own party or just one level of government but not the other, one might suspect that trust was simply another mask for partisanship. If it reflects political culture, then it must be a characteristic posture in regard to a wide range of political objects. In B.C., that appears to be the case; and although one cannot be sure about other provinces where comparable questions were not asked, this is probably what we would find.

For B.C., at least, trust is a coherent and characteristic outlook. The 1979 B.C. survey asked people eight questions involving trust (described in the Appendix), four about politicians and civil servants in the provincial arena and the same four about federal politics. Thus, respondents had the opportunity to express differentiated patterns of feelings about the two arenas or about politicians compared to civil servants. Some people did so; but the vast majority of respondents expressed almost identical levels of trust for all objects, or identical levels of mistrust. Hence, for purposes of analysis, one can safely combine all of these answers into a single indicator of the degree of trust in government in general.[19]

One might, at first glance, assume that efficacy and trust would be strongly correlated. After all, people who feel unable to influence politics might also feel mistrust about political operations, and those who are very trusting might as a result feel that political leaders would be responsive to them or to people like them. On the other hand, one could give plausible reasons why there would be little or no relationship between the two scales. Although trust might lead to feelings of efficacy, it might also result in feelings of apathy, of a lack of need to do anything because political figures are benign. Likewise, mistrust might generate a sense of concern or even of outrage at what politicians are up to; thus, it could stimulate or reinforce a sense of efficacy.

As it happens, there is a positive relationship between these two scales, but it is very modest. In the national studies reported by Simeon and Elkins, the correlation is positive in all regions of Canada but varies slightly from province to province.[20] In the 1979 B.C. survey reported here, the correlation is a modest +.30 (Pearson) or +.23 (tau B). From these results, we can conclude that both aspects of our reasoning are correct: for some people efficacy and trust reinforce each other, while for other people, mistrust may spawn a greater sense of efficacy; but, on balance, the former is slightly more common overall.

Since the two scales, although slightly related, are hardly redundant or tapping the same orientation, it is useful to combine them to create several types of citizen views. This leads a step further into the analysis, so that we can see not only the proportions of people who have certain attitudes but also how these are related to other attitudes and to certain kinds of political behaviour.

To create these "citizen types," each scale was divided at the mid-point, and then the two dichotomies were cross-classified to describe four types of citizens. One could, of course, divide each scale into three levels (high, middle, and low) and thereby create nine types. If one does, it turns out that the "extreme" types (high on both, low on both) reveal patterns of association with the variables reported below which are essentially the same as when one uses only four types. Thus, the simple typology will be used for convenience.[21] The creation of the types may be seen in Table 13, along with the numbers of people in each type. The slightly larger numbers in the high-high and low-low categories reflect the fact that the scales are positively correlated, as noted above. Each type has been given a name for easy reference. "Supporters" are, perhaps, the classic citizens of democratic theory, trustful but efficacious. "Critics" are suspicious of government but watchful and efficacious. Those low on efficacy but trusting are called "deferentials." And those who are suspicious or mistrustful and inefficacious are labelled "disaffected" for obvious reasons.

Helpful as it may be to know about the proportions in each type, the

TABLE 13

FOUR CITIZEN TYPES IN B.C., 1979

		Efficacy	
		High	Low
Trust in Government	High	Supporters N = 296	Deferentials N = 159
	Low	Critics N = 189	Disaffecteds N = 273

greater interest is in the way these types differ or are similar in attitudes and in political behaviour. For one thing, are these types found more often in one party than in others, or do the parties partake equally of all types? For another, do these citizen types differ in predictable ways? For example, one would expect that the disaffected would be relatively less likely to partici- pate in politics because of their mistrust and low sense of personal efficacy.

Table 14 describes the partisan shares of these citizen types. There one finds the proportions of each type in each party, where "party" is assessed by respondents' own partisan self-identification. Focusing on the NDP and Social Credit parties, since the numbers of Liberals and Conservatives are so small, one notes some differences but all types occur in substantial numbers in both parties. The differences are not unexpected. The NDP has a higher proportion of people who are disaffected and a lower percentage of supporters. This reflects a political reality which affects the scales. Since Social Credit had formed the government for the preceding period (1975-79) and for 1952-72, it is hardly surprising that fewer NDP identifiers or voters were supporters and that more were disaffected. Although the scales should ideally refer to political objects generally, it is inevitable that some partisan assessments creep in. Nevertheless, very substantial proportions of NDPers are supporters and of Socreds are disaffected; and they have equal propor- tions of critics and deferentials.

TABLE 14

PARTISAN DISTRIBUTION OF CITIZEN TYPES, 1979
(horizontal percentages)

Provincial party identification	Citizen types				
	Supporters	Critics	Deferentials	Disaffected	N
Liberal	33	27	17	23	64
Conservative	32	20	26	22	50
NDP	30	19	16	36	326
Social Credit	37	22	20	21	276
Other, none	29	21	15	36	201

The four citizen types vote in somewhat different proportions. Although many of the disaffected do vote, their rate of abstention in the 1979 provincial election, for example, was three times that of the supporters. This propensity is more easily seen if we percentage the cases in a different way: of all the people who report *not voting* in the 1979 provincial election, 46 per cent were "disaffected."

We have argued that political culture should reflect a general pattern in a population, rather than people of different backgrounds holding different views. For example, controls for several social and demographic variables did not diminish interprovincial differences on efficacy, trust, or the citizen types. Likewise, within B.C., there are very few differences among social groups in the proportions of citizen types. It is true that educational attainment (years of schooling) drops off somewhat as one moves from supporters to critics to deferentials to disaffected; but all educational levels are represented in all types. There are no significant differences, however, among citizen types in terms of social class, age, whether born in Canada or elsewhere, whether born in B.C. or in other provinces, in length of residence in B.C., or in length of residence in the local area or neighbourhood. Therefore, these political orientations are learned, but all social groups seem equally capable of learning any type.

POPULISM AND MORALISM

In discussing the hypothetical European visitor to B.C. above, emphasis was placed on fundamental similarities underlying the apparent differences between the major provincial political parties. This section describes the political cultural foundations of this deep consensus; and the next section explores and characterizes the axis of partisan—or sub-cultural—differentiation. The subtle interplay of similarities and differences has been well stated, for these parties at least, by Premier Bill Bennett. Shortly after becoming premier, he was quoted as saying: "No party of the extreme right or the extreme left can survive. We are a populist party slightly to the right of centre. The NDP is a populist party slightly to the left."[22] Populism tempers NDP and Social Credit differences on many potentially contentious issues such as the seven listed above, makes them attractive to the vast majority of British Columbians as is evident from the trends in vote shares outlined in Chapter 3, and makes them "blind" to many institutional, policy, and ideological options available to non-populist parties. However, as the next chapter demonstrates, populism is also a source of division within each party.

Populism in North America originated as an agrarian reform movement in the United States in the late nineteenth century.[23] The first major group was called the People's party, a name which accurately summarized its tone or outlook—people, the little people, mattered more than institutions, especially rich and powerful ones like banks and railroads or even legislatures. This outlook found ready acceptance in the Canadian prairie societies of the first third of this century.[24] The deeply felt grievances against banks, the Canadian Pacific, and "eastern interests" more generally rallied prairie farmers to the ranks of several populist parties, including the United Farmers of Manitoba, United Farmers of Alberta, the Progressives, and most importantly for this analysis, the Co-operative Commonwealth Federation (now NDP) and Social Credit.

Its agrarian origins and supporters made the movement naturally suspicious of urban sophistication and led to a glorification of direct action by the people, especially the hardy and self-reliant farmers.[25] Both features have given populism a strong flavour of conservatism—small town and rural isolationism in world affairs, a moral and religious cast to its outlook, and a yearning to nurture and sustain old-fashioned values of thrift, honesty, and rectitude. The emphasis on "little people" and the "grass roots," however, has given many populist ideas a liberal flavour, most noticeably in their concern for humane treatment of ordinary folk and equality derived from a belief in the dignity of each person and of hard work.

Some scholars have therefore suggested that populism should be seen as embodying elements of liberalism and conservatism, while others have written it off as simply confused or contradictory. Another school of thought argues that there are really two types of populism—a "left" version and a "right" version.[26] The next section will return to this latter argument as it might apply to B.C. Here it is important only to note that populism appeared to participants as a consistent and reasonable outlook on political matters, whether called liberal, conservative, or something else. Analysis of public opinion data in the United States has found in recent decades a cluster of policy issues which might be called populist and which, although only loosely connected, appear to have more coherence than alternative clusters defined more strictly (from a scholar's point of view) as either liberal or conservative.[27]

Populism, like all predispositions which gain wide recognition, has thus become a label covering several distinct elements which may occur in different combinations. No longer exclusively rural or agrarian, populism crops up in diverse manifestations. At the core of all populist outlooks, however, are two related beliefs. There is a suspicion of "experts" and a concomitant trust in "ordinary people" and commonsense. In addition, there is a preference for "action," getting down to work rather than wasting time talking, and preferably simple, concrete, commonsense actions rather than the complicated schemes of experts or intellectuals.

A fair assessment of populism might conclude that it is not "really" an ideology but a mood or sentiment or style of politics. The distinction loses its force, however, when we consider populism as one pillar of the B.C. political culture, manifesting itself in ideological form as campaign rhetoric and legislative debate but also in styles of conduct and habits of thought, as assumptions or premises which are "taken for granted" by most active participants in both major parties. It is "cultural" also in that the outlook is so widely shared; and that outlook does not, as a rigid ideology would, entail very specific policies, legislation, or overarching goals. It defines a range of admissible policies and hence removes from serious consideration many other policy options.

That these views are common to both major parties and important in shaping at least some political actions is easy to demonstrate. For one thing, both parties have a long history of grass-roots activism. The NDP and the CCF before it have made a fetish out of democratic control in the party. Social Credit grew out of a tradition which thought that even political parties were dangerous instruments which could too easily lose touch with ordinary voters. Likewise, both parties—for all their use of experts, royal commissions, and other inquiries—frequently manifest signs of distrust of them. They each have set up commissions and then ignored their findings or recommendations. They have each been suspicious of universities and professors, while providing money for them. One sign of both parties' suspicions of city people and "sophisticates" concerns the emphasis on providing educational services where people are rather than having students come to Vancouver or Victoria. Hence, both parties have sponsored community colleges, technical institutes, correspondence courses, satellite campuses, and most recently the "Knowledge Network" (modelled on Britain's Open University). Clearly, education is favoured but given a populist, home-town slant.[28]

Keeping in mind these many facets of populism, the 1979 B.C. survey endeavoured to assess the extent and intensity of these feelings and beliefs. The principal measure is a Populism Scale, consisting of a number of agree-disagree items and some of a forced-choice format.[29] (See the Appendix for details.) Each respondent can thus be assessed for the degree of sharing in this major system of ideas or feelings. Similarly, one can examine groups in the population to see who shares these ideas the most and who the least. In particular, do the supporters of the NDP and Social Credit parties differ on this scale?

Although certain types of people differ in predictable ways on populism, the parties do not. Higher status occupational groups, higher income groups, the highly educated, and urban dwellers all score significantly lower on populism than the obverse groups. Yet no difference at all exists between the major parties. Even when one compares specific sub-types, such as blue collar workers or managers, across the two parties, no differences in mean scores appear. (See Chapter 5, Table 25 for the figures.) We may thus conclude that populism is a shared trait, common to both of the successful parties in B.C., even if there is a range within each party in the degree of enthusiasm for these outlooks.

Another common pattern in populist thinking, shared by Social Credit, the CCF, and the NDP, concerns moral demands. Current supporters of Social Credit and the NDP probably have different reasons for their feelings about moral rectitude—the former because of the religious convictions and fundamentalist affiliations of its members, which are now uncommon among NDPers. But one must recall the role of the Social Gospel in Social Credit and CCF origins; and one must not forget that many prominent CCF leaders (including J.S. Woodsworth, M.J. Coldwell, and Tommy Douglas) were Christian preachers, albeit of a slightly different ilk than "Bible Bill" Aberhart.

Moral fervour is alive and well in both major parties, whatever the lapses by some of their members, in the puritanical attitudes towards consumption of alcoholic beverages. Like most Canadian provinces, sales of liquor are tightly controlled by the B.C. government; and also like most, opportunities to drink on Sunday are extremely limited. The fact that the government profits enormously (hundreds of millions of dollars in taxes per year) from its beer, wine, and liquor monopoly may be another of those contradictions at the heart of Canadian identity. It may instead reflect the political consensus that drinking should "hurt," that high taxes restrict demand, and that the more profit the government makes, the more it can spend on rehabilitation. In either case, the NDP and Social Credit are fully at one on "demon rum" as a public concern.

Another manifestation of moralism derives perhaps from the nature of politics itself. Politics has frequently been characterized as "immoral" because it involves compromise, expediency, and self-interest, and particularly when there is corruption. Hence, many people find politics threatening, especially in a polarized political system which emphasizes ideological differences. The "loyal opposition" can easily come to be viewed as "the enemy," and then compromise and "give-and-take" pose threats to one's cherished values. This version of "we-they" thinking is all the more likely when the political culture is suffused with moral indignation from its populist roots; and after decades of rhetoric about "free enterprise" versus "godless socialism," everyone knows who the enemy is.

Two scales were constructed to assess these "moralism" demands.[30] One of them, called "Moral Rectitude," asks a series of questions about the demands made on political leaders. It attempts to assess the willingness to impose high moral demands on political élites, perhaps even higher than on ordinary citizens. A low scorer on this scale, on the contrary, professes to care only about getting the job done rather than politicians' methods or ethics. The second scale, called "Willingness to Compromise," isolates people who are willing to give up some principles in order to further others, to find solutions even when they do not fully measure up to one's ideal standards. The other end of that continuum, of course, highlights people unwilling to give up any principle in any degree. (Both scales are described in the Appendix.)

In Table 15, both parties contain a wide range of views on these matters. Yet the overall outlook of the two parties is quite similar. Although there is a significant difference among the three federal parties on "Compromise," there is no significant difference between the NDP and Social Credit at the provincial level. On "Rectitude," none of the partisan differences are significant either federally or provincially.

TABLE 15

SCORES ON "WILLINGNESS TO COMPROMISE"
AND "MORAL RECTITUDE" BY PARTY
(% across; mean scores)

	"Willingness to Compromise"					
Provincial party ID	*Lowest*	*Medium low*	*Medium high*	*Highest*	*Mean scores*	*N*
Liberal	7.9	23.8	42.9	25.4	2.84	63
Conservative	11.1	24.4	40.0	24.4	2.78	45
NDP	21.1	22.6	35.0	21.4	2.51	323
Social Credit	14.3	25.7	35.7	24.3	2.67	272
Federal party ID						
Liberal	7.5	25.1	43.5	23.8	2.83	239
Conservative	17.4	22.8	39.0	20.7	2.61	241
NDP	25.0	22.8	30.8	21.4	2.41	224
	"Moral Rectitude"					
Provincial party ID	*Lowest*	*Medium low*	*Medium high*	*Highest*	*Mean scores*	*N*
Liberal	29.7	20.3	31.3	18.8	4.30	64
Conservative	30.6	20.4	32.7	16.3	4.24	49
NDP	29.0	30.2	27.1	13.7	4.12	328
Social Credit	28.0	24.5	30.1	17.4	4.20	282
Federal party ID						
Liberal	33.6	20.5	28.7	17.2	4.12	244
Conservative	26.2	24.6	31.3	17.9	4.28	252
NDP	29.1	29.1	28.2	13.7	4.15	227

Without pretending that these scales capture all there is to political style or populism, they are nevertheless sufficient to draw several conclusions and suggest several speculations. First, the parties are quite similar in these respects, whatever differences one may note in regard to other matters. Second, there is a wide range of outlooks, styles, or ideological combinations within each party. This may explain some apparent inter-party differences. As leaders change, or as circumstances cause the rise or fall of certain groups' fortunes in a party, the "public face" of the party may emphasize one style more than the other party does. Dave Barrett was more populist than his predecessor, and Bill Bennett is probably less so than his father was. What does not seem to have changed, however, is the existence in both parties of the full complement of populist and moralistic outlooks. Both parties share the same range of styles and in roughly comparable degrees. Thus, to remain appealing to British Columbians—and true to their own beliefs as well, perhaps—the activists, candidates, and leaders dare not stray too far from the modal outlooks shared by the supporters of all the parties.

Third, with these outlooks so deeply embedded, one can speculate about some reasons for intense conflict to grow out of apparent consensus. With a large component of each party holding to populist views, the remaining areas of disagreement must be played up to distinguish one's own party from an opponent. Also, with so many in each party espousing an unwillingness to compromise and wanting to impose severe moral standards, leaders must give at least the appearance of toughness, of standing up for "motherhood" and all things good. Yet it must be added at once that according to Table 15 each party contains roughly equal proportions who are willing to compromise and who are relatively tolerant about moral standards. Thus, normal political deals can be consummated, even if they must be publicly announced as principled victories.

Without passing judgement on these patterns and styles, we may note that they are conducive to a politics of accomplishment.[31] They allow considerable latitude to leaders sensitive to public concerns and to the political ethos of the province and who are creative in the ways they describe what they have done. Consensus has its uses, and one of them is to take some matters out of active discussion, to help everyone to take certain things for granted, and thus to move on to the areas of remaining disagreement. In B.C., the real ideological gulf between the major parties centres on individual versus collective responsibility and risk-sharing and not on populism or moralism.

INDIVIDUAL AND COLLECTIVE RESPONSIBILITY

Liberalism and conservatism are ideological labels which mask a variety of orientations. They encompass generalized postures towards change and tradition, civil liberties and civil rights, economic equality, free enterprise and government regulation, and social planning. All of these aspects find some degree of resonance in British Columbia. An aspect of these ideologies which has particular relevance in the context of B.C., however, concerns individual versus collective responsibility for social and economic matters.

Virtually all residents of B.C. agree about prosperity, economic development, social well-being, improved health care and education, minimum welfare benefits, and individual betterment or advancement. Unfortunately, like all broad social goals, these frequently conflict. Individual economic improvements, for example, may be bought at the cost of other people's detriment. Likewise, owing to increased taxes, expenditures on health, education, and welfare — while providing benefits widely acknowledged — divert money from other uses, such as capital formation or higher real wages. Besides, agreement on goals leaves ample scope for disagreements over the means to achieve them and over the party best able to carry out the means.

In assessing the "trade-offs" among political goals and costs, two major orientations may be identified. One focuses on each individual's responsibility to do his best, take care of himself and family, and aid the common good by being a productive member of society. The other emphasizes the risks one runs in an individualistic and competitive economic system; it focuses on collective sharing of certain risks and collective benefits which can perhaps be attained only by co-ordinated actions. The latter view acknowledges that many individuals "fail" or fall behind through no fault of their own, because of illness, accident, or handicaps. Since these misfortunes can, in principle, afflict any given person, the latter view stipulates that these risks should be shared collectively. Generally this involves some form of governmental intervention, but it could in principle involve private forms of collective support such as unions or professional associations.[32] The individualist perspective — being both optimistic and fatalistic — retorts that these are the breaks, and each person must bear the costs and consequences whether positive or negative.

As may be seen, these two outlooks may coincide closely with liberalism and conservatism, but the matter is more complicated than that. Many of the benefits to be gained by collective means are individual in nature: welfare support in bad times, workers' compensation after on-the-job injuries, and educational opportunities. They are often collective, too, since clean air and water can, for example, only be attained by assuming collective responsibility and collective actions. On the other side, "free enterprise" advocates argue that collective benefits arise from the unco-ordinated actions of individuals; this is Adam Smith's "invisible hand" at work.

The 1983 sitting of the B.C. Legislative Assembly produced a bitter debate on Bill 3, the Public Sector Restraint Act, which is one of the cornerstones of Premier Bennett's package of "restraint" legislation brought down in conjunction with the July 1983 budget speech. The use of "legislation by exhaustion"—all-night sittings of the legislature to speed up passage of legislation—brought charges of "fascism" and "dictatorial" tactics from the Opposition.[33] Yet one may see in this tactic an example of the populism of the Social Credit caucus: direct action rather than dithering endlessly through the niceties of normal legislative procedure. Likewise, the content of much of the proposed legislation reflects the individualist strand in B.C. political culture. Bill 3 will reduce the job security of civil servants and other public employees, thereby (the government says) making it more difficult for people to get a "free ride" at the public's expense and "getting government off the back" of the public and businesses; all of that will in turn enhance collective well-being and prosperity. Likewise, abolition of the Rentalsman's Office and of the Human Rights Commission will put everyone on equal footing—no special favours or protection, according to the government. The Opposition, of course, portrays these (and other) bills as draconian, as shifting collective responsibilities onto the shoulders of individuals, and indeed of individuals least able to bear them.

The strong emotions aroused by the legislation might be viewed as a result of the bill's violation of political cultural norms. In fact, the Government withdrew some of the most objectionable features of Bill 3, such as the provision that employees could be fired "without cause"; and this may indicate that they overstepped cultural bounds. It also created a new code and enforcement structure for the protection of human rights, but one which critics have described as the weakest in Canada. The basic argument, however, appears to be a dispute well within the range of the acceptable in B.C. political culture. It is a classic instance of an individualist-oriented party acting on its beliefs and strenuously opposed by the party oriented to greater collective responsibility. To those who agree with the "restraint" program, it is the application of firmly entrenched principles of B.C. political culture. To its opponents, it is the working out in practice of the dark side of the political culture.

Whatever the complexities and cross-currents, when people are forced to make hard choices, as the premier claims he is doing now, they evince characteristic orientations towards individual or collective responsibility. These differ in degree depending on which risks should be shared and which personal costs should be compensated by collective benefits through taxation or government regulations. The 1979 B.C. survey tried to assess these gradations of feeling between the polarities of individual and collective responsibility by means of an attitude scale. Of course, the scale could not anticipate the exact contours of today's legislation, so it refers to general situations and the "trade-off" between individual and collective responsibilities for several types of situations. (For details, see the items listed in the

Appendix.) We can make no claims that this scale is ideal, that it is unidimensional (since it probably could not be), or that other provinces or countries might not require a modified measure. Its utility in the B.C. context will be clearly demonstrated. Later chapters make use of this scale in various ways, and thus here only an overview of these attitudes and their relationship to partisan and social sub-cultures are provided.

Table 16 summarizes the distribution of respondents on all points of the scale from most individualistically to most collectively oriented. It also indicates the way these have been combined to produce four major groups or quartiles. Tabular presentations will use the quartiles, and the mean scores will always be based on the full range of scores.

TABLE 16

DISTRIBUTION OF BRITISH COLUMBIANS
ON "INDIVIDUAL VERSUS COLLECTIVE RESPONSIBILITY"
(frequencies, percentages)

	Raw scores	Frequency	Percentage	Quartiles
Individualist	0	1	0.1 ⎫	
	1	29	4.1 ⎬	130
	2	100	14.1 ⎭	
	3	165	23.3	165
	4	208	29.4	208
	5	139	19.7 ⎫	204
Collectivist	6	65	9.2 ⎭	

The first thing to note about these results is that people take widely different positions. This orientation divides the population into a wide array of groups who differ on where responsibility should lie. It is a fundamental source of ideological cleavage. At the same time, most respondents do not take extreme positions but find themselves slightly more collectively oriented or slightly more individualistically oriented. This accords with the party positions as enunciated by Premier Bennett in the quotation above. The parties reflect the divergence of orientations and appeal to somewhat different groups, but they must recognize that the population consists of views spread along the whole continuum rather than being located only at the extremes. The "logical" mid-point of the scale is "3," exactly half-way between zero and six; and the actual mean for this sample (3.7) is slightly in the collectivist direction. In fact, more than seven out of ten respondents fall in the categories of three, four, and five. The rhetoric of "free enterprise versus socialism," on the other hand, implies a much more polarized distribution.

Table 17 presents the distribution of views on this measure for each provincial party.[34] The patterns are clear: the NDP is significantly more "collectively" oriented than any other party whether we look at mean scores or the proportion in the most collective quartile; Social Credit is very "individually" oriented; and all parties contain at least some people of each outlook. At the same time, all four party averages fall well within the range (three to five) which encompasses the overwhelming majority of the population; and the average for the population lies almost exactly mid-way between Social Credit and the NDP.

TABLE 17

PARTISAN DIFFERENCES ON
"INDIVIDUAL VERSUS COLLECTIVE RESPONSIBILITY"
(% down; mean scores)

Quartile scores	NDP	Conservative	Liberal	Social Credit
Most individualist	8	27	22	27
Medium individualist	19	27	31	26
Medium collectivist	29	19	25	33
Most collectivist	45	27	22	13
Mean scores	4.26	3.46	3.51	3.27
N	251	37	49	231

NOTE: Party measured by provincial party identification; mean scores based on full range of scores rather than quartiles.

The fact that Social Credit and the NDP diverge in the expected way accords with several features of each party. Social Credit purports to be more business-oriented, and businessmen like to claim they are individuals who stand on their own feet, take their risks and profits, and oppose government "tampering" with the economy. The NDP, on the other hand, is labour-oriented, and the labour movement has always acted on the assumption that "solidarity" is the key to success. Likewise, if we examine the candidates put forward or elected by each party, they correspond to these outlooks: small businessmen are common in Social Credit circles but rare in the NDP, and members or leaders of unions tend to gravitate to the NDP rather than to Social Credit.

From these facts, one would conclude that social classes differ in predictable ways on the question of individual or collective responsibility. Workers, especially those who are unionized, should be collectively oriented, either because of necessity or because they have learned from union activities that that is expedient. Middle class people, especially those in businesses, should have more of an individualist outlook, since that is how the free enterprise system works: profits are the positive inducement but losses are the risk one must accept, otherwise the system does not work.

As Table 18 indicates, however, there are relatively small differences between the classes. This may be seen from the mean scores at the bottom of the table. When we examine the interaction of class and partisanship, three conclusions stand out. First, in the Liberal, Conservative, and NDP parties, the middle class respondents are more collectivist than are those who identify with the working class, while for Social Credit identifiers the two main classes are equally individualist. Second, the NDP supporters are more collectivist than the supporters of any other party regardless of which class we examine; this is also true of the groups who do not think in class terms. Third, the difference between the NDP and each other party is equal to or greater than the differences between classes in any one party.

TABLE 18

CLASS AND PARTISAN DIFFERENCES IN
"INDIVIDUAL VERSUS COLLECTIVE RESPONSIBILITY"
(mean scores)

Provincial	Self-designated social class		
party identification	Middle class	Working class	None
Liberal	3.89	2.89	3.43
	(19)	(9)	(21)
Conservative	3.90	3.38	3.17
	(10)	(8)	(18)
NDP	4.43	4.24	4.18
	(61)	(98)	(91)
Social Credit	3.29	3.30	3.23
	(103)	(43)	(82)
Overall mean scores	3.74	3.87	3.65

NOTES: (a) Cell entries are mean scores on "Individual versus Collective Responsibility" scale; number of cases in parentheses. (b) "Middle class' combines people who said they were "upper middle" or "middle" class. (c) "Working class" combines people who said they were "working" or "lower" class. (d) "None" combines people who denied there were classes and those who said they never think of themselves in class terms.

How can these patterns occur? The next two chapters address this question in more detail, but we can anticipate some of the argument here. Although the patterns are complex, they reflect some simple principles. Note that in the NDP there are many more working class identifiers than middle class identifiers, whereas the opposite is the case for the other three parties. This would be expected, given what we know of the social and political appeals of the parties. Note also that one would expect middle class people who are attracted to the NDP to be more collectively oriented or to learn that norm after joining. Likewise, workers attracted to Social Credit (or Liberal or Conservative parties) should be more individualist than other workers or should come to espouse that view after joining. As further corroboration, note that the *most* collectivist group in every non-NDP party is still less collectivist than the *least* collectivist group in the NDP.

While it may be surprising that the social classes overall do not differ in mean scores on individual versus collective responsibility, this is less surprising if we think about this orientation as a cultural norm for the province as a whole. In that light, it appears reasonable to conclude that it is a general orientation widely spread throughout social groupings, in this case classes and even groups who deny class or do not think of themselves in that way. Although the data are not presented, analysis has revealed that many other social and demographic groups exhibit no differences in mean scores on this measure of ideology. For example, there are no significant differences among groups defined by interest in politics, trust in government, populism, union membership, gender, whether employed by government or in the private sector, income, or province of birth. There are some differences among groups defined by age, education, marital status, and religion; but the patterns are not easily interpretable. For example, the very young and very old are slightly more collectivist than those in between. Also, married and widowed respondents are more individualist than the single, divorced, or separated. Education differences are complex: the higher the education (years of schooling), the more *polarized* the group is over this ideology, but the average score hardly varies.

In short, orientation to social risk-sharing appears to be a cultural norm in B.C. which exists equally in virtually all groups and all sectors of society. The variations are essentially partisan: the NDP and Social Credit parties define two sub-cultures on this ideological cleavage, although we have seen they are in agreement on other aspects of style and ideology. Since the vast majority of British Columbians perceive this difference, although generally describing it as "free enterprise" and "socialism," the cleavage is clearly a central aspect of B.C. political culture and the parties compose their policies and rhetoric to fit the cultural setting. The analysis in Chapter 6 reinforces this conclusion. The principal sources of variation on the ideological cleavage revealed there—employment in the natural resource sector and residence in working class neighbourhoods—reflect the kinds of settings which one would expect to affect the transmission of sub-cultural values.

There are at least three ways of accounting for this axis of controversy within the broader cultural consensus. First, it may simply represent a disagreement over specific choices within the range of the acceptable for B.C. political culture, disagreements which have become institutionalized in two partisan sub-cultures. Second, one might argue that individualist and collectivist positions derive from two variants of populism. As John Richards and Larry Pratt have argued, "left populist" and "right populist" variants took hold in Saskatchewan and Alberta, respectively.[35] It appears reasonable to argue that both variants have firm roots in the partisan sub-cultures of British Columbia.

Third, Daniel Elazar has argued persuasively that:

> the United States as a whole shares a general political culture that is rooted in two contrasting conceptions of the American political order. . . . In the first, the political order is conceived as a marketplace in which the primary public relationships are products of bargaining among individuals and groups acting out of self-interest. In the second, the political order is conceived to be a commonwealth — a state in which the whole people have an individual interest — in which the citizens co-operate in an effort to create and maintain the best government in order to implement certain shared moral principles.[36]

These two fundamentally different conceptions of political order have been manifested, according to Elazar, in three distinct sub-cultures with regions and localities varying in the balance among the three.[37] For certain purposes, it may be useful to view B.C. political culture in terms of this framework — where two of the three sub-cultures exist in virtually equal strength. The "individualistic" sub-culture corresponds closely to the Social Credit-individual responsibility orientation identified above, although without the clear populist base found in B.C. Elazar's "moralistic" sub-culture, by its emphasis on collective and communitarian values, resembles the collective responsibility orientation of the NDP in B.C. The third sub-culture, which Elazar labels "traditionalistic," seems negligible in B.C. Ambivalent about both marketplace and commonwealth, adherents of the traditionalistic sub-culture prefer an élitist, hierarchical, paternalistic political order. In terms of origins if not always of current outlook, Liberals and Conservatives might be placed in this category; if so, that might explain in part their inability to maintain more than a foothold in the provincial arena.

It is not necessary to prefer one of these three accounts of the basis of "individual versus collective" orientations — the sub-cultural interpretation receives some empirical support later on. Perhaps all three are correct or just different ways of saying the same thing. All three agree, implicitly, that these two orientations which appear so opposed are in reality two sides of the coin of B.C. political culture. To understand B.C. politics today, one must understand the ways in which views about individual and collective responsibility permeate the political system and the ways in which intense conflict has been built on a foundation of common political styles, citizen types, and populism. That has been the aim of this exploration of B.C. political culture. The next chapter shows how the central ideological dimension affects and even reverses the conventional linkage between social class and partisanship — at least in the provincial political world.

5

The Imperatives of Social Class

To most students of comparative provincial politics British Columbia has been a refreshingly simple province to understand. Constantly renewed by immigration from abroad and by migration from other provinces, and overwhelmingly British in origin and Protestant in religion, it is relatively free from the grip of history and the ethnic and religious conflicts which shaped politics in other provinces. As a consequence, most attempts to explain the province's cleavage pattern have used variations on the theme of economic determinism. Even the anti-Orientalism so characteristic of the province for much of its history has been viewed as a predictable response to the use of Oriental immigrants "by the employing class to break strikes and lower wage rates in mining and other employments."[1]

Weakness of tradition, population flux, and the resource dominated economy have been cited by several scholars as factors accounting for the development of a bipolar political culture and a class-based party system. As Gordon Galbraith put it:

> One set of attitudes, one pole, emphasized individual achievement and economic growth. It finds its social centre of gravity among white collar workers, professionals and businessmen. Its political vehicles have been the Conservative Party, the Liberal Party, the Social Credit League, and at times all three. The second set of political attitudes emphasizes distribution of existing wealth and social egalitarianism. It finds its centre of gravity among trade unionists, and blue collar workers generally. It has found its political expression first in the Co-operative Commonwealth Federation, then in the New Democratic Party.[2]

For Galbraith it is "status anxiety" created by the experience of immigration which accounts for the need to find a place in a new society; and a simplified economy—with relatively weak manufacturing and agrarian sectors—which constrains the alternatives. His views mirror closely those of Martin Robin, the best-known analyst of the province's political history, who sees in B.C. "the persistence of the negative community, aggravated by the spirit of acquisitive individualism and by...strong regional and class sentiments."[3]

The analysis in the previous chapter poses a challenge to this interpretation which is pursued in this chapter and the next. The ideological division does exist. British Columbians do differ in the importance they attach to individualistic and collectivist values, but most of them are found near the centre when their positions on a variety of issues are taken into account. Second, while a good number of voters occupy the extremes on this dimension, there is little relationship between those locations and subjective social class position, nor a strict link between ideology and a class hierarchy based on occupational status.

There is little doubt that, compared to other provinces, a strong relationship exists between social class and partisanship in British Columbia. Yet until now, very little evidence has been available to explore the links between class and ideology or to test the view of some observers that class conflict has completely obliterated other divisions or that it pervades all aspects of life in the province.[4] Labour disputes may have been more bitter and protracted than elsewhere in Canada,[5] but a large proportion of the labour force is not unionized or is found in public sector and white collar unions which do not draw upon the same historical memories as blue collar workers. The economy is resource-based, and resource industries are dominated by large corporations and large unions, but direct employment in these industries accounts for only 10 per cent of the labour force.[6] In other words, our understanding of British Columbia partisanship requires updating to take account of the structural changes associated with the growth of state activity and the creation of new occupational groups.

Robin offers some qualifications of his own regarding the traditional view. He considers region to be a major cleavage[7] and acknowledges that "a remnant of the labour vote — older craft unionists, unorganized workers, dual unionists and chronic oppositionists — had always escaped [the socialists'] political grasp."[8] He also argues that Social Credit economic development policies have helped to divide the working class. W.A.C. Bennett advertised Social Credit as the "party of progress," the best guarantee of high-paying jobs and economic prosperity.[9] Still, these are presented as minor variations on the main theme of class division.

There have been some dissenting voices. Edwin Black takes some of the same factors cited by Galbraith and Robin — "the absence of both traditionalism and a shared past, as well as...the continuous striving of successive waves of immigrants to better themselves materially"[10] — but arrives at a different conclusion about the strength of ties between class and party. B.C. as a frontier community has encouraged populism, characterized by "an extreme orientation towards action" and "a lack of respect for traditional procedures," but these attitudes, he feels, characterize the supporters of both Social Credit and the CCF/NDP. This conclusion is supported by the analysis in the preceding chapter.

The most explicit challenges to the interpretation of B.C. politics as class politics have come from Mark Sproule-Jones and Peter Ward. Sproule-Jones argues that the extent of class voting has been exaggerated and that the parties themselves have created their followings without "an intermediate structure of group influence."[11] Social Credit, however, has had the most success in winning adherents to its "sponsored conceptual ideology," a compound of populism, free enterprise, and development boosterism. Unfortunately, Sproule-Jones downplays the extent of class voting evident in his own data and is unable to provide direct evidence for his own interpretation.[12]

Ward's argument goes to the heart of the economic determinist argument that "the rapid expansion of industrial capitalism" produced a self-conscious working class at an early stage in B.C. history.[13] In fact, according to his evidence, support for the trade union movement prior to 1939 was weak or at least not particularly strong compared to that in other provinces, and parties based on the working class had limited electoral support. Nor have the factors identified by Ward as responsible for weak class loyalties prior to 1939 — seasonality and mobility in the labour market, individualistic motives among workers on the frontier, and the strong and widespread desire for upward social mobility — completely disappeared.[14]

Trade unions appear to have coped with the organizational problems presented by seasonality and mobility through the development of industry-wide bargaining. However, rewards for workers in the mining frontier and in the woods remain high, as do the physical and financial risks. Moreover, economic development in the province, whatever its effects might otherwise be, has produced the highest industrial wages in Canada and the prospect of rapid economic advancement.

The arguments and counterarguments could be continued, but by now the major positions should be clear. All agree that the pattern of economic development and labour-management relations in B.C. has been unusual if not unique by Canadian standards. Population change through migration and immigration has been so dramatic that at any given time a majority of the province's residents have come from somewhere else. At this point students of B.C. politics part company. Some argue that the severing of ties to old communities and the irrelevance of tradition in the new led to self-definitions based on the most obvious shared characteristic — position in the class hierarchy. Others argue that opportunities for upward social mobility or even the perception that such opportunities exist have contributed to a weak sense of class identification, at least among the working class, a tendency which working class organizations must continually fight. Still others view the partisan battle in British Columbia as a clash between right and left populism rather than between free enterprise and socialism.[15] Only a few have attempted to explore the partisan implications of changes in the province's occupational structure.[16]

The class polarization perspective is compelling given the current provincial party system. But the picture of the provincial economy and occupational structure on which it is based needs to be re-examined given current realities. The analysis of B.C. political culture in Chapter 3 shows only a weak link between class, as traditionally measured in voting studies, and ideology. The remainder of this chapter and the next are devoted to alternative ways of measuring social class and to analysing the links between class, ideology and voting in British Columbia. The story which emerges is rather different from any of those presented so far. It is particularly destructive of the simple equation of middle class-right wing Social Credit and working class-left wing NDP. It will demonstrate the utility of using a more elaborate conceptualization of social class, one which better reflects the structure of the modern economy.

CONSCIOUSNESS OF CLASS IN BRITISH COLUMBIA

The conceptualization and measurement of social class have long been the focus of scholarly debate. For political scientists, increased use of the sample survey as a research technique led to heavy reliance on "subjective" measures—measures which asked voters to define their class positions themselves. They absolve the researcher of the need to choose among a variety of "objective" measures which are often only weakly related to each other. Subjective class also seems to approximate the elusive concept of "class consciousness"—individuals who consider themselves to be working (or middle or upper) class are expected to have specific (and within classes, similar) sets of attitudes. The major analyses of class voting in Canada have tended to use subjective measures, though not exclusively.[17]

The category of objective indicators can be further subdivided into measures of socioeconomic status—usually occupation, income, and education—and those linked to Marxist theories regarding relations of power and exploitation in the capitalist economy. A number of modern Marxist typologies exist which differ in detail but most commonly emphasize the existence of sharp divisions among class groups (rather than the continuum implied by status measures such as income and education) and the importance of the relationship between the individual and the locus of ownership or control in the work-place. Marxist approaches have been further refined to take account of new middle class groups and the expansion of state employment.[18]

Whatever their theoretical perspective, proponents of objective measures argue that subjective awareness of class position is irrelevant to expectations regarding behaviour. As Anthony Giddens puts it:

> [Among members of a given class] there will tend to exist a common awareness and acceptance of similar attitudes and beliefs, linked to a common style of life . . . . [This does not require] a recognition that these attitudes and beliefs signify a particular affiliation, or the recognition that there are other classes. . .[19]

The British Columbia Election Study was explicitly designed to allow the detailed analysis of the class positions of B.C. voters using a variety of measures. Subjective class and socioeconomic status measures are the focus in this chapter to facilitate comparison with the conceptions of class used in previous writing on British Columbia and most studies of Canadian voting. In the following chapter a more elaborate perspective is employed, one based on a combination of socioeconomic status indicators and measures similar to those used by Marxist theorists.

Relatively few British Columbians are willing to classify themselves in class terms, a fact which seems startling given the image of the province. When asked whether they consider themselves to be upper middle, middle, or working class, 40 per cent were unable to do so or specifically disputed the relevance of social classes. When the 60 per cent who selected a class label were asked whether their class position is important to how they think of themselves, only 22 per cent said yes.[20] In other words, only 13 per cent of our sample accepted a class label *and* considered class to be important to their self-definition. Precise comparisons with other provinces are difficult because no other study has employed the same sequence of questions. Instead, respondents normally are asked to choose a label if they did not do so spontaneously. However, it is instructive to note that in the 1979 National Election study, only 43 per cent of respondents (39.1 per cent in B.C.) answered "yes" to a question asking whether they ever thought of themselves as members of a social class.[21] Thus, consciousness of class is apparently low in Canada, and B.C. voters do not represent an exception to the rule.

While the intensity and pervasiveness of felt class antagonisms must be questioned, subjective class position *is* related to partisanship in B.C. A majority of the self-identified working class votes NDP and majorities of the upper middle and middle classes vote Social Credit (Table 19). Moreover, and this can be considered as partial validation for the decision not to force respondents into class groups, party shares within the "no class" group are virtually identical to those in the electorate as a whole.

TABLE 19

1979 PROVINCIAL VOTE BY SUBJECTIVE SOCIAL CLASS
(vertical percentages)

Provincial vote	Subjective class				
	Upper middle	Middle	Working	None[1]	Total
Liberal	0.0	3.9	2.2	2.0	2.5
Conservative	3.2	5.3	5.6	5.9	5.5
NDP	35.5	35.0	57.5	43.5	44.3
Social Credit	61.3	55.8	34.1	48.6	47.5
	(31)	(206)	(179)	(255)	(671)

1. Respondents in this column reported that they never think of themselves in class terms or rejected the idea that social classes exist.

Restricting analysis to the small minority who feel class is important does not appreciably change the relationships in Table 19 except for the percentage of the subjective working class voting NDP. The figure in the table (58

TABLE 20

SUBJECTIVE SOCIAL CLASS AND PARTY SUPPORT OVER TIME[1]
(vertical percentages)

	Social class			
	Upper middle	Middle	Working	Total
1966:				
Liberal	72.7	29.0	12.7	24.2
Conservative	9.1	8.6	7.6	7.9
NDP	0.0	10.8	32.9	20.0
Social Credit	18.2	51.6	46.8	47.9
	(11)	(93)	(79)	
1972:				
Liberal	13.0	7.9	5.0	6.4
Conservative	8.7	6.6	1.4	6.8
NDP	30.4	49.7	63.8	51.2
Social Credit	47.8	35.8	29.8	35.6
	(23)	(151)	(141)	
1975:				
Liberal	8.3	5.6	4.2	4.6
Conservative	16.7	10.1	4.8	9.1
NDP	25.0	33.1	57.0	41.6
Social Credit	50.0	51.1	33.9	44.7
	(24)	(178)	(165)	

1. 1966 figures are based on a question about how the respondent voted in the "last provincial election" included in the 1968 national election study. The figures for 1972 and 1975 are based on specific questions about those elections included in the 1979 B.C. survey.

per cent) jumps to 68 per cent among workers who are class-conscious in the sense indicated. Class-conscious middle class voters are no more likely to vote Social Credit than those who are not.

Most of the electorate is reluctant to define itself strictly in terms of class. But among those who do there is a clear relationship between subjective class and partisanship. Moreover, the relationship is probably stronger than it has ever been now that only two parties represent meaningful choices to the electorate. Table 20 shows a class-vote relationship similar to the present one in the 1975 election and one which represented greater polarization than existed in 1972. While results based on recall (four years for the 1975 election and seven years in the case of 1972) must be interpreted with caution, 1972 does seem to represent a turning-point, especially when compared to the election of 1966. However, the figures also show substantial working class support for Social Credit no matter which election is considered, and a respectable middle class vote for the NDP in the 1970s.[22]

TABLE 21

SOCIOECONOMIC STATUS AND PROVINCIAL PARTY SUPPORT
(horizontal percentages)

	1979 provincial vote				
	Liberal	Conservative	NDP	Social Credit	
Annual family income					
less than $10,000	1.1	6.6	58.2	33.0	(91)
10,000-14,999	1.3	6.5	53.2	39.0	(77)
15,000-24,999	1.8	3.6	47.9	46.7	(167)
25,000-34,999	2.4	1.6	40.3	55.6	(124)
35,000 and over	6.3	4.5	31.3	58.0	(112)
Education					
Elementary or less	0.0	6.7	46.7	46.7	(45)
Some high school	2.3	4.2	41.9	51.5	(260)
Some post-secondary	0.7	6.0	44.8	48.5	(134)
Some university	4.2	6.3	45.6	43.5	(237)
Occupation					
Managerial/professional	3.3	5.8	44.2	46.7	(242)
Other white collar	4.6	4.6	32.8	58.0	(131)
Blue collar	1.1	5.7	52.1	40.7	(263)
Farmer	0.0	0.0	27.8	72.2	(18)
Approximate total[1]	2.6	4.2	45.4	47.6	

1. Marginal frequencies differ slightly among the three parts of the table because of differing amounts of missing data. These figures are based on the vote distribution by income.

There is little question about the current relationship between class and party support even though classes are not politically monolithic, but nor is there much evidence that class labels are crucial symbols for large numbers of voters. Of course, individuals who did not consider class to be important and even those who question or reject class distinctions may be "unconsciously" guided by class in their voting decisions. This is a different version of the class conflict perspective and cannot be tested without some form of objective measure of social class.

Table 21 has been constructed using three measures of socioeconomic status—family income, educational level, and occupational status. The question naturally arises whether these measures have independent effects or whether they simply tap the same dimension in slightly different ways.[23] The best way to answer that question is with multivariate analysis, but let us look at the simple relationships first.

The poorest discriminator is education. Very little difference appears among educational groups in the attractiveness of the major provincial parties.[24] Family income provides the most striking contrasts, with Social Credit and New Democratic support patterns by income level being almost mirror images of each other. Differences by occupation are apparent but not nearly so striking because the grouping in the table shows a nearly even division among managerial and professional groups between Social Credit and NDP supporters, respectively.[25] The conventional combination of managerial and professional groups into a single category seems justifiable. It simply combines adjacent positions in a hierarchy (self-employed professional, employed professional, high level manager, semi-professional, technical, middle management, and supervisory) created on the basis of income and educational levels associated with different occupations. However, partisan differences do not follow the same hierarchy.

These anomalies and the recent history of party policies in British Columbia point to the need for a more refined view of the class-party relationship. The Social Credit party has had a reputation for suspicion, if not outright hostility, towards traditional élites, particularly lawyers, doctors, and educators. The nearly complete alienation of public school teachers prior to the 1972 election was probably a major determinant of the party's defeat then and threatened them again in 1983. Shortly after the election, a variety of upper status workers and public sector employees, including teachers, professors, and lawyers, joined hands with organized labour in a broadly based coalition to oppose the government's legislative program. That program, advertised as a program of economic restraint, was quickly denounced as an unprecedented attack on the protection of human rights, academic freedom, collective bargaining, community control over education, medicare, the poor, and the handicapped. The adoption of the label "Solidarity" by the coalition, given the struggle in Poland at the time, provides a clear indication of the strength of feelings involved. It also hearkened back to an earlier era when labour solidarity was developed as a defence against the power of capital abetted by political élites.

Despite its historical roots, the NDP has been remarkably successful in attracting professionals and semi-professionals to its ranks. One is more likely to find a schoolteacher than a trade unionist running for election to the legislature under the NDP banner. Dave Barrett was trained as a social worker; his immediate predecessor was a lawyer. Barrett's successor was a schoolteacher. As shown in Chapter 3, the NDP's growth in the 1960s and 1970s was closely linked to the growth of employment in the public sector. Nor has the NDP always had its way with the working class. Social Credit development policies were continually justified by W.A.C. Bennett by pointing to the blue collar jobs they would create, a practice continued by his successor.

The private sector managerial élite, in contrast, represents the kinds of abilities the Social Credit government prides itself on possessing and an attachment to the free enterprise system to which party leaders make regular and passionate obeisance. The media, only partly in jest, described the Social Credit caucus elected in 1975 as a party of used car dealers. The restraint program introduced in 1983 was justified as an attempt to free resources for job creation by the private sector and to give managers in the public service the same power over their employees as private sector management possesses.

Members of traditional élites now occupy prominent leadership roles in the modern Social Credit coalition, many of them recruited from Liberal and Conservative backgrounds during the seventies realignment. However, the size of the professional occupational category is linked with growth of the public sector, a favourite target of the Social Credit government. That factor combined with the partisan division between managerial and professional groups in the electorate suggests that attitudes towards the role of the state may be partly responsible for the level of middle class support obtained by the NDP. The fact that 40 per cent of the blue collar group voted Social Credit in 1979 and that the party has always had a respectable blue collar following suggests another—working class populism—although as we shall see, populism represents at least as great a strain within each party as it does a difference between them.[26]

IDEOLOGICAL DIVISION IN THE ELECTORATE

Sixty per cent of B.C. voters feel that provincial elections should be contests between free enterprise and socialism. Despite the fact that most professional observers consider this imagery to be a Social Credit tactic aimed at discrediting and isolating the NDP, this statistic varies only slightly by party—63 per cent of Social Credit voters agree, but so do 59 per cent of NDP voters. Respondents were not asked to define these terms, but they were presented, in a large battery of items, with questions which tap differences in those ideologies as presented to the electorate: attitudes towards government regulation of business, the role of government in ensuring an adequate standard of living, the degree of community responsibility towards senior citizens, the position that the unemployed could find work if they wanted to, tax-supported medical care, and the degree of responsibility individuals have for their own well-being.

The attitude scale created from responses to these questions was described in the previous chapter. Scores range from 0 to 6, with higher scores representing greater support for collective solutions. The scale probably taps more than one dimension, but we do not wish to argue that the two provincial parties rigorously adhere to opposite positions on a single ideological dimension. Supporters of the two major provincial parties are sharply differentiated by positions on the scale. Social Credit voters score on average 3.3 and New Democrats 4.2.[27]

TABLE 22

SOCIAL CLASS AND POLITICAL IDEOLOGY
(horizontal percentages)

	Individual/collective responsibility scale score[1]			
	Individualist (0-2)	Neutral (3,4)	Collective (5,6)	Mean score
Subjective class				
upper middle	24.1	55.2	20.7	3.4
middle	19.1	50.7	30.1	3.8
working	12.6	55.3	32.1	3.9
none	21.0	52.0	26.9	3.6
Family income				
less than $10,000	15.1	50.5	34.4	4.0
10,000-14,999	12.0	58.7	29.3	3.9
15,000-24,999	16.4	55.2	28.4	3.7
25,000-34,999	26.4	52.8	20.8	3.5
35,000 and over	26.1	47.7	26.1	3.6
Occupation				
managerial/professional	20.3	49.0	30.7	3.7
other white collar	19.0	57.7	23.2	3.6
blue collar	15.9	54.4	29.6	3.8
farmer	17.6	58.8	23.5	3.5

1. These categories were created by grouping respondents on the basis of their scale scores into (approximately) the most individualistic 25 per cent and the most collectively oriented 25 per cent, leaving 50 per cent in the middle or "neutral" category.

TABLE 23

1979 PROVINCIAL VOTE BY OCCUPATION AND INDIVIDUAL/COLLECTIVE RESPONSIBILITY
(vertical percentages)

	Occupation									
	Managerial/professional			White collar			Blue collar			Overall mean
Ideology[1]:	Indiv.	Neut.	Collect.	Indiv.	Neut.	Collect.	Indiv.	Neut.	Collect.	score[2]
Provincial Vote:										
Liberal	4.9	2.9	3.0	8.7	1.5	4.2	2.9	0.8	1.6	3.4
Conservative	7.3	5.8	6.1	0.0	7.4	4.2	2.9	6.4	3.3	3.6
NDP	24.4	38.5	62.1	8.7	33.3	58.3	22.9	50.4	77.0	4.2
Social Credit	63.4	52.9	28.8	82.6	57.4	33.3	71.4	42.4	16.4	3.3
	(41)	(104)	(66)	(23)	(68)	(24)	(35)	(125)	(61)	

1. See notes to Table 22 for an explanation of ideological categories.
2. Difference in means by party significant beyond .001 level.

More important for explanatory purposes is the fact that position on this scale is only weakly related to subjective social class and socioeconomic status measures with the exception of family income (Table 22). For ease of display we have collapsed categories of the scale into "individual" (scores 0 through 2), "neutral" (3 and 4), and "collective" (scores 5 and 6). However, the means appearing at the ends of the rows are based on the full 7-point scale. The difference in means by income level is statistically significant; those based on subjective class and occupation are not.

The set of attitudes tapped by the scale plays an important role in interpreting the class-vote relationship (Table 23). In the case of every occupational group, those scoring at the individualistic end of the scale are much more likely to vote Social Credit than those at the collective responsibility end. For example, individualistic blue collar workers are nearly 4½ times as likely to vote Social Credit (71.4 per cent versus 15.4 per cent) as their fellow workers who endorse collective action. Table 24 utilizing mean scores based on the full scale reinforces this conclusion: attitudinal differences within occupational groupings are strongly associated with choice of party; there are only minor differences *within* parties based on occupation and none are statistically significant.

In contrast, populist attitudes may contribute to strain within the parties rather than a difference between them.[28] While Social Credit may benefit from working class populism, blue collar supporters of that party are no more populist than their counterparts who vote NDP (Table 25). Moreover, members of upper status occupational groups in both parties are significantly less populist than their lower status co-partisans.[29]

Attitudes towards a prominent state role in social policy and economic regulation are an impressive source of division within occupational groups. Nevertheless, occupation still has an independent effect on party choice (see Table 23). No matter how similar their attitudes might otherwise be, all ideological categories except the most individualistic within the managerial/professional group are stronger supporters of Social Credit than

TABLE 24

MEAN INDIVIDUAL/COLLECTIVE RESPONSIBILITY SCORES
BY PARTY AND OCCUPATION
(NDP and Social Credit voters only)

	Occupation		
Provincial vote	*Managerial/professional*	*Other white collar*	*Blue collar*
Social Credit	3.4	3.2	3.3
NDP	4.2	4.1	4.2
significance level for difference between parties	.001	.001	.001

TABLE 25

MEAN POPULISM SCORES BY PARTY AND OCCUPATION
(NDP and Social Credit voters only)

	Occupation		
Provincial vote	*Managerial/professional*	*Other white collar*	*Blue collar*
Social Credit	3.4	4.0	4.4
NDP	3.5	4.4	4.3
significance level for difference between parties	N.S.	N.S.	N.S.

their blue collar counterparts. Blue collar workers, the most individualistic aside, are also somewhat more likely to support the NDP, than equivalent ideological groupings within the upper status occupational group. And other white collar workers are the strongest Social Credit supporters of all. The next section contains an evaluation of the strength of ideology relative to income and occupational status differences and other voter characteristics as determinants of the choice between Social Credit and the NDP. In the next chapter the sources of ideological differences among voters are explored in more detail.

MULTIPLE INFLUENCES ON PROVINCIAL PARTY SUPPORT

The limited acceptance of self-definition in terms of social class in British Columbia may make it easier for individuals within objectively different socioeconomic groups to support the same policy options. It is also possible that some individuals view Social Credit and the NDP from a perspective which is unrelated to class or ideology. The appeal made by Social Credit when W.A.C. Bennett was leader emphasized traditional values and the importance of religion, and the denunciation of socialism then as now often used the adjective "godless" to describe the left. Populism has links with religious fundamentalism. Although the justification for it seems weaker given the predominance of British ethnic origins in B.C., ethnic division could be a factor in provincial party support given its significance in federal politics and the cultivation of certain ethnic groups by the parties. The NDP has a strong following among union members and, as was shown in Chapter 3, has had greater success than Social Credit in recruiting younger voters. This section will evaluate the importance of class and ideology by developing a model of voting choice which takes into account the diversity of individual experience. The first step in that development is an exploration of partisan differences among religious and ethnic groups comparable to that presented for voters categorized by their social class position.

There are clear differences in the attractiveness of the major provincial parties to members of different religious and ethnic groups. If we look only at those who vote Social Credit or NDP, the difference in party support ranges by 34 percentage points for religious groups and 23 percentage points in the case of ethnic origin. The details are presented in Table 26, where the groups are arranged in order of increasing Social Credit support. The previous section demonstrated the importance of income differences and ideology, and differences among groups on these dimensions also appear in the table. Since the parties do not make overt appeals on the basis of religion or ethnicity and since neither source of division has figured prominently in the recent history of the province, it seems natural to look for economic or ideological explanations of the religious/ethnic voting patterns.[30]

Not much help is obtained in the case of ethnic origin. Neither income averages nor collective responsibility scores differ in a way consistent with an ordering by Social Credit voting. The reported range in Social Credit support (the exact complement of NDP support given the construction of the table) is greatly affected by the values at the two extremes. Excluding those groups reduces the range to less than 5 percentage points. The ethnic distribution is also skewed strongly towards British origins, further restricting its explanatory power.

The picture is very different in the case of religion. The distribution is less skewed, and the ideological and partisan positions of the different religious groups are precisely aligned. Those with no religion are least sympathetic to Social Credit and, on average, have the most collectivist attitudes. Members of the fundamentalist religions are overwhelmingly Social Credit voters and most individualistic,[31] and variation among religious groups in income levels is not associated with variations in party support.

TABLE 26

ECONOMIC, IDEOLOGICAL, AND PARTISAN DIFFERENCES AMONG RELIGIOUS AND ETHNIC GROUPS IN B.C.

	Mean family income[1]	*Mean collective resp. score*	*Per cent Social Credit*[2]	*Per cent of eletorate*
Religious group				
none	3.0	4.0	37.4	21.0
Baptist	2.5	4.0	38.1	3.2
Lutheran	3.4	3.9	44.0	4.0
United Church	2.9	3.7	56.0	28.6
Anglican	3.1	3.6	56.1	16.1
Roman Catholic	3.0	3.5	63.1	13.8
fundamentalist[3]	2.7	3.1	83.3	5.5
Ethnic group				
Eastern European	3.1	3.5	41.7	7.4
French	2.7	3.6	45.5	3.6
North European	3.1	3.8	48.8	6.5
British	3.0	3.7	53.0	62.3
German/Austrian	2.9	3.9	53.8	6.2
Dutch	2.7	3.9	63.6	3.6
Overall means	3.0	3.7	51.6	

1. Mean income calculated after dividing sample into income quintiles and assigning numbers 1 to 5 from lowest to highest income group.
2. Groups are arranged in order of increasing Social Credit percentage of the combined NDP and Social Credit vote in 1979.
3. Fundamentalist religions were considered to be Pentecostal, Mennonite, Dutch/Christian Reformed, Salvation Army, Jehovah's Witness, and Mormon.

Having explored their separate effects, we are in a position to test the relative importance of religion, ethnic origin, social class, and attitudes regarding individualistic or collective policy options in accounting for the choice between Social Credit and the NDP. The procedure followed in constructing Table 27 was to estimate the differences in the probability of voting Social Credit associated with religious, ethnic, age, social class (occupation and income), and ideological differences in the electorate.[32] Union membership was considered as well. When these characteristics are combined statistically, religious and ethnic differences do not appear to affect the choice between Social Credit and the NDP. Occupation, income, ideology, age, and union membership do. The irrelevance of ethnicity was expected given the pattern reported in Table 26, and the fact that religion does not appear significant confirms our suspicion that the partisan differences associated with religion are primarily a function of attitudinal and, perhaps, socioeconomic differences among religious groups. The possibility

TABLE 27

DETERMINANTS OF PROVINCIAL PARTY SUPPORT

Dependent variable: probability of voting Social Credit rather than NDP in 1979[1]		
Explanatory variables[2]	Effect Co-efficient[3]	T-ratio
family income	.29 (.06)	5.21
middle age	.35 (.14)	2.45
union membership	−.56 (.14)	−4.15
individual/collective responsibility times:		
managerial/professional	−.33 (.05)	−6.54
white collar	−.26 (.06)	−4.32
blue collar	−.39 (.05)	−7.26
Constant	.49 (.24)	2.00

$\hat{R}^2 = .24$

Likelihood ratio test with 6 degrees of freedom 119.97

N = 456

1. To emphasize NDP/Social Credit differences, this table has been prepared by eliminating voters for other parties.
2. Family income is a five point scale which divides the electorate (approximately) into quintiles; middle age has the value 1 for those between ages 40 and 59, 0 otherwise; union membership has the value 1 if any union members in the household, 0 otherwise. Each of the other variables is the product of a dummy variable for occupation and the individual/collective responsibility score.
3. Effects of the explanatory variables were estimated using Probit analysis. Standard errors for each co-efficient appear in parentheses. A t-ratio greater than 1.96 marks a level of statistical significance greater than .05.

that doctrinal differences among religions are themselves a source of differences in individual/collective responsibility attitudes is intriguing, but it will not be examined here.

For simplicity, Table 27 has been restricted to NDP or Social Credit voters.[33] While a variety of statistics appear in the table to attest to the technical adequacy of the results, the key figures for explanatory purposes appear in the column labelled "Effect Coefficient." The size and sign (positive or negative) of these coefficients measure the effect on the probability of voting Social Credit of each characteristic listed under the "Explanatory Variable" column. It appears that the probability of voting Social Credit increases with income, is higher among the middle-aged, and is lower among union members.[34] The interpretation of the other three coefficients is slightly more complicated because the variables with which they are associated have been constructed to take into account the pattern revealed in Table 23—while, on average, the occupational status groups differ in their level of support for the parties, there is considerable variation *within* each group because individuals differ ideologically. The three coefficients are all negative as would be expected given that they measure the effect of increasingly *collective* attitudes on the probability of voting Social Credit, but the relative sizes of the coefficients indicate that, for a given ideological position, the white collar group has the highest probability of voting Social Credit, followed by the managerial/professional group, and then blue collar workers.

The combined effect of occupation and ideology becomes clearer when the procedure used in constructing the table is used to estimate the probability of a Social Credit vote by individuals with given social characteristics and ideological positions. For example, an individual with a median family income, who is middle-aged, not a union member, who is engaged in a professional occupation, and who occupies a position near the centre (scale score of 3) on the individualism/collectivism dimension has a .76 chance of voting Social Credit.[35] The probability of a Social Credit vote by an other-

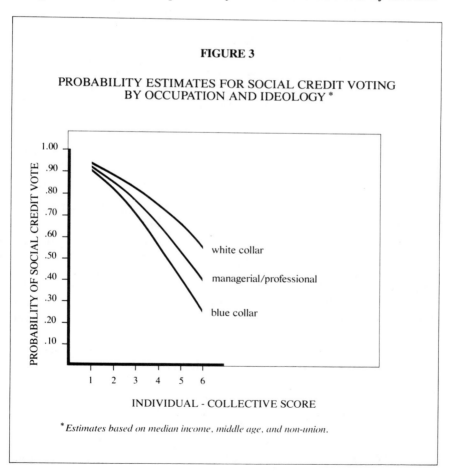

FIGURE 3

PROBABILITY ESTIMATES FOR SOCIAL CREDIT VOTING
BY OCCUPATION AND IDEOLOGY *

white collar

managerial/professional

blue collar

INDIVIDUAL - COLLECTIVE SCORE

Estimates based on median income, middle age, and non-union.

wise similar individual, but with extreme collectivist attitudes (a score of 6), would be only .39.

Figure 3 is a graphical representation of several such calculations. It shows quite clearly the joint effects of ideology and occupation on the the individual's vote. The strong effect of ideology is readily apparent. The probability of a vote for Social Credit decreases sharply with increased collectivist attitudes, but at a different rate depending on an individual's occupation (age, family income, and union membership have been held constant at middle age, median income, and non-union in preparing the figure). A graph of the pattern of NDP vote probabilities would be just the mirror image of Figure 3.

The statistical tools needed to explore the underpinnings of party support are complex, but the story they tell is relatively straightforward. There are a large number of ways in which individuals may differ, differences which are potentially relevant to the choice among parties. However, when a large number of potential differences are considered simultaneously, occupation, age, level of economic well-being, union versus non-union, and left versus right emerge as the major divisions in provincial politics. Social Credit is the party most favoured by the ideological right and the NDP by the left, but each has developed an appeal beyond the class boundaries normally associated with those positions.

CONCLUSION

Social class has a place in explanations of B.C. partisanship, but a simple working class/middle class dichotomy no longer gives an accurate guide to partisanship. Social class position is not an important part of the self-definition of most British Columbians, nor are they more eager to define themselves in class terms than other Canadians. Nearly 30 per cent of those with family incomes less than $10,000 annually voted Social Credit in 1979; the same proportion in the above $35,000 group voted NDP. The managerial and professional occupational group divides between Social Credit and the NDP rather than uniting behind the party of the right.

The value cleavage identified as the core of provincial politics does exist. A clear majority of provincial voters feel that elections are and should be a battleground between free enterprise and socialism. In this sense other accounts of the province's politics are correct. But the conclusion that class position as traditionally considered is completely responsible for the relative attractiveness of the two alternatives cannot be sustained. Support for the different bundles of policies represented by B.C. versions of the two ideologies cuts across occupational lines and helps to account for such apparent anomalies as lower class support for Social Credit and upper class support for the NDP.

When considered as occupational status groups, social classes appear internally divided on many of the questions which separate the major provincial parties. The result is a complex and subtle class-party relationship. The transformation of the economy and social structure of the province associated with realignment in the seventies have also made the traditional picture of class conflict in the province obsolete. Even if provincial social divisions once simply pitted workers against owners (a position which enjoys strong but not unanimous support in the literature on B.C.), such divisions are now cross-cut by differences between employment in the public and private sector and between old and new industries and occupations. Individuals can still be classified into different social classes on objective grounds, but the contexts within which blue collar and white collar groups work are increasingly differentiated, and require a more elaborate classification scheme. These contextual differences are, in fact, sources of ideological differences found within class groups. Their effects are examined in the next chapter.

6

The Context of Partisanship

The analysis of provincial political culture in Chapter 4 showed that ideological differences at the mass level are only weakly related to the subjective class positions or socioeconomic characteristics of voters. Yet as we have just seen, ideological differences exert a powerful influence on the choice between parties in provincial elections.[1] Given election campaigns which stress fundamental choices, a governing party whose very existence is testimony to the fear of socialism, and a social democratic party which portrays Social Credit as little more than a front for unrestrained capitalism, ideology is bound to affect voting decisions. But how are these attitudes developed and sustained? And how can these perspectives be linked to the structural changes underlying the realignment of the 1970s? In order to answer these questions a more elaborate conception of social class is needed, one which makes distinctions between the traditional, resource-based economy and the modern economy characterized by the growth of the service sector and government employment. We also need to go beyond broad structural divisions to identify social settings and work-place characteristics which facilitate the transmission of political ideas and partisan influences or help to generate competing ideological perspectives. These are the goals of this chapter.

While reducing the significance of direct employment in the resource economy, economic development has not eliminated its political significance. Provincial government revenues rise and fall sharply with fluctuations in the well-being of forestry and mining. We have also seen that the growth of the NDP to an electoral position rivalling that of Social Credit is linked to the economic development of the interior and to the spread of large-scale industry based on the exploitation of the province's natural resources. According to economists, the export-dependent, boom or bust character of the resource sector is particularly likely to generate working class militancy and insecurity. When times are good, employers are unwilling to jeopardize production by resisting demands for wage increases. They are also more able to pay. When times are bad, employer resistance to worker demands runs up against expectations generated by previous concessions and by the urge to keep in step with workers in industries such as construction and manufacturing which are less cyclical.[2]

Industrialization of the interior also coincided with the spread of trade union membership providing valuable organizational support for the NDP in previously unrewarding areas at election time. Social Credit's reputation as a party unfriendly to organized labour makes the appeal of trade union leaders to the self-interest of workers that much easier.

The development orientation of Social Credit may counter-balance these factors to some extent. NDP critics frequently condemn the deals arranged with private capital or question the environmental impact of mega-projects. But each such project adds to Social Credit's reputation for the ability to create blue collar jobs. Gambling for riches on the resource frontier may also appeal to the individualistic streak in the province's political culture—a phenomenon which the previous chapter has shown appears among blue collar workers.

The growth of public sector employment has produced another potential source of division within social classes and of cohesion across class lines. Social Credit and the NDP hold sharply contrasting views on the utility and desirability of state sector activity, and, as a consequence, the NDP should be better able to attract the support of public sector employees whether through an appeal to self-interest or to attitudes favouring collective solutions to social and economic problems. However, public sector workers suffer from stereotypes regarding waste and inefficiency in the public service and the link between taxes and wages. While they now have the right to strike in British Columbia, here, as elsewhere, the exercise of that right is readily portrayed by government and the media as an act against the public interest. A poll commissioned by the Vancouver *Sun* in 1983, during heated public and legislative debate over the Social Credit restraint program, revealed considerable public ambivalence about the role of government. On the one hand, only 27.5 per cent of the public disagreed with the need to reduce the size of the public service; on the other hand, large majorities opposed cutbacks in social welfare programs, increased user fees for medicare, and abolition of the Human Rights Commission.[3]

The potential for conflict within class groups divided into public and private sector employment is particularly apparent during periods of economic decline. Public sector workers are normally less likely to suffer from unemployment, a source of resentment to add to the image problems they already have among private sector workers. This cleavage was clearly exploited by Social Credit during the 1983 election campaign. They promised to continue restraints on public service wages in order to free up resources which could be used for job creation by the private sector, the avowed source of "real" jobs. Premier Bennett defended restrictions on public sector collective bargaining introduced after the election on the grounds that they merely put public and private sector workers on the same economic footing. It would make it easier for the government to institute lay-offs.[4]

The private/public sector distinction also divides the middle class. An expanded social policy role for government produced thousands of new jobs in the areas of health, education and social welfare during the 1960s and 1970s. At the same time as new expectations were being generated about the proper role for government, new groups of workers were created whose self-interest is linked to an interventionist and activist state sector. But the ranks of the middle class have also been swollen by the addition of large numbers of workers providing financial and other support services in the private sector.

Division of the population into industrial sectors, between metropolis and hinterland, between private and public sector, and by distinctions within traditional occupational groupings provide relatively crude ways of distinguishing between environments which may generate different ideological perspectives and political choices. The theoretical justification for such divisions rests on the assumption that living and working in similar environments creates shared experiences and communities of interest which may extend to political matters.

For example, industrialization of some parts of the hinterland has produced single-industry company towns, settings where working class consciousness and militancy may be especially pronounced. Sociologists attribute these characteristics to the carryover of authority relationships in the work-place to the structure of social interaction in the community—the superior economic position of management in the plant brings with it social and political superiority in the community, especially if housing and amenities are provided by the company.[5] Even if this particular pattern did not emerge, we would expect residential segregation to influence political attitudes and partisanship. Whenever the social contacts of individuals at school, in community centres, or shopping areas are confined to people with similar class backgrounds, the potential exists for the development of similar outlooks on political and social issues.

Direct neighbourhood effects may occur during election campaigns as lawn signs sprout and bumper stickers appear advertising neighbourhood biases. The bias of political advertising and political discussion in the neighbourhood will favour the neighbourhood political majority, helping to reinforce the loyalties of those already predisposed in that direction and helping to sway those who are not.

Some neighbourhood segregation by social class does exist in British Columbia. Vancouver civic politics is structured by parties and voting patterns which reflect political and social divisions between the east and west sides of the city. In one-quarter of the neighbourhoods represented in our sample, at least 40 per cent of the adult population had a grade 10 education or less according to census figures. One-third of the blue collar families in our study lived in those neighbourhoods. Given the absence of comparative data, it is difficult to decide whether neighbourhoods are unusually homogeneous in British Columbia or not; however, it is clear that many blue collar workers and their families live in areas where most of their social contacts will be with those of the same class.

Such influence processes are not confined to the neighbourhood. Organizations such as trade unions may exert a double-barrelled effect, indirectly through political education of the rank-and-file and directly via solicitation of support for the party of organized labour. From the analysis in this chapter, it appears that the second effect may be more powerful, perhaps because the closed shop is the norm in the province, limiting the self-selection of workers into trade unions on the basis of left-wing attitudes, and in B.C., as elsewhere, only a minority take an active part in union political education programs.

Some of the social and economic settings described here should theoretically sustain a consensus on economic, social and political issues within the working class and generate support for the NDP. Others offer potential sources of division. Not all workers are unionized. Nor are all work-place settings alike in terms of authority relations, organization of work, and physical danger. Moreover, most workers live in metropolitan areas, not single-industry towns. Within those areas, some live in working class neighbourhoods; others do not. Most individuals will also be part of several social networks.

Forces working against a consensus on political and economic questions also affect the middle class. The upper status occupational label conceals a range of work-place experiences. Some individuals are involved on the management side of the bitter confrontations which occur in some industries. Others are themselves employees, some unionized, some not. Nor does position in the work-force exhaust the sources of politically relevant experiences on this side of the objective class divide.

These, in brief, are some of the contexts within which the province's voters live and work. The next section examines them for signs that they are associated with variations in party support in the ways outlined. Following that is an exploration of the links between context, political attitudes and partisanship.

WORK-PLACE SETTING, RESIDENTIAL SETTING, AND PARTISANSHIP

The presence of trade unions is probably the most obvious contribution of work-place setting to the attitudes and partisanship of blue collar workers. Unlike the case in some other western economies, union membership as a percentage of the work-force has remained high in B.C. (nearly 50 per cent), in part because of high rates of unionization in the growing public and service sectors, although it has dropped about five percentage points from its peak in 1958. Trade unions in the province look back over a long history of struggle, and the main trade union federation, the B.C. Federation of Labour, has been particularly sensitive to any threats to the economic power of unions. Efforts to generate blue collar support for the NDP such as that launched by the Canadian Labour Congress during the federal campaigns of 1979 and 1980 are routine in B.C.

But even unionized work settings may differ in the degree of union militancy and labour-management conflict. Assembly line jobs are normally more alienating work experiences than industrial occupations which allow individual initiative or autonomy in work scheduling. Workers in dead-end jobs may also be more alienated and thus more receptive to appeals from the left than those with prospects for advancement. Workers in declining industries are probably more concerned with the relative sensitivity of parties to unemployment or job retraining than similar workers in expanding industries. Even the broader economic environment—location in a single-industry town, in a city with many large-scale, heavy industries, or in a primarily non-industrial service centre—may be relevant to divisions within the working class.[6]

The attitudes of those in upper status occupations may also be affected by work-place context. A lawyer employed by the provincial Ministry of Industry will probably view a powerful public sector with more equanimity than one employed by MacMillan-Bloedel. A forest industry executive may have a different perspective on the free enterprise system than an executive in a regulated industry like communications or utilities.

These examples have been chosen with a view to comparing individuals in different sectors who have roughly equivalent education and job skills, but it is undoubtedly the case that some inter-industry differences in attitudes within the same occupational group are produced by factors only indirectly related to the work setting. Income is probably the most obvious example. Professionals such as lawyers and economists can normally draw higher salaries in the private sector than by working for government; tradesmen's wages differ in the service, manufacturing, and primary sectors. Of course, individuals with the same educational background may choose between government or private sector employment, or among industrial sectors, on the basis of attitudes developed before entering the labour force, a possibility it is impossible to investigate without following individuals through time. Income differences can be measured, and income is an important predictor of the vote in British Columbia. However, we will ignore this and other individual level differences until we have established the prima facie validity of the argument that differences in political choice are associated with differences in context.

Despite the significance attached to them here, the political implications of differences between economic sectors in stability and desirability of employment or of possible conflicts of interest between employees in the public and private sectors have rarely been studied. An analysis of job satisfaction, attitudes towards government expenditures on social welfare, and political attachments in the United States turned up few differences between workers in the "core" (the monopoly sector containing large-scale, capital-intensive, highly profitable firms providing stable employment and generous benefits) and the "periphery" (the competitive sector characterized by small-scale, labour-intensive firms, seasonal work, high turnover of firms and jobs, and low wages).[7] A British study which added the distinction between public and private sectors was unable to detect any consistent sectoral effects on voting separate from those expected given a higher rate of unionization in the public sector in that country.[8] However, a third study, also using British data, does provide evidence of sectoral effects, independent of class and unionization, but confined to public servants from middle-class family backgrounds.[9] Recent work in Canada has demonstrated that a connection exists between class background and political ideology, but reports only a tenuous connection between ideology and partisanship. Moreover, the authors of that study did not explore differences between employment in the private and public sectors as a source of ideological or partisan differences.[10]

Several theoretically significant divisions were measured in this study. People can be classified according to whether they work in the private sector or in the public sector, whether directly employed by government or by publicly funded institutions such as universities, hospitals, and public schools, or by a Crown corporation. We know what trade unions they belong to and the sizes of firms for which they work. The divisions of economic interest associated with type of corporation and the kinds of markets they operate in can be approximated by a modified version of the standard census classification of industrial sectors—primary, manufacturing, construction, transportation/communication/utilities, retail/wholesale trade, financial services/real estate, educational/medical services, and public administration.[11] This division has the further advantage of representing a first approximation to a division among work-place settings on the basis of the kind of internal work relationships they are likely to exhibit. The divisions overlap. For example, a given individual can be both a trade unionist and a public sector employee. But the consequences of overlap can be examined statistically.[12]

An exact specification of work relations in particular jobs is not attempted here—the amount of research required to establish reliable generalizations would be immense.[13] Nevertheless, some speculation is possible, recognizing that exceptions undoubtedly exist. Four sectors contain high ratios of blue collar to white collar and managerial/professional employees; primary, construction, transportation/communications/utilities, and manufacturing. The primary division identifies the sector where large-scale corporations confront large trade unions and where there has been a long history of industrial strife associated with safety, working conditions, and job security. The line between management and labour is sharp and rarely crossed by most workers.

The construction industry contains both large and small contractors but is characterized by the hiring of specialized trades and unskilled labour for discrete tasks on particular job sites. An individual worker may perform the same task but for a wide variety of employers over time. While some may aspire to become independent contractors themselves (an occupation fraught with insecurity), most will have their work-place contacts confined to a small number of members of the same trade.

Most blue collar employees in the transportation, communication, and utilities fields do not work under the direct gaze of supervisors when on the job, but are despatched to jobs by those keeping a record of productivity. Upward mobility is possible to technical supervisory positions, but rarely to the higher management levels.

The manufacturing sector covers such a wide range of firm sizes, physical hazards, and processes that generalization is difficult. Nevertheless, the distinction between management and labour is likely to be distinct and the setting should at least be conducive to frequent contact among workers. Even in the absence of a high degree of unionization and despite some differences between sectors, blue collar workers in those settings should be more receptive to parties making appeals to the interests of labour than blue collar workers in other environments.

The other sectors (retail/wholesale trade, financial services/real estate, educational/medical services, and public administration) include mainly white collar and upper status jobs and, in most cases, physically pleasant work settings. Because of this and because of the diversity of settings *within* sectors, if we find variations in partisanship *between* these sectors, they are more likely to reflect the direct impact of unionization and the attitudes of managers and professionals towards government activity rather than alienating work settings per se.

Work-place setting does cut across occupational status divisions (Table 28).[14] Blue collar support for the NDP in 1979 ranged from a low of 37.5 per cent in the "retail and wholesale trade" sector to nearly 65 per cent in "public administration." The average level of blue collar support for the NDP (55.1 per cent) is also surpassed by workers in primary and construction occupations. Support is somewhat below average in the case of blue collar "educational/ medical" workers, but the small number of cases may be a factor. With the exception of blue collar workers in public administration, the expected higher level of NDP support in sectors dominated by blue collar occupations did appear. Moreover, despite the diversity within public and private sectors, the table confirms the apparently greater attractiveness of the NDP to blue collar workers in the public sector. There is, then, a private sector blue collar

TABLE 28

WORK-PLACE CONTEXT AND THE 1979 PROVINCIAL VOTE BY OCCUPATION
(labour force members only)[1]

Work-place context		Blue collar (% NDP)		Managerial professional (% NDP)	
Union membership					
CLC Affiliate	67.1⎫	64.9	(76)	55.9	(59)
Non-CLC	57.1⎬		(21)		
Non-union	⎭	46.0	(113)	43.3	(127)
Industry sector					
primary		61.5	(39)	54.5	(11)
manufacturing		52.5	(40)	46.2	(13)
construction		60.0	(20)	42.9	(7)
transportation/utilities/					
communication		55.3	(38)	33.3	(15)
retail, wholesale trade		37.5	(24)	27.3	(22)
financial services, real estate		—	(1)	50.0	(8)
educational, medical services		50.0	(10)	53.8	(65)
public administration		64.7	(17)	40.0	(20)
miscellaneous		58.8	(17)	57.9	(19)
Size of firm					
10 or fewer employees		56.5	(46)	52.5	(40)
11-50		48.6	(37)	35.0	(40)
51-100		38.9	(18)	35.3	(17)
101-500		64.3	(28)	50.0	(20)
501-1000		50.0	(22)	57.9	(19)
more than 1000		67.6	(34)	45.5	(22)
Employer type					
private		52.9	(157)	41.7	(84)
public		60.4	(53)	52.0	(102)

1. Numbers in parentheses are the totals for the subgroup on which the percentage, for example, there were 76 blue collar workers in CLC affiliated unions, of whom 67.1 voted NDP in 1979.

constituency which might favour Premier Bennett's efforts to "tame" public sector employees.

Union membership and even type of union affiliation help to structure support for the NDP among blue collar workers. Any type of union membership is associated with an above average level of NDP vote. But membership in a union affiliated with the Canadian Labour Congress, hence with the militant B.C. Federation of Labour, carries with it a much higher level of NDP support than union membership alone.[15] Size of firm as measured by number of employees, however, bears an equivocal relationship to NDP support among blue collar workers. Larger firms are more likely to be characterized by impersonal relationships between management and labour, usually mediated by union leaders, hence one would expect them to contain a higher percentage of NDP voters then smaller firms. Moreover, the larger the firm the more likely it is that an individual's contacts at work will be confined to fellow blue collar workers. Blue collar workers in the largest firms do have the highest level of NDP support, but the lowest level is found in the median category (51-100 employees). Dichotomizing firms at 100 employees would produce the "expected" relationship (50.4 per cent NDP in small firms versus 61.9 per cent in large), but at the expense of ignoring the obvious departures from linearity.

There has been little previous study of work-place variations in the attitudes and behaviour of those in upper status occupations.[16] In B.C., given the public positions of the two main parties on the role and size of the state, the fact that managers and professionals in the public sector find the NDP more attractive than their counterparts in the private sector was expected. However, a finer division reveals some surprises. The average level of support for the NDP among managers and professionals is 46.7 per cent. Support for the party is somewhat higher than this in the primary and educational/medical services divisions. The latter group contains a large number of unionized professionals (such as teachers and nurses) and is also a group whose economic well-being is dependent on a high level of government support for the services they provide. The figure for primary occupations, however, seems large given the history of labour-management conflict in the industry and the fact that Social Credit has been more willing than the NDP to provide government financing of the industry's infrastructure. Again, the figure may be affected by the small number of cases available in that sector.

The Social Credit party makes a strong appeal to businessmen, an appeal reflected in the much below average level of support for its major opponent among managers and professionals employed in retail and wholesale trade. The low level of upper status support for the NDP within the transportation/communication/utilities sector is more interesting. The NDP might be viewed with suspicion by upper status employees of regulated private companies, such as B.C. Telephone, whose "provincialization" is periodically demanded. Labour-management relations in the telephone company have also been extremely bitter in recent years, with the NDP normally siding with labour. However, the grouping of industries also includes Crown corporations such as B.C. Hydro, whose personnel have a stake in the size and growth of the public sector. Again, as expected given the analysis in Chapter 4, the B.C. political climate defies simple categorization. A Social Credit government led by W.A.C. Bennett created the corporation while continuing to extol the benefits of free enterprise. Social Credit has also been more willing than the NDP to protect the corporation from regular public and legislative scrutiny. No such explanations come readily to mind to account for the below average levels of NDP support among managers and professionals employed directly by government (40.0 per cent in public administration), except to note that many of them are employed by the federal government, whose employees, as employees, do not have a direct stake in the size of the *provincial* state. At that level one is also more likely to find managers who have been recruited because of their sympathy for Social Credit's view of the role of government.

TABLE 29

GEOGRAPHICAL CONTEXT AND 1979 PROVINCIAL VOTE BY OCCUPATION
(labour force members only)

	Blue collar (% NDP)		Managerial professional (% NDP)	
Region				
metropolitan	43.8	(146)	39.5	(177)
hinterland	62.4	(117)	56.4	(62)
Riding				
Vancouver Centre	63.6	(22)	58.3	(24)
N. Vancouver, Seymour	42.9	(28)	34.9	(43)
Burnaby-Willingdon	60.0	(25)	40.7	(27)
Surrey	40.0	(30)	55.6	(18)
Central Fraser Valley	28.6	(14)	31.3	(16)
Oak Bay-Gordon Head	25.9	(27)	30.6	(49)
Prince Rupert	64.4	(45)	50.0	(20)
Comox	63.3	(30)	64.5	(31)
Kootenay	69.6	(23)	60.0	(5)
Cariboo	47.4	(19)	33.3	(6)
Neighbourhood social context *(% with Grade 10 education or less)*				
9.2-24.2	35.5	(31)	37.7	(69)
24.3-32.2	51.7	(58)	54.1	(37)
32.3-41.0	60.3	(58)	58.1	(43)
41.1-81.3	61.9	(63)	45.9	(37)

Provincial geography has been an important determinant of the character of provincial politics. Barriers to communication, competition between regions for government favours and life-style differences have all left their mark. Are regional differences in economic self-interest important enough to drive a wedge between voters in the same social class? Patricia Marchak argues that they are—"the workers in the Vancouver-Victoria region benefit from the dominance of [the metropolis over] the resource hinterland. The workers of the hinterland cannot depend on the workers of the metropolis to join them in class action when the benefits are unequally distributed."[17] Upper status workers may also be divided in terms of metropolitan/hinterland residence. "Those in government service, for example, may be members of the policy-directing class in class terms, yet be so located in regional terms that their hinterland status involves them in conflict with members of their own class in the metropolitan regions."[18]

Table 29 has been prepared to allow the examination of metropolitan-hinterland differences within lower and upper status occupational groups, but it also contains a breakdown by provincial riding within regions. Hinterland (Prince Rupert, Comox, Kootenay, and Cariboo) blue collar workers evince a much higher level of NDP support than their metropolitan counterparts. Managers and professionals in the hinterland are also stronger NDP supporters, a finding which may help to explain higher support for the NDP among upper status workers in the primary sector noted earlier. A riding-by-riding breakdown indicates that the hinterland pattern is consistent across the region with the possible exception of Cariboo riding, but the diversity within the metropolitan grouping belies any simple regional division. While the lowest levels of blue collar NDP support are found here (26 per cent in Oak Bay-Gordon Head, a posh Victoria suburb), so are some of the highest—nearly 64 per cent in Vancouver Centre and 60 per cent in Burnaby-Willingdon. Upper status support for the NDP also varies within the metropolitan area—even exceeding blue collar support in Surrey, a large Vancouver suburb.

One possible clue to the diversity within regions is provided by the final breakdown in Table 29, which groups respondents by the objective class level of the neighbourhoods in which they live.[19] Numerous studies have shown that people whose neighbours have a different class status than their own often vote for the party favoured by the community majority even when it differs from the normal preference of their own social class.[20] The low levels of blue collar support for the NDP in the upper status ridings of Oak Bay-Gordon Head and North Vancouver-Seymour may reflect this phenomenon. The table does indicate that blue collar support for the NDP is low in neighbourhoods which contain relatively few poorly educated people (and thus, we would argue, few blue collar workers) and increases with the proportion of the neighbourhood population having low educational levels.

A complementary pattern holds, in part, for managers and professionals. However, in the most blue collar neighbourhoods, NDP support drops to the average level for the upper status group as a whole. Put simply, blue collar voters in middle class settings were likely to support Social Credit. Middle class voters in working class neighbourhoods were unlikely to support the NDP. At least one researcher reports a similar result based on data from the United States. He argues that the failure of middle class voters to respond in the same way as voters in the working class reflects a tendency of members of a social minority to *resist* neighbourhood influence when minority standing becomes pronounced: "the assimilation process predominates up to the point that group members are in a minority position threatening to their own identity or status. At that 'tipping point,' members of the minority turn inward in an attempt at preserving their own identities."[21] This is an intriguing possibility, but when factors other than neighbourhood characteristics are taken into account, the anomaly disappears in B.C.

The standings of the parties among class groups in different industrial settings, in different types of neighbourhoods, or in different parts of the province are important in themselves, because election outcomes may turn on such groupings. Election platforms are designed to tailor party appeals to segments of the electorate where an electoral reward might be generated. Campaigns are organized around the known voting patterns in neighbourhoods and the presumed voter characteristics which produce them. However, a fuller understanding of the impact of context on partisanship requires analysis of how the effects are produced, the effects of overlapping contexts, and the relative significance of context given other attributes of individuals.

MULTIPLE CONTEXTS, POLITICAL ATTITUDES AND PARTISANSHIP

Explanations which identify context as a factor in the choice between parties generally point to the effect of different settings on political attitudes and definitions of individual self-interest. Marchak argues, for example, that workers in different regions of the province, those in oligopolistic or competitive markets, or those employed in the private or public sectors have a direct stake in the willingness of government to curtail corporate power.[22] Murphy and Morris offer a more complex explanation suggesting that the variation across industrial divisions in the strength of class-vote relationships in the United States may stem from the persistence of crude manual/non-manual distinctions in the minds of those employed in industries where technological change has made the "head versus hands" distinction nearly obsolete; differential distributions of bureaucratic and entrepreneurial jobs; mobility characteristics; and the rate and nature of unionization.[23] A Vancouver area study by John Leggett has shown that involvement in unskilled occupations and occupations particularly vulnerable to unemployment contribute (albeit weakly) to greater class consciousness among blue collar workers and that union membership has a strong effect.[24] Finally, Johnston and Ornstein discovered that lower rates of pay, lower skill levels, union membership, undesirable or physically demanding jobs, and poor working hours are all linked to more left-wing attitudes within the working class.[25]

We have already shown that the positions of voters on the individual versus collective responsibility dimension are strongly related to party choice (Chapter 5), but that ideology is only weakly related to social class measures except for income. Given the foregoing, differences in the conditions under which people live and work, which our identification of contexts is intended to capture, are an obvious place to look for sources of attitudinal variation. Hints of a contribution exist in the tendency of voters, whatever their occupational status, to favour the NDP if they work in the public sector, and Social Credit if they work in the private sector.

It is also conceivable that some contexts may exert a more direct effect on party choice or, at least, an effect which is independent of the central attitudinal dimension. Those who fall into the middle levels of individual/ collective responsibility, for example, should be more susceptible to influence by the majority preference in their work-place or neighbourhood than the more committed. The ranks of union members undoubtedly include many for whom ideological questions are not particularly salient but who are convinced of the appropriateness of NDP support by the example of more militant co-workers or union leaders.

Finally, we cannot ignore the possibility that apparent differences between settings are really the result of differences between contexts in the characteristics of the individuals who live and work within them. Differences between sectors in the income levels of similar occupations and in rates of unionization are potentially the most significant. For example, blue collar workers in construction are more likely to vote NDP than those in retail and wholesale trade, but more of the former are union members. Social Credit does better among professionals in the private sector than in the public sector, but private sector professionals are paid better. Since we know that both union membership and income affect voting, we cannot be certain that contextual effects exist until we test competing explanations of this sort.

The previous chapter has identified the most important predictors of party choice in British Columbia—income, union membership, occupation, and ideology. However, it also revealed the existence of ideological differences within occupational status groupings. Some of these differences may be related to the structural differences explored above—industrial sector, private or public employment, or differences within occupational groups associated with differing skill levels or the distinction between managerial and professional employment. Some of these differences may have an effect on the choice between parties which is independent of personal ideology.

The presence of large numbers of voters in B.C. whose attitudes place them close to the centre makes this a distinct possibility.

Tables 30 through 32 contain the results of the examination of the attitudes and behaviour of the three main components of the labour force: blue collar workers, managers and professionals, and white collar workers.[26] The analysis was conducted separately for each class group because so much of what has been discussed to this point relates to differences within classes defined according to occupational status. Each table contains two sets of results. The first column lists the effects of individual characteristics and structural factors on ideology.[27] Numbers with positive signs identify factors linked to left-wing attitudes (higher individual/collective responsibility scores); negative signs, to right-wing attitudes. The numbers were produced using multiple regression, a technique which allows one to evaluate the relative explanatory power of a large number of individual and structural characteristics. Some characteristics, "employment in resource industry," for example, are represented by dichotomies. In such cases, significant coefficients are produced when members of the group identified this way differ ideologically, on average, from those not in the group.

The second set of results shows what happens when an attempt is made to predict voting choice from the voter's ideological position, and/or individual characteristics (such as income), given his or her neighbourhood or work environment. Proceeding in this fashion helps to identify sources of ideological differences within each class group—we know ideology is a powerful determinant of partisanship—but it also serves to measure the effects of context and individual characteristics on the vote which exist independently of ideological position.[28] For example, the results in the first column of Table 30 show that differences in the class composition of neighbourhoods and employment in the resource industry are the best predictors of ideological differences among blue collar workers. However, the second column tells us that the probability of a blue collar vote for the NDP is also affected by union membership and income, even when ideology is taken into account.

Each of the tables is accompanied by a diagram of the direct and indirect effects on voting of the factors considered, which should make the results easier to understand. The major role of ideology in political choice justifies placing it in the centre of each figure. Sources of ideological differences among voters appear above or beside the ideological dimension, linked to it by arrows which also contain measures of the magnitude and direction of their effects.

The vote is represented as the result of a combination of factors at the bottom of each figure. The impact of ideology on the vote is indicated by another arrow. Again the magnitude and direction of impact are represented numerically.

Finally, each figure contains additional factors, individual and contextual, linked directly to political choice independently of ideology such as union membership and income noted above in the case of blue collar support for the NDP. For the "Other White Collar" grouping (Table 32 and Figure 6), income has an effect on ideology (higher income is associated with right-wing attitudes) *and* on the vote. No attempt has been made to develop a causal model of the relationships described. The arrows in each diagram represent plausible paths of influence, but no account has been taken of the ways in which the background variables affect each other, nor have other possible sources of attitudinal and partisan differences been considered.[29]

Let us look at blue collar workers first. The political attitudes of this group differ considerably when work-place contexts are considered separately. Mean scores (not shown in tabular form) on the individual/collective responsibility scale range from 3.1 in the retail and wholesale trade sector to 4.3 in educational/medical services. Part of this difference may reflect the degree of unionization in the two sectors (union members average 4.0 on the scale, non-union workers 3.7) or public/private sector differences (public sector/blue collar workers score 4.1, private sector workers score 3.8). However, when personal characteristics and overlapping contexts are taken into account (as in Table 30 and Figure 4), only two contexts remain significant—educational composition of the neighbourhood and employment in the resources sector. Blue collar workers living in blue collar neighbourhoods are more likely to express left-wing attitudes than fellow workers in neighbourhoods where blue collar workers are fewer in number. We saw earlier that higher incomes are linked to individualism. Blue collar workers in resource industries are well paid, but differences in attitudes associated with variation in work setting persist when income is controlled. The direction of the difference in attitudes is important. The negative sign indicates that, on average, blue collar workers in the resources sector are more individualistic than their counterparts in other types of employment. The finding probably identifies a receptive blue collar audience for the resources mega-projects favoured by Social Credit. Residence in a blue collar neighbourhood has the anticipated (and opposite) effect on political attitudes in the working class—support for collective policy options is reinforced.

Conspicuous by its absence is a role for union membership in the development of a sense of collective responsibility. However, the second column of Table 30 shows that union membership does make a direct contribution to NDP support among blue collar workers. Since differences by industrial sector and region (metropolitan versus hinterland, and comparisons between ridings) were also tested for their direct impact on NDP support, we are forced to conclude that regional and institutional divisions within the working class may exist as Marchak speculated. But except for the link between individualism and employment in the resource industry, they are apparently income and union membership differences in disguise.

Figure 4 charts the hypothesized influence pattern. The direction of the relationship of neighbourhood social composition and industrial sector to ideology, and of ideology, union membership, and income to the vote is indicated by the sign of the number on each arrow. The numbers themselves measure the relative impact of the factors once they have been standardized to take account of different units of measurement (the technical term is "beta coefficient").[30] For example, income takes on possible values from 1 to 5 (lowest 20 per cent to highest 20 per cent of the population) whereas the proportion of the neighbourhood with grade 10 education or less ranges from 9 per cent to over 80 per cent.

Using this method of comparison, the effects of neighbourhood and employment in the resource sector on ideology appear to be comparable in magnitude (.20 and −.15, respectively), whereas ideology has a substantially greater impact on the vote than either income or union membership (.35 compared to −.14 and .21).

The same technique was extended to managers and professionals and to white collar workers: personal and contextual differences were tested for their effects on ideology and, together with ideology, tested for their impact on voting for the Social Credit party. Simple tabular analysis pointed to significant attitudinal differences between industry groups and between private and public sectors,[31] but multivariate analysis reveals a more complex underlying pattern, especially in the case of the upper status occupational groups.

TABLE 30

CONTEXTUAL AND INDIVIDUAL SOURCES OF NDP SUPPORT
AMONG BLUE COLLAR WORKERS[1]
(labour force members only)

	Dependent variable	
Explanatory variables	*Individual/collective responsibility*	*NDP provincial vote in 1979*
Working class neighbourhood	.021 (.008)***	.0004 (.003)
Employed in resource industry	−.466 (.252)**	.013 (.101)
Union member	—	.206 (.078)***
Family income	—	−.051 (.029)**
Individual/collective responsibility	—	.148 (.032)***
Constant	3.154 (.311)***	.041 (.190)
N	153	153
R²	.05	.20

1. Entries are regression coefficients with associated standard errors in parentheses.
 ** Significant at .05 level (one-tailed)
*** Significant at .01 level (one-tailed)

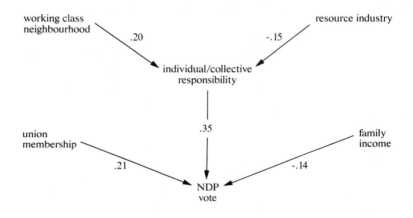

FIGURE 4

**DIRECT AND INDIRECT SOURCES OF NDP SUPPORT
AMONG BLUE COLLAR WORKERS***
(LABOUR FORCE MEMBERS ONLY)

working class
neighbourhood   resource industry

              .20   -.15

                        individual/collective
                        responsibility

union   .35   family
membership   income

        .21   -.14

                        NDP
                        vote

*The numbers appearing in this figure are beta coefficients which allow one to compare the
relative effects of each explanatory variable on the dependent variable – in this case, the effect on
ideology and the vote.*

For managers and professionals (Table 31 and Figure 5), two contextual differences appeared when individual socioeconomic differences were controlled. Employment in the construction industry or one of the resource industries is associated with more individualistic attitudes. These, in turn, are associated with a higher level of Social Credit support. Employment in the private sector generally is strongly associated with Social Credit support even though that distinction is not significantly related to the ideological dimension. Income also makes a contribution to Social Credit support. Finally, the significant difference in support for Social Credit between professional and semi-professional workers and others in upper status occupations suggests that it is not status or income per se which determine party choice in the province. Whether by virtue of the training they undergo or predispositions which lead them to choose a professional career, members of this occupational group are more likely to endorse interventionist solutions to society's problems. Even when these attitudes have been taken into account (see the second column of Table 31), professionals and semi-professionals are less likely than other members of the upper status occupational group (mainly owners, managers, technicians, and supervisors) to vote Social Credit.[32]

Figure 5 provides an assessment of the relative impact of each factor on ideology and the vote like that already described in the case of blue collar workers. Employment in the construction or resource sector is linked to greater individualism compared to other sectors, with similar effects in both. No other factors were statistically significant. Ideological position (beta = −.15), a professional or semi-professional job (beta = −.18), and employment in the private sector (beta = .15), in turn, have similar effects on voting, but income level is even more important (beta = .25).

Once again it should be noted that the numbers represent the net effect of each characteristic—for example, the lower probability of a Social Credit vote among professionals assumes income, ideology, and sector (private or public) have been controlled. Concretely, the results point to the effects of occupational self-interest *and* ideology on partisanship.

The white collar group bears more cautious interpretation because the numbers available for analysis are relatively small compared to the other two

TABLE 31

CONTEXTUAL AND INDIVIDUAL SOURCES OF SOCIAL CREDIT SUPPORT
AMONG MANAGERIAL AND PROFESSIONAL WORKERS[1]
(labour force members only)

	Dependent variable	
Explanatory variables	*Individual/collective responsibility*	*Social Credit vote in 1979*
Employed in construction industry	−1.218 (.566)***	−.013 (.201)
Employed in resource sector	−1.171 (.526)***	.111 (.188)
Professional or semi-professional	—	−.181 (.081)**
Employed in private sector	—	.149 (.082)**
Family income	—	.101 (.031)***
Individual/collective responsibility	—	−.055 (.028)**
Constant	3.885 (.115)***	.337 (.179)**
N	152	152
R²	.06	.17

1. Entries are regression coefficients with associated standard errors in parentheses.
 ** Significant at .05 level (one-tailed)
*** Significant at .01 level (one-tailed)

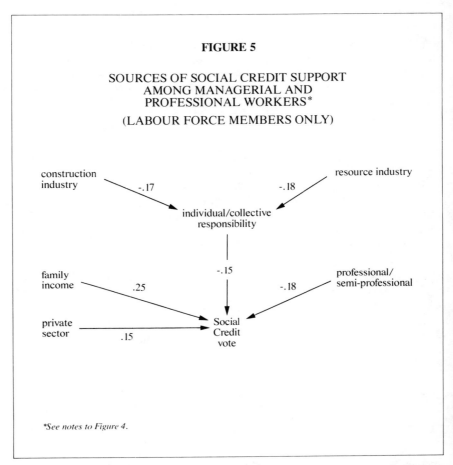

FIGURE 5

SOURCES OF SOCIAL CREDIT SUPPORT
AMONG MANAGERIAL AND
PROFESSIONAL WORKERS*

(LABOUR FORCE MEMBERS ONLY)

*See notes to Figure 4.

groups (Table 32, Figure 6). Only income has a significant effect on attitudes (but also on the vote), but, again, employment in the private sector makes an independent contribution to Social Credit support. As was true of all the other occupational groups, ideology is a key factor affecting the vote, but in this case income and sector (public or private) have comparable effects.

CONCLUSION

The British Columbia political and economic environment lends itself to the use of dichotomies: free enterprise versus socialism; management versus labour; working class versus middle class; metropolis versus hinterland; and

TABLE 32

CONTEXTUAL AND INDIVIDUAL SOURCES OF SOCIAL CREDIT SUPPORT
AMONG WHITE COLLAR WORKERS[1]
(labour force members only)

	Dependent variable	
Explanatory variables	*Individual/collective responsibility*	*Social Credit vote*
Family income	− .317 (.094)	.096 (.039)***
Employed in private sector	—	.232 (.113) **
Individual/collective responsibility	—	−.092 (.040)***
Constant	4.513 (.321)***	.424 (.234) **
N	94	94
R²	.11	.18

1. Entries are regression coefficients with associated standard errors in parentheses.
  ** Significant at .05 level (one-tailed)
 *** Significant at .01 level (one-tailed)

Social Credit versus NDP. Yet these phrases obscure as much as they reveal. Neither management nor labour is politically monolithic. Social classes whether defined in traditional ways in terms of occupational status or using subjective classifications are internally divided on policy questions and party choice. The electorates of the two parties do differ in class terms, but the conditions under which class-party relationships are formed do not fit dichotomous explanations.

On the whole, blue collar workers in British Columbia are relatively well off financially. Industrial wages are the highest in Canada. Yet economic security is not assured. The provincial economy is heavily dependent on the volatile export market with its attendant impact on employment. Employment in the export-oriented forest industry is also highly seasonal. Moreover, the cost of living in the major metropolitan centres may offset the benefits of blue collar employment. Nevertheless, there are signs in our data that wealthier blue collar workers and those employed in the resources sector are less likely to possess political attitudes which support NDP social and economic policies. Residential segregation works against that trend, however, since blue collar workers living in neighbourhoods populated by blue collar families are less likely to support individualist social and economic arguments.

Union membership plays a crucial role in our analysis, a role which underscores the direct impact of union political mobilization rather than the inculcation of attitudes supporting interventionist policies. In fact, the figures reported in Chapter 5 suggest that blue collar supporters of the NDP are slightly less supportive of interventionist solutions than upper status New Democrats.[33] These results have profound implications for the approach the NDP makes to its traditional supporters and to its new ones. A "social

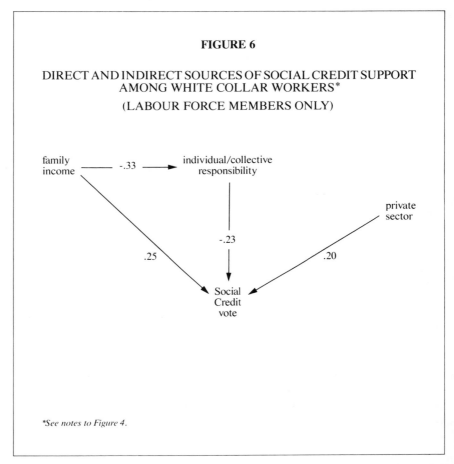

FIGURE 6

DIRECT AND INDIRECT SOURCES OF SOCIAL CREDIT SUPPORT
AMONG WHITE COLLAR WORKERS*

(LABOUR FORCE MEMBERS ONLY)

*See notes to Figure 4.

welfare" party image may cost it support in the working class unless it retains its image as the party of organized labour. However, that image has been downplayed by the party since the 1960s as it searched for supporters amid the ruins of the provincial Liberal and Conservative parties.

Party support patterns of upper status voters are no less fascinating because of what they reveal about the reception of the revitalized Social Credit party. The party is still linked to its past. Accounts of Social Credit support in the 1950s and 1960s stressed its ideological appeal to captains of the resource industry, an appeal which persists among upper status employers and employees in the resource sector. The individualistic character of construction industry management is also reflected in our data. The appeal of Social Credit to the private sector is also evident. Even when income and attitudes are taken into account, upper status workers in the private sector are differentially attracted to the party. The final ghost of the past appears in the case of professional and semi-professional workers. The modern Social Credit party has yet to surmount the lack of ideological sympathy and relative political hostility of this group.

The analysis based on survey data provides a single snapshot of the province, limiting the extent to which one can talk about change and the causes of change. Yet the analysis has revealed attitudinal variations and party support patterns which are anchored to and sustained by the province's social structure and political economy lending strength to its conclusions. Together with the results in the preceding chapter, it has shown how important ideology is as a source of partisan division in provincial politics and has traced the impact of a complex social and economic environment on that division. The impact of social class on partisanship has been clarified by looking at the sources of division within traditional class groups associated with the growth of the public sector, the relative decline of employment in the resource economy, and changes in the character of the white collar work-force.

With this chapter we leave, for now, the world of provincial politics. Federal politics takes place in a world containing additional bases for conflict between parties. The two worlds do overlap, but divisions between left and right in the federal party system are overshadowed, if not eclipsed, by alienation and disaffection from the federal government. Coalitions of provincial voters dissolve to form anew with different members. To understand this transition, we first need to examine the psychological ties which bind British Columbians to the national political community. That is the subject of the next chapter.

7

Allegiance and Discontent in British Columbia

David J. Elkins

One can only speak of alienation from something that one has reason to be attached to anyway.[1] Alienation is similar to a heresy. Something can be heretical only if it lies within a system of belief. Buddhism is not a Christian heresy; it is a complete religious system in its own right. Alienation, by analogy, can be understood as involving a dual relationship of acceptance and rejection: rejection of one part of a political system by another part; feeling left out of something into which one is in fact integrated to a significant degree; feeling "alien" in a place where one has every right to feel at home.

This duality has usually been ignored in accounts of "western alienation," the focus of attention here. Western alienation will be understood as an attitude or set of attitudes about the place of western provinces (and especially B.C.) in the Canadian confederation. It involves beliefs about the appropriate distribution of powers and jurisdictions between the federal and provincial domains of politics, feelings about nation, province, and locale, expectations about policy responsibility and performance, fears about being left out of significant political decisions, and the balance between national and regional or provincial loyalties and identities.

Western alienation, therefore, has a bright side, even if that side is often overlooked in the concern for its potential dangers. For people in B.C. or elsewhere to express concern about their place in Canada and their grievances against real or imagined slights, they must feel that they are a part of Canada. In this sense, the real enemy may be indifference to Canada. One need not worry about whether Canadians are alienated from Germany, Jamaica, or Japan, because Canadians are only remotely and very hypothetically part of those political systems. One may worry about whether Canadians are alienated from aspects of Canada precisely because they are Canadians. Ironically, given its usual connotations, alienation helps to unite British Columbians with other Canadians in appraising the alternatives presented in the federal party system. In other words, despite the peculiarities of the provincial political world, the federal one is much less idiosyncratic. This chapter provides the foundation for this argument, which is then pursued through an analysis of federal voting in the next two chapters.

Western alienation is a misleading term in two ways. The data in this chapter demonstrate that alienation in any fundamental sense hardly appears among British Columbians. They are unquestionably critical of many political events and personalities, but their allegiance is strong. Their discontentments focus on incumbent leaders and on policies and hardly at all on the system of parliamentary democracy or on Canada as a nation.

The word "western" is equally misleading, implying as it does that this phenomenon is common throughout the four western provinces.[2] The evidence in this chapter and elsewhere in the book shows that British Columbia differs from the prairie provinces in important respects. Other data suggest that the prairie provinces are not uniform in regard to this political phenomenon. For all these reasons, readers must understand that the phrase "western alienation" is used because it is the currently popular slogan, not because it has any analytic value in itself. Indeed, it is a phrase which has several dangerous connotations, a point to be addressed after the data have been examined.

If alienation always involves rejection or feeling apart from something, it will generally also entail allegiance to something else.[3] One of the central tasks of this chapter concerns the specifications of the objects rejected and of the objects to which allegiance is felt. Western alienation involves a positive concern for certain political units smaller than Canada and, at least in British Columbia, a concern for Canada in general. While such alienation may prove to be an annoyance from a Canada-wide perspective, its elimination might have negative side-effects which many would deem equally harmful, such as alienation from the locale in which people live and work. To reduce alienation from the federal government, some deem it necessary to increase alienation from provincial governments. Presumably, the goal should not be the destruction of local pride or rivalry, however, but the harnessing of local pride to national purposes. Indeed, an attachment to provincial or local units of government need not be in conflict at all with strong attachment to the federal government or to Canada as a whole. The conflict may occur on particular issues or over specific leaders without entailing a definitive attachment to one "side" and rejection of the other.

We know from previous research that Canadians have loyalties towards more than one order of government.[4] Except for some supporters of the Parti Québécois, most Canadians who feel warmly towards their province or region also feel very warmly towards Canada and the federal government. Obversely, people who do not regard Canada or the federal government warmly are also, by and large, relatively cool towards their own province. They are not identified with any part of Canada. (Again, some Péquistes prove to be an exception.) Therefore, to try to strengthen national feelings and support for the federal government by undermining local loyalties may turn out to be self-defeating.[5] As Gibbins has argued about Albertans, so for most Canadians, political alienation may consist in feeling rejected by the system one admires rather than wishing that one's provincial sub-system were less Canadian.[6]

THE MEASURE OF ALIENATION

The B.C. survey in 1979, which has been used throughout this book, contained several items used to assess respondents' feelings about federal and provincial governments and B.C.'s place in Canada. They are listed in the Appendix. Although they were intended to measure these sentiments in B.C., the scale created from them serves as a concrete indicator of what has frequently and nebulously been called western alienation.

A brief examination of the attitude items should dispel some possible misconceptions about the extent of alienation in B.C. Whatever may be the case elsewhere or at other times, these items reveal little that could prove comforting to leaders hoping to mobilize British Columbians to separate from Canada.[7] For example, 66 per cent of the sample disagree with the statement that "the federal government has all but forgotten B.C."; 69 per cent think of themselves as Canadians first and British Columbians second; and 70 per cent say that "B.C. is much better off in Confederation than out of it." Of course, there are signs of some degree of alienation. This is especially notable in the large proportions who think the provincial governments could do a better job of many things that the federal government now does (45 per cent), who believe that "our MPs lose touch with the people who elect them" (62 per cent), and who express the view that "local questions just don't get the attention they deserve in Ottawa" (47 per cent).

Any given person can express agreement with a particular item which seems to reflect alienation, and yet not feel alienated. Hence, one should never rely on any one fallible indicator of an attitude. Instead one should use a battery of items on the assumption that although each item is imperfect, many items together are reasonably reliable and accurate. To be scored as "high" on this measure of alienation, a respondent had to give a definite response in the alienated direction (not a "don't know") on at least four of the seven items. Only 221 individuals did so; the rest were less alienated.

We must emphasize that this scale, like all attitude scales, is a *relative* measure of alienation. People who score "high" are deemed to manifest more of the trait in question than people who score "low." No inference is possible, however, about the *absolute* level of feelings for any respondent or for the sample as a whole. This is especially important to remember in contemplating the political implications of the data. Are people who score "high" on B.C. alienation, for example, likely to support the separation of B.C. from Canada? One cannot know, since high scorers might fail to act on their feelings because of other attitudes, social pressures, or lack of opportunity, as well as because their alienation—although "high" on this measure—may not represent extreme or deep-rooted feelings. This chapter contains data about associated attitudes which help to assess the intensity of these feelings of alienation and of possible actions which the alienated might be induced to undertake. If one wishes to use these data to plan governmental policies or actions designed to "reduce alienation," one must consider carefully the overall pattern of responses and not simply the absolute level of the scores obtained.

The relative proportions of B.C. residents who express negative feelings about something is an important measure of the seriousness of that type of alienation. Ironically, as we shall see, the most prevalent strain of discontent concerns former Prime Minister Trudeau. His departure from Canadian politics will probably reduce some of the negative feelings expressed by these respondents. Thus, while the significance of pathways to alienation can be measured partly by the numbers of people affected, equally we must weigh the degree of tractability of the reasons. As the example of anti-Trudeau feelings suggests, common or numerically frequent expressions of alienation may also be transient. It is much harder to deal with alienation, even if it is infrequent, if it derives from intractable features of Canadian life or from features that most citizens cherish. Who wants to reduce the alienation of ethnocentric residents by forcing French Canadians to assimilate fully or by giving up the bilingual goal for Canada? Who wants to reduce the alienation felt by avowed separatists by dismembering Canada? Aside from the fact that such actions might alienate people who are not now alienated, the reduction in alienation where it does occur must be purchased at a price few would wish to pay.

The aim in this chapter is not, however, to offer solutions to the problem of alienation. As should be clear by now, we are not convinced that alienation is the problem it is thought to be, at least in British Columbia. To the extent that alienation stems from policy disagreement or leadership assessment, attention should focus on policies and leaders rather than on alienation; if alienation derives from more fundamental concerns about the legitimacy of the federal government, tinkering with policy or changing leaders will probably do no good. Similarly, the goal of eradicating all alienation is unattainable, if alienation is in part a reflection of the *complexity* of society and the necessary contradictions inherent in positive government ("welfare state") as opposed to the nineteenth-century "watch-dog state."[8]

THE ALIENATED PATRIOTS

Perhaps it is best to dispel first the most common myth, the simplest explanation. The interchangeability in the media and in many political speeches of the phrases "western alienation" and "western separatism" suggests the first hypothesis: those people who score highest on this measure of alienation do not like Canada; they wish to sever all (or most) ties with Canada, whether the dividing line be the Rocky Mountains, the Canadian Shield, or the Ottawa River. The data for B.C. flatly disprove any simple equation of alienation and separatism.

Table 33 summarizes evidence about how much respondents who differ in degree of B.C. alienation like and dislike Canada and B.C.[9] Several general features stand out. First, there is no significant difference in the degree of *liking* Canada among the four levels of alienation. Second, the degree of liking is very high everywhere: 85-90 per cent of all respondents give either a "9" or a "10" on the amount that they like Canada. Third, there is very little *disliking* of Canada, judging by the very low mean scores. Although the alienated respondents score slightly more disliking than the less alienated, the differences are not large and the mean scores are uniformly low. Fourth, the patterns for liking and disliking British Columbia are similar: slightly more liking of B.C. by the alienated; slightly less disliking of B.C. by the alienated; very high scores in all groups for liking B.C.; and very low dislike scores in all groups.

This general pattern should occasion no surprise. One can be alienated from aspects of Canada and still hold in high esteem the country as a whole. Indeed, there are probably few people with no criticisms to make, even among the most patriotic. Presumably one test of whether alienation might pose a threat to Canada concerns the degree of liking and disliking of other political systems. Some spokesmen for western separatism look to the United States; instead of the West or a given province becoming a sovereign state, these people urge a transfer of loyalty to the United States. Some people, of course, emigrate from Canada each year without advocating the transfer of political sovereignty of provincial units. The relative attractions of Canada and other countries, then, are worthy of consideration.

Table 34 reveals that residents of B.C. like the United States, Britain, and France less than they like Canada; and they also have higher dislike scores for these countries than for Canada. To the extent there are any differences in liking or disliking among people with differing levels of alienation, the

TABLE 33

FEELINGS ABOUT CANADA AND BRITISH COLUMBIA
BY LEVELS OF B.C. ALIENATION
(% down)

		B.C. Alienation				
		1=low	*2*	*3*	*4 = high*	*Significance of chi-square test*
Like	0 - 8	12.1	8.5	13.5	14.3	
Canada	9	15.0	11.7	14.0	13.4	p = .26
	10	72.9	79.8	72.5	72.3	
Like Canada mean score		9.52	9.67	9.58	9.28	
Dislike Canada	0	54.1	55.2	58.5	55.3	
	1 - 2	32.4	28.7	26.1	22.8	p = .01
	3 - 10	13.5	16.1	15.4	21.9	
Dislike Canada mean score		1.19	1.19	1.20	1.69	
Like B.C.	0 - 8	15.8	9.4	12.1	9.5	
	9	17.8	13.5	12.1	9.9	p = .14
	10	66.4	77.1	75.8	80.6	
Like B.C. mean score		9.35	9.49	9.63	9.46	
Dislike B.C.	0	50.8	54.3	59.4	59.2	
	1 - 2	33.2	29.6	27.0	24.6	p = .07
	3 - 10	16.0	16.1	13.6	16.2	
Dislike B.C. mean score		1.31	1.18	1.06	1.33	
N =		222	195	160	221	

more alienated respondents are *less* favourable towards each of these three countries than are the respondents who express little alienation.[10] Alienation in B.C., therefore, cannot be explained by the lack of positive feeling for Canada or by the relative attractiveness of other countries.

Gibbins and others have argued that a major theme of "western alienation" in Alberta concerns a feeling of rejection by powerful interests outside Alberta. Many Albertans, it seems, are alienated because they feel rejected by Ottawa, by Ontario, or "the east." Albertans, to some degree, feel alienated because they are unable to be as much a part of Canada as they would like or as much as they think they deserve.[11]

B.C. respondents were not specifically asked about the types or the degree of integration they favoured, and one wonders how much any of them have thought about their province in that way. Our data demonstrate, however, that even British Columbians who score high on the alienation scale want to remain Canadians and may also demonstrate that they wish to be more involved in Canadian political life than they are.[12] Be that as it may, these data certainly undermine any implication that the alienated in B.C. are a reserve army waiting to be mobilized for the cause of separatism.[13] Even the alienated can be patriots.

TABLE 34

LIKE AND DISLIKE U.S., BRITAIN, AND FRANCE BY LEVELS OF ALIENATION
(mean scores; N)

B.C. Alienation	United States		Britain		France		Minimum
	LIKE	DISLIKE	LIKE	DISLIKE	LIKE	DISLIKE	N =
1 = low	7.1	3.3	7.3	2.8	5.4	4.1	199
2	6.6	3.8	6.7	2.9	4.8	4.6	173
3	6.7	3.8	6.9	3.1	5.1	4.3	147
4 = high	6.8	3.6	6.4	3.3	4.4	4.9	191
(Significance of F-test=)	(.103)	(.189)	(.004)	(.198)	(.001)	(.030)	

ALIENATION AND THE DISTRIBUTION OF POWER

If alienation does not reflect a rejection of Canada, it may nevertheless mark a feeling that the federal government is remote, that provincial governments are more important, or that the distribution of powers within our federal system places too great an emphasis on the federal order to the detriment of the provincial or local governments. Thus, alienation could involve a fairly sophisticated view of constitutional niceties; and it could also reflect a reaction against government in general, analogous perhaps to the "tax revolt" in California.

The first type of evidence concerns who should be responsible for what kinds of policies or issues. Respondents were asked to name the three issues most important to them; they were then asked to discuss what these issues meant and what solutions, if any, they would suggest. Finally, they were asked, "Who do you think should be responsible for handling this matter, the federal government in Ottawa, the provincial government in Victoria, your local government, private citizens like yourself, or some other group?" Presumably, respondents who are alienated because of federal government dominance or incompetence would be unlikely to urge that the federal government should be responsible for the salient issues they have mentioned. To test this hypothesis, we summed the number of times responsibility by each major government or group was mentioned; for each respondent there could be zero, one, two, or three issues for which the federal government (or some other) should be responsible.

The more a respondent prefers that "his" or "her" issues be under provincial control, the more alienated he or she scores. Nevertheless, there is no significant difference in alienation as the number of references to the federal

TABLE 35

MISTRUST OF GOVERNMENT BY LEVEL OF ALIENATION
(% across; mean scores)

		B.C. alienation				
		1 = low	2	3	4 = high	N =
Proportion	most	12	21	23	44	124
of politicians	some	23	22	20	36	385
in Victoria who	not many	31	21	20	28	344
are crooked	none	33	26	18	22	72
Proportion of	most	13	17	23	47	140
politicians in	some	23	21	21	35	413
Ottawa who	not many	33	24	19	25	307
are crooked	none	27	31	22	20	64
Proportions of	most	30	23	20	27	462
civil servants in	a few	19	24	22	35	357
Victoria who	hardly any	21	10	21	47	98
are competent	none	20	25	5	50	20
Proportions of	most	30	24	21	26	452
civil servants in	a few	20	24	22	34	355
Ottawa who	hardly any	23	9	17	51	100
are competent	none	16	16	11	58	19
Mistrust of Ottawa mean score[1]		10.1	10.5	10.9	11.8	F-test: p<.00001
Mistrust of Victoria mean score[1]		9.8	10.1	10.4	11.1	F-test: p<.00001
Mistrust of Government mean score[1] (combines Victoria and Ottawa mean scores)		19.9	20.6	21.3	22.9	F-test: p<.00001

1. Low scores indicate more trust; higher scores signify less trust.

government increases; and more respondents assign responsibility to the federal than to the B.C. government.[14] Although the few respondents who want local or private control of these issues are significantly more alienated, the small numbers who favour this decentralized control mean that these relationships cannot explain alienation in B.C.

In short, alienation seems to be in part a reflection of positive orientation to provincial powers, but it is unrelated to federal powers and hardly affected by feelings about other jurisdictions. These conclusions are sufficiently counter-intuitive that further tests seem desirable. It should be noted, however, that they are compatible with the data in the previous section which found the alienated to be no less nationally oriented than the unalienated and to be equally allegiant to province and nation.

What could account for these relationships between alienation and jurisdiction over important issues? Are some levels of government more trustworthy than others? Are people more involved with one level than another?

Would involvement make them more favourable to that government or does familiarity breed contempt? Or are the alienated simply withdrawn from politics generally?

Table 35 summarizes the evidence on several aspects of trust in government in general and in regard to the federal and provincial orders in particular. Three patterns deserve our attention and bear on the questions above.

First, trust and alienation are negatively related, although not very strongly. Many of the most trustful respondents still exhibit moderate amounts of alienation, and many of the least trusting individuals nevertheless are not at all alienated. To the degree that they are negatively related, these measures form an understandable syndrome. Whether mistrust or alienation is causally prior to the other is, of course, not proven. Second, virtually identical patterns of trust (or mistrust) and alienation are evident for both the federal and provincial governments. Although at each level of the B.C. alienation scale the degree of mistrust is slightly higher for Ottawa than for Victoria, none of those differences proves to be statistically significant.

Third, trust or mistrust seems to derive equally from feelings about politicians and about civil servants, from concerns about competence and about rectitude. (Not shown in Table 35 are other items included in the overall Trust Index which explore these other possible combinations of personnel and activity.)[15] In short, alienation can be assumed to increase with (or perhaps as a result of) lack of trust that either level of government or its personnel are competent, fair, and just.

These findings about trust in government help to clarify the finding that assignment of responsibility for major political issues to the federal government was unrelated to feelings of alienation. Trust does not reside solely or even primarily at one level of government, and yet alienation is differentially related to federal and provincial responsibility for issues. Thus, attributions of responsibility could hardly have been made in terms of which government is more trustworthy.

One might hypothesize that alienated respondents are generally withdrawn from politics, that they follow politics less closely, and that they are less likely to pay attention to campaign coverage in the mass media. These expectations are strongly refuted by the data. There is no significant difference between respondents high or low on the measure of B.C. alienation in terms of media consumption or how closely they follow politics. To the extent there is any difference, the alienated may be slightly more likely to pay attention to politics than the less alienated.

One explanation for the observed relationship between alienation and issue responsibility would hypothesize that differential attention to federal or provincial politics might be related to alienation, even though there is no general withdrawal from politics by the alienated. As it turns out, this cannot account for the relationship of alienation and issue responsibility. When we examine the level of government which the respondent follows closely, fairly closely, or not very closely, there is an increase in proportions who follow federal and provincial politics closely as the score on the B.C. alienation measure increases; there is a concomitant decline in the proportion who follow closely international politics. The most alienated respondents divide their attention equally among these types or levels of government and politics. As hypothesized in note 10, this evidence suggests that the alienated respondents are generally well informed and more critical of several kinds of political objects.

There are, however, other measures which reveal differential attachments to the federal and provincial orders of government, but the patterns are quite complex and do not serve to explain alienation in a simple manner. In Table

TABLE 36

ORIENTATION TO LEVEL OF GOVERNMENT BY DEGREE OF B.C. ALIENATION
(% across)

		B.C. alienation				
		1 = low	*2*	*3*	*4 = high*	*N =*
In 1979, in which	federal	31	21	19	29	546
election were the	provincial	15	22	23	40	252
stakes higher	both equally	24	23	21	33	174
	neither	0	0	17	83	12
Level of	federal	35	25	16	24	216
government felt	provincial	19	21	23	38	576
closer to	both equally	29	21	22	29	105
	neither	26	28	17	30	98
Level of	federal	31	23	17	29	242
government with	provincial	23	21	21	35	445
more effect on	local	15	23	17	45	60
you personally	all equally	24	25	21	30	115
	federal and provincial	25	22	22	31	96
	provincial and local	24	20	36	20	25
Index of	1 = most					
provincial	federalist	41	26	14	19	156
orientation	2	31	25	19	25	194
	3	28	23	22	27	169
	4 = most					
	provincialist	19	25	27	34	187
"The federal						
government should	agree	24	23	21	32	830
ensure that each						
province provides	disagree	29	20	21	31	146
a minimum standard						
of public services."						

36, one can examine the degree of alienation evinced by people with different orientations to government.

There are two strands to the argument. First, most people thought the federal election of 1979 was "where the action was," but only 216 out of 546 felt closer to the federal government. Most people felt closest to the provincial government, but a minority of them (252 out of 576) thought that the provincial election, which occurred in the same month, was as important as the federal election in 1979. There appears to be a *disjunction* between perceptions of crucial decisions and where one might like the decisions to be made. Second, feeling closer to the provincial government, thinking its election more important, and believing it has more impact on one personally all are associated with elevated scores on B.C. alienation.[16] Surely, the natural conclusion must be that alienation is not a rejection of the federal government as such, but a positive orientation to provincial government. In Table 36, one finds that over 85 per cent of the people agree, for example, that "equalization" or enforcement of minimum national standards is the duty of the federal government; and agreement with this view has nothing to do with alienation. Alienation, therefore, derives in large part from *frustration* of provincial actions rather than from federal activities as such.

Let us recapitulate all the patterns together. Alienation is not related to lack of involvement in politics. Alienation does not depend on degree of attention to federal politics or assignment of responsibility to it. Alienation is lessened by thinking federal politics is important, by judging its elections crucial, and by feeling closer to it. Alienation is markedly higher among people who believe federal politics is important but feel closer to provincial politics and judge the provincial government to have a greater impact on their daily lives. Although speculative, one interpretation of these patterns concerns the belief that some provincial activities (such as health, job creation, and resource development) are frustrated by the actions of a federal government whose choice in the 1979 and other elections was important but distant or beyond local control. From the point of view of British Columbians, federal elections are often "decided" by the larger numbers of seats in Ontario and Quebec, not by B.C. voters; and yet the outcome often has important consequences for decisions made by the provincial government in B.C.

In conclusion, alienation rests only in small degree on estrangement from federal politics. Alienation as assessed here lacks a separatist base to the degree that *in the abstract or without regard to specific issues*, it does not mean a rejection of the federal level. Alienation in B.C., thus, may reflect a judgement that the federal government has done some things wrong, rather than a feeling that it is illegitimate or that it can do nothing right. Alienation is not inherently anti-government nor is it inherently anti-federal government, even though a few people may be alienated for these particular reasons.

ALIENATION AND PARTISANSHIP

Two questions, apparently similar but quite distinct, arise in examining how alienation relates to partisanship. First, how alienated are the supporters of different parties? Second, how do the alienated as a group differ from the non-alienated in their evaluation of each of the political parties?

If alienation derives in large part from the belief that the federal government has frustrated some provincial policies of direct relevance to the majority of British Columbians, the people who oppose the party which has taken these actions should be more alienated than supporters of the governing party. Such is clearly the case whether we examine groups classified by vote or by party identification. At the time of this survey, the Progressive Conservatives controlled the federal government. The Clark government, however, could not have been closely identified with the perceived federal intrusions on provincial domains, since that party had been in opposition from 1963 to 1979 and had been in office for only a few weeks when the interviews were conducted.

When one examines scores on B.C. alienation by people who identify themselves with one federal or provincial party or another, one pattern stands out above all others: regardless of level of government, Liberals are less alienated by a sizeable margin.[17] (The same results obtain if one focuses on actual vote reported for the 1979 or 1980 federal election or the 1979 provincial election.) Although less striking, other aspects of partisanship deserve brief mention. First, there is almost no difference among the non-Liberal parties in their mean scores, all being much more alienated than the Liberal supporters. Second, people with no party identification resemble the non-Liberals in average levels of alienation.[18]

Partisans differ in degree of alienation, but some Liberals are quite alienated and some non-Liberals are not alienated. Hence, one must reverse the analysis in order to see how the alienated and unalienated, regardless of which party they support, evaluate each of the political parties. The answer is simple and predictable.

As alienation increases, there is a marked and very significant decline in positive rating of the Liberals and an increase in negative ratings. If one subtracts the negative from the positive scores, the least alienated have a net positive orientation, while the most alienated have a distinctly negative net orientation. For the federal Conservatives and NDP, on the other hand, there is a very slight but not significant increase in liking as alienation increases and no difference on the dimensions of disliking. Overall, all four levels of alienation yield net positive orientations to both non-Liberal parties. These same patterns occur also at the provincial level, where alienation is related to feelings about the B.C. Liberal party but not to feelings about the other parties. People who are alienated seem to generalize their negative assessments to a local party just because it bears the label of a federal party perceived to have neglected B.C.

TRUDEAU AND ALIENATION

The central focus of the 1979 election, according to all commentators, was leadership. In particular, two questions were foremost in the minds of the electorate: how can we get rid of Trudeau? and can Joe Clark handle the job? The clear implication of these questions for the types of alienation examined here is this—negativism. If the alienated are animated by dislike of the Liberal party, that is in part because of the linking of its policies with "the Northern Magus" who had led it for so many years.[19] If Clark had been perceived as a strong leader or at least not a weak leader, the negative feelings about Trudeau could have been translated into positive feelings about an alternative government. After a few months in office, however, the Clark government managed to lose the advantage of even this degree of negativism towards Trudeau and turned it into reluctant—ambivalent— acceptance of another Trudeau/Liberal government. Of course, the major vote shifts were in Ontario, and the question for this analysis is: how were British Columbian attitudes about alienation structured around the party leaders and Mr. Trudeau in particular?

The simple answer is revealed in Table 37. It summarizes respondents' likes and dislikes within each level of the B.C. alienation scale in regard to the three leaders of the federal parties. As with the Liberal party, evaluations of the Liberal leader differ greatly among the levels of alienation. Clark and

TABLE 37

EVALUATIONS OF THE FEDERAL PARTY LEADERS
BY LEVELS OF B.C. ALIENATION
(means and standard deviations)

Leader evaluated			Whole sample	B.C. alienation				Sig. of F-test
				1 = low	2	3	4 = high	
Trudeau	likes	mean	4.99	5.74	5.17	4.65	4.33	p<.00001
	dislikes	mean	5.03	4.19	4.76	5.30	5.96	p<.00001
Clark	likes	mean	4.99	4.85	4.92	5.20	5.04	p=.6262
	dislikes	mean	4.81	4.77	4.72	4.65	5.03	p=.6147
Broadbent	likes	mean	6.04	6.17	5.69	5.97	6.27	p=.1919
	dislikes	mean	3.71	3.72	3.86	3.60	3.63	p=.8443
Approximate N = (N varies by leader due to some missing data)			798	222	195	160	221	

Broadbent, however, receive uniform evaluations regardless of how alienated the respondents are. Alienation appears to be significantly based on negative perceptions of Trudeau and to be reduced by positive perceptions of him. Alienation appears to bear no relationship to reaction—positive or negative—to the other leaders.

These data make plain that alienation in 1979 was closely related to feelings about Trudeau. Part of the relationship, however, could be the result of the partisanship of the respondent, which we have seen to be strongly related to alienation, since the alienated are more anti-Liberal party in general. Hence, Table 38 serves to specify the independent influence of Trudeau on these feelings of alienation.[20]

As expected, Liberal identifiers expressed much less dislike for Trudeau or for the Liberal party than did Conservative or NDP identifiers, regardless of the amount of felt alienation. The important result, however, concerns the relationship within each party between alienation and attitudes towards Trudeau. In every case, greater degrees of alienation are associated with greater dislike of Trudeau and of the Liberal party. The alienated Liberals— most of whom voted for Trudeau, after all—still rated their dislike of him nearly twice as high as the least alienated group. The range of negative sentiments about Trudeau within Liberal ranks was considerably greater (3.79—2.30 = 1.49) than for Conservatives (.66) or the NDP (1.03). Although Trudeau seems to be an independent stimulus to alienation among British Columbians, the effect of his personality or politics appears greatest *among his own potential supporters.* Among the least alienated Liberals, there was more dislike for the party than the leader, while among the more alienated, the negative views of Trudeau outpaced those for the Liberal party.

TABLE 38

MEAN SCORES ON "DISLIKE TRUDEAU" AND "DISLIKE FEDERAL LIBERAL PARTY" BY FEDERAL PARTY IDENTIFICATION AND BY ALIENATION

Party identification	Alienation	Mean dislike score for:	
		Trudeau	*Federal Liberal Party*
Liberal	1 = low	2.30	2.95
	2	2.58	2.86
	3	3.08	2.84
	4 = high	3.79	3.64
Progressive Conservative	1	6.29	5.82
	2	6.13	5.73
	3	6.90	6.93
	4	6.95	6.40
New Democratic Party	1	5.26	5.49
	2	5.79	6.06
	3	5.38	5.73
	4	6.29	6.93
		(Ns range: 39-86)	(Ns range: 39-84)

When we examined the ratings for Clark and Broadbent, in contrast, we found no relationship between level of alienation and positive or negative feelings. Just as for the sample as a whole, a control for party identification or for vote revealed no relationship between alienation and the evaluation of the leaders of the Conservative or NDP parties. Only Trudeau and the Liberal party consistently aroused negative feelings differentially among the four levels of alienation.

Parties differ, therefore, in how they evaluate each other and in how they rate each other's leaders. But only the Liberal party and Trudeau serve as targets of negative sentiment specifically related to alienation as measured here.

IDEOLOGY AND ALIENATION

Many commentators on western alienation assert that it reflects a conservative ideological orientation. Gibbins, for example, argues that alienation and conservatism in Alberta form a relatively unified ideological structure, and his data provide some evidence for that conclusion.[21] Several of the authors in a book on western separatism point to the uses of alienation or separatism as a "short-cut" to the achievement of a new, more conservative or free enterprise economic and social order.[22] Just as there are partisan differences in degree of alienation, we might therefore expect ideological differences in our sample of British Columbians to be closely related to alienation. The fact that the expected relationship with conservatism is absent is one more piece of evidence for the view that "western" alienation has a different character in different provinces.[23] There are two major measures of ideological orientation in the B.C. survey which are relevant here. One, which has figured prominently throughout this book, is the measure of "Individual versus Collective Responsibility." The other is the measure of populism which was discussed in Chapter 4. The brief answer is this: individual versus collective responsibility has no relationship with B.C. alienation by any of several statistical tests.[24] Within partisan groups defined by party identification or by vote, the relationship is also non-significant. This finding points to a clear separation between the federal and provincial party systems in the minds of voters, and that forms the basis for the analysis in the next chapter. Populism, on the other hand, is strongly and positively related to B.C. alienation.[25] In the sample as a whole and within each partisan group, greater alienation is associated with greater populist sentiment.

This pattern has interesting implications. Most observers and historians have agreed that most western protest movements have had a populist basis. Likewise, this measure of populism is strongly related to alienation among all partisan groups. The fact that B.C. alienation bears no relationship at all to individual versus collective responsibility means that in B.C. this form of populist protest has no connection with the main expression of liberal or conservative ideologies or that it has equal connection with both elements of ideology. Therefore, the protest movements of the past, if similar to "western alienation" today, may not have represented a generalized ideological context but one focused on specific issues and specific grievances, the topic to which we now turn.

POLITICAL ISSUES AND ALIENATION

Western alienation has a long history. It has traditionally been associated with certain issues and particularly with certain policies and actions of the federal government. These have included freight rates and transportation policy in general, tariff barriers favourable to industry in central Canada, the lack of government action in regard to marketing raw materials and in regard to extreme fluctuations in commodity prices, and the imbalance between central Canada and the west in industrial development opportunities. This is not the place to debate the accuracy of popular evaluations,[26] but we can address the question of whether these policies and activities have current relevance in the eyes of our alienated respondents. We can likewise examine whether any new issues have gained prominence as sources of alienation and whether these explain why the alienated are so much more negative than the less alienated about Trudeau and the Liberal party.

First, the traditional grievances were hardly ever mentioned by respondents as prominent concerns. For example, only eleven people gave as one of their three most important issues topics which could be interpreted as grievances about tariffs, whereas forty-two people had favourable things to say about tariffs. Not a single person mentioned freight rates, and the few people who discussed transportation were primarily exercised about the lack of rapid transit facilities in Vancouver and about the price of gasoline. To the extent that industrial policy was broached, it concerned the lack of federal policy about foreign investment more than favouritism towards Ontario or Quebec. Of course, this is a sample in British Columbia; a comparable study in the Prairies or Atlantic Canada might reveal greater discontent about these matters. Nevertheless, for residents of B.C., alienation seems unrelated to the long-standing policy grievances of the West. This is perhaps further evidence that western alienation may not be western in scope or uniform throughout the western provinces.

Second, several other issues do have a clearer place in the pantheon of western grievances. In particular, issues such as fisheries policy, control of off-shore resources, energy development and pricing, and the whole area of economic growth loom relatively large in the sample. Federal cultural and language policies provide additional sources of grievance for large segments of the population, linked to alienation for some but not for others.[27] These concerns are not, however, exclusively the preserve of disgruntled British Columbians. Although the alienated respondents were somewhat more likely to express pure criticism, the less alienated were likely to propose federal initiatives in these areas as well as to criticize federal policy. In short, many areas of concern stimulated our respondents to chastize the federal government, but they then called for *better federal policies* as least as often as they demanded that the federal government leave these matters to provincial or private control.

Third, in aggregating responses across all issues mentioned, each person was scored in terms of whether his preferences clearly favoured actions which would centralize policy and government activity, which would decentralize them (to the provincial level or to the subprovincial and local level), or which did not take a clear position on this dimension. Those respondents who favoured some degree of centralization outnumbered the decentralizers by 168 to 102, with the rest being neutral or unclear about their position. The "centralists" tend to have lower scores on B.C. alienation than those with no position or those who are "decentralizers." The latter group, however, is quite evenly spread across all levels of the B.C. alienation scale, suggesting that their alienation is not explained solely by their views on where decision-making should occur. On some issues the alienated prefer federal action, and on other issues they advocate provincial or local action. Again we see that alienation based on a judgement that the government has handled some issue badly must not be generalized to a wholly negative assessment of that government.

Fourth, each party consists of people who represent all of the points of view just outlined. Some Liberals, for example, are quite alienated, even though as a whole they are the least alienated group. The alienated Liberals are alienated in part because they focus on traditional or current grievances and favour decentralization of policy. Many Progressive Conservatives and NDPers, on the other hand, score quite low on our measure of alienation; and this relates to their focus on grievances not specific to the west or not related to one level of government and to their favouring more centralized structures or policy, at least on some matters of government activity.

Finally, there is a shrewd or canny quality to many issue positions enunciated by our sample, and this quality bodes ill for any conclusion that the alienated are passionate or hot-headed fanatics. Many people, for example, prefer that certain activities be under joint provincial and federal control, suggesting a lack of "we-they" thinking. Others bemoan the fact that matters are under federal control but recognize that there is no feasible alternative since nation-wide co-ordination is necessary. Not all respondents exhibit such "balanced" thinking, but many do; and many of the alienated are just as shrewd, balanced, and ambivalent as the least alienated. One does not readily build successful protest movements or separatist organizations around recruits with these habits of thought.

CONCLUSION

Alienation generally refers to a condition of *estrangement from something*; but in complex societies like Canada, with an extensive division of labour, regionalism, and social heterogeneity, everyone must be alienated from something. The fact of alienation, therefore, is only of passing interest in itself. Of greater importance is the specification of the objects from which people feel alienated. Of greatest importance is the interpretation to be placed on the social and political meaning of alienation.

This analysis of western alienation in British Columbia has uncovered several ways in which political motives underlie expressions of alienation. In particular, these motives constitute quite common types of political orientation—feelings about parties, leaders, and issues—and are not in large measure expressions of hostility toward Canada or its basic institutions. The variety of alienation examined here does not to any significant degree put in question the existence of national unity or the legitimacy of the federal government. Indeed, it may be inappropriate to call these feelings "alienation." Feelings of estrangement which focus specifically on the party responsible for most governmental performance in the recent past and on its long-time leader should perhaps be termed discontent or partisan opposition rather than alienation.

Although one might, in the abstract, wish there were less alienation or none at all, one can be optimistic and positive in light of this evidence. There are problems—economic, social, and political—and it would be surprising and disturbing to find that no one was alienated, disaffected, disgruntled, or critical.[28] Instead we have found evidence that a wide variety of Canadians in B.C. can express reasoned disagreement with their federal government, its leader, and his party without calling into question their affection for Canada or their belief that in other ways the federal government can be trusted to perform many activities passably well. Moreover, alienated British Columbians tend to support the Progressive Conservative party rather than withdraw from federal politics or turn to separatist alternatives.

One must emphasize that we are talking about the full variety of British Columbians. There are no significant and interpretable demographic or sociological differences between the alienated and not alienated respondents. To the extent it occurs, alienation can be found equally in all parts of the province, among all socio-economic strata, throughout the multitude of groups defined in terms of ethnicity, province of birth, education, age, and religion.[29] Alienation of the sort assessed here is not a dark and foreboding force lurking in pockets of ignorance, economic disadvantage, or personal failure; nor is it an expression of élitist conservatism. It is arguably a political response to political problems.

One must not be overly optimistic, however, and jump uncritically from Cassandra to Pollyanna. Many respondents, whether alienated or not, voiced opinions which were judicious and balanced, and it behooves us to be equally even-handed about alienation as a phenomenon in Canada. In conclusion, therefore, we wish to suggest three ways in which alienation may continue to be a problem worthy of the attention of scholars and political actors, even if it is not a problem as severe as many accounts imply. Western alienation in British Columbia does not threaten the foundations of the polity, but it is a sign of citizen grievances.

First, the summary of issue concerns revealed that there are genuine concerns about what the governments of this country have been doing or not doing. The sense of alienation, muted though it is, stems in part from a reasoned discontent with several significant areas of policy and performance. These concerns could fester if political leaders, parties, and governments fail to deal with them; but they can be contained and perhaps reduced if governments act appropriately. That is, after all, how it should be. Democratic theory suggests that the people should voice their concerns, and voting should reflect their judgement about who can best deal with these problems. Those elected then should attend to the problems and only secondarily focus on the apparent alienation which the voters evince.

Second, we must emphasize that these data refer only to British Columbia. We believe that they have some applicability to other provinces, but the intensity of grievances may be greater elsewhere, the specific issues may be different in other provinces, and obviously evaluations of the parties and leaders vary widely in other parts of Canada. Two lessons may be drawn from this belief. Policies which are undertaken to quell the feelings of alienation in one part of Canada may exacerbate them in another place. After all, part of the discontent in B.C. or elsewhere in the west derives from an assessment of policies which were partly designed with the hope of stemming the tide of discontent among residents of Ontario and especially Quebec. In addition, policies are not always intended to help or to hinder regional or provincial groups, nor should they be. They are often undertaken to deal with problems specific to types of individuals wherever they live, and different parts of Canada feel their impact differently because of the varying proportions of people of particular types in the various regions and locales. Regionalism and alienation are, to that extent, incidental and inevitable by-products of national policies.

Finally, alienation probably derives more from doing things than from not doing them. To the extent that government undertakes responsibility for ever wider aspects of life, it draws the fire of critical assessments which in earlier so-called "simpler" times were directed at a broad spectrum of institutions. Surely that is fair and proper. But it is too easily forgotten in our haste to analyse growing discontent with government, whether federal, provincial, or local. As leaders, parties, and governments arouse expectations that problems can and will be solved, they run the risk of failure, of alienating some by helping others, and of making compromises which leave no one feeling satisfied although few are fully left out.

As Schaar has sagely noted in his extensive analysis of the United States:

> It is true of course that variety of loyalties militates not only toward freedom but also toward conflict. Indeed, the basic problem of such a system is that of adjusting competing loyalties within some common frame of reference. As society grows more complex, so does the problem. With this we come to the everyday work of politics. The claims of these competing loyalties must be adjusted, and this has become the chief task of government in the modern liberal democracies.[30]

Alienation in British Columbia exists; it deserves some attention. But it deserves attention mainly because it reveals that people care about Canada, about British Columbia, and about the actions of government, not because it is a serious problem which can be eradicated without changing the activities which have given rise to it over a long period of time. We have argued that "alienation" is probably an inappropriate label for the phenomena outlined in this chapter. Better would be words like discontent, policy grievances, or partisan rivalry. Such words would be better because they are more precise. They would also be better because it is easier to accept that people can have such feelings and still consider themselves fully Canadian. As long as "western alienation" is the phrase we use, however, we must constantly remind ourselves that alienation and allegiance can be found in the same person, and that allegiance and discontent may reflect a reasoned posture and a balanced assessment of political objects.

Having demonstrated that British Columbians are truly Canadians, we can now turn our attention to the ways in which federal and provincial concerns intersect in the province. This is the subject of Chapter 8. Our analysis of alienation has also shown how the attitudes it represents link British Columbians to other Canadians beyond the province's borders. In fact, British Columbians are self-consciously members of the Canadian political community and, as such, participate in the same party system and issue space as do other Canadians, despite the apparent isolation of the world of provincial politics. These links are explored further in Chapter 9.

8

The Federal Connection

British Columbia is widely perceived to be a province cut off emotionally as well as physically from the rest of Canada. As R.M. Burns put it: "Under most of its leaders in recent times British Columbia has been chiefly concerned with its own affairs and the pursuit of its own destiny, rather than with establishing itself as a vital and integral part of the Canadian nation."[1] Pierre Trudeau once described British Columbians as people who dwell at the foot of the mountain but never climb to the top. British Columbia has never really produced a prime minister or even a leader of one of the major national parties although it did provide seats for Sir John A. Macdonald and T.C. Douglas when they suffered electoral setbacks in their home provinces. John Turner attempted to use his ties to the province to help rebuild the national Liberal party in 1984. His efforts did produce a prime minister from British Columbia, but only for the short time between his swearing in as the member for Vancouver Quadra and his resignation as prime minister. For their part, British Columbians apparently[2] share with other western Canadians a feeling that their views have a limited impact on national affairs because of their small share of Canada's population and, as we saw in the last chapter, because substantial numbers feel that the federal government has lost touch with their problems and aspirations.

Yet, despite the peculiarities of its provincial party system and the parochialism of some its leaders, B.C. has never completely abandoned its interest in the divisions represented by the dominant federal parties. The Progressive Conservative party has been the major beneficiary of that link most recently, but the province's voters have exhibited strong Liberal sympathies in the past. Conservative ascendance and Liberal decline are both linked to feelings of alienation which developed after 1968, independently of developments in the provincial party system.

The provincial and federal elections in May 1979 were close in time but distant in psychological space. Voters moving from the provincial political system to the federal entered an arena with different party histories, different coalitions of voters, and different strategic circumstances. Issues of inflation, unemployment, and economic mismanagement were prominent in both campaigns, but the federal election also provided an outlet for feelings of alienation from Ottawa and ratification or rejection of the constitutional and language policies of the federal government.

Twelve days after maintaining the provincial government in power (albeit with a reduced majority), the province's voters[3] returned to the polls to assist in the defeat of the federal government. The provincial Conservative party had bravely contested 65 per cent of the seats in the provincial legislature but was rewarded with barely 5 per cent of the vote. The federal Conservatives,

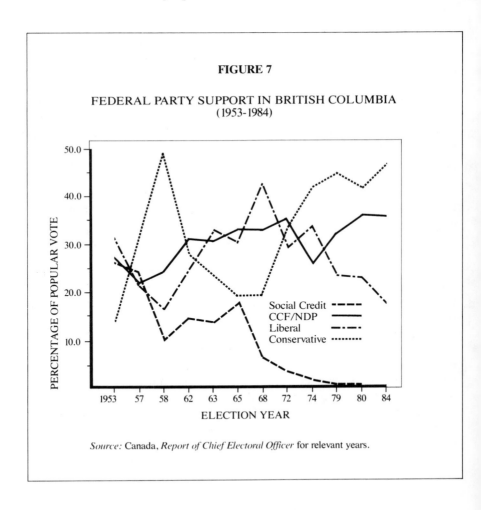

FIGURE 7

FEDERAL PARTY SUPPORT IN BRITISH COLUMBIA
(1953-1984)

Source: Canada, *Report of Chief Electoral Officer* for relevant years.

on the other hand, were jubilant. With nearly 45 per cent of the vote (Figure 7), their best federal showing since the 1958 Diefenbaker landslide, and the lion's share of the province's parliamentary delegation (nineteen of twenty-eight seats), they made a major contribution to the short-lived Clark government.

The 1980 election destroyed Conservative euphoria, but the province remained a Conservative stronghold despite a small vote drop and seat losses to the NDP. The Liberal party, which had a minor presence in the provincial election (it ran only 5 candidates), made a brave effort federally but was crushed, winning 23 per cent of the vote and electing but one candidate. The decline in Liberal popularity did not end there. In February 1980, the party managed just 22.2 per cent and their only Member of Parliament from British Columbia was defeated. In September 1984 they sank to a level not seen since the 1958 Diefenbaker landslide—16.4 per cent.

The analysis in this chapter is based mainly on the survey of the 1979 federal election. The results of that election in British Columbia helped to deprive the Liberals of the reins of power in Ottawa, if only temporarily, but their poor showing in the province was expected. New Democrats must have been much more disappointed. As a provincial party they received 46 per cent of the vote, the highest level in their history, and reduced the Social Credit majority from seventeen seats to five. As a federal party, less than two weeks later, they finished a distant second to the Conservatives with just under 32 per cent of the vote. This was better than their 1974 performance, but, as can be seen in Figure 7, it was not much different from their long-term average. The NDP was the only party to contest all seats at both electoral levels in the province, and since provincial and federal election campaigns proceeded virtually simultaneously, their experience dramatically illustrates the separation of federal and provincial contexts.

In all, approximately 65 per cent of those who voted in both elections in 1979 voted differently. Table 39 details their political journeys. Despite the coincidence of federal and provincial campaigns and the short time-lapse between the two elections, the NDP was able to deliver only 64 per cent of its

TABLE 39

VOTER MIGRATIONS, 1979
(vertical percentages)

Federal vote	Provincial vote				
	Liberal	Conservative	NDP	Social Credit	Total
Liberal	87.5	13.9	12.6	27.5	21.8
Conservative	12.5	80.6	22.3	69.3	48.0
NDP	0.0	2.8	63.7	2.3	29.0
Social Credit	0.0	2.8	0.0	1.0	0.6
Other	0.0	0.0	1.5	0.0	0.7
	(16)	(16)	(278)	(309)	

provincial supporters to the federal party. The remainder distributed themselves between the federal Conservatives and Liberals in a ratio of just under
two to one. Transfers to the federal NDP from other provincial parties were
almost negligible with the result that almost 96 per cent of federal NDP
support came from those who had voted NDP in the preceding provincial
election.

The federal Conservative party *is* the provincial Social Credit party for
many voters. Nearly 70 per cent of those who voted for the government in the
provincial election went on to support the federal Conservatives. The Social
Credit to federal Conservative transfer rate is higher than the NDP transfer
rate between levels, and may seem to justify the suspicion expressed in some
quarters that a "deal" existed between federal Tory and provincial Social
Credit leaders. Provincial Tories charged that the federal party deliberately
ignored them and expected Social Credit support for Conservative federal
candidates in return. In fact, the account of provincial political history
presented in chapters 2 and 3 shows that Conservative weakness at the
provincial level dates back to 1952, the first provincial election following the
termination of coalition government. It is unlikely that support from the
federal party in 1979 would have made any difference.

The magnitude of voter shifting *between* levels confirms the fact that the
province has a two-party system provincially and a three-party system federally.
However, a comparison of changes *within* levels, vote shifts from the previous election (1974 in the federal case and 1975 provincially) reveals another
important difference between the two contexts. Party choice in the 1979
federal election represented a change from 1974 for 32 per cent of those who
voted in both elections. The comparable figure for switching between the
1975 and 1979 provincial elections was only 19 per cent. As one would
expect, the federal Liberal party was the main victim, abandoned by nearly
53 per cent of its 1974 supporters who also voted in 1979. Even more
ominous and, we would argue, indicative of the importance of short term
forces in the 1979 federal election, was the defection rate among those who
normally consider themselves to be federal Liberal identifiers (Table 40).
Over one-quarter of those who identify with the federal Liberal party voted
Conservative in 1979 and an additional 8.7 per cent voted NDP, a defection
rate nearly three times greater than that for the NDP and over 5.5 times
greater than the Conservative defection rate. In 1980, the party fared even
worse among its own identifiers: only 52.1 per cent voted Liberal, 29.6 per
cent voted Conservative, and 18.3 per cent voted for the NDP (results not
shown in tabular form). Again the contrast with the provincial context is
illuminating. In the May 1979 provincial election Social Credit and the NDP
received the support of all but 5.3 per cent and 2.4 per cent, respectively, of
their provincial identifiers. In short, the provincial election was marked by

relatively stable voter alignments; the federal election by a good deal of switching. The federal Liberal party, in second place among party identifiers, finished third at the polls.

TABLE 40

IMPACT OF PARTY IDENTIFICATION ON FEDERAL VOTE, 1979
(vertical percentages)

Federal vote	Federal party identification				
	Independent	Liberal	PC	NDP	Total
Liberal	26.7	64.1	2.3	4.2	23.2
Conservative	46.7	26.6	93.0	8.5	46.6
NDP	25.0	8.7	4.2	86.7	29.0
Social Credit	1.7	0.0	0.5	0.0	0.5
Other	0.0	0.5	0.0	0.6	0.9
	(60)	(184)	(214)	(165)	

FEDERAL AND PROVINCIAL POLITICAL SETTINGS IN BRITISH COLUMBIA

As devastated as the Liberals were, their federal defeats in 1979 and 1980 represented a level of support not much worse than their best showing (23.3 per cent in 1952) in provincial elections since the break-up of coalition (compare figures 1 and 7). Provincial Conservative support also peaked (at 15.2 per cent) in the first election after coalition. The federal Conservatives have surpassed this figure in every election since 1957, despite considerable variation over time. Examination of the ebb and flow of support for these two parties strongly suggests that their provincial and federal fortunes are not strongly linked, an observation confirmed by statistical analysis. The correlation between federal and provincial vote shares for both Liberals and Conservatives over the period 1949-74 is effectively zero.[4] This separation dates at least from the collapse of the federal two-party system in 1921 in the case of the Liberals. For the Conservatives, provincial and federal fortunes were apparently connected from 1921 until the formation of the provincial coalition (as indicated by a correlation of .60). At the present time, only Quebec rivals British Columbia in the distinctiveness of provincial and federal party systems, although Saskatchewan and Alberta were also companions during the elections of the 1950s and 1960s.[5]

History has rendered a harsh judgement on Conservative participation in the coalition which governed the province from 1941 to 1952. As the junior partner in a union where the Liberal party always supplied the premier, they could rarely claim credit for government initiatives and accomplishments. The coalition's formula for contesting elections effectively discriminated against the Conservatives. Sitting Liberals and Conservatives were automatically nominated as coalition candidates in 1945 and 1949, giving an edge to the Liberals who entered the coalition with more members (twenty-one versus twelve), although that may have helped only to determine the relative ratio of defeat in 1952. As Conservative provincial organization atrophied, federal leaders of the party, dependent on support of the provincial organization in contesting federal elections, exerted increasing pressure on their provincial counterparts to withdraw from coalition, only to be rebuffed.[6] The legacy of bitterness thus created did not end with coalition[7] and helped to create divisions within the provincial party itself. In fact, W.A.C. Bennett's successful flirtation with Social Credit came after being defeated in challenges for leadership of the provincial Conservative party.

Yet the impact of coalition cannot be the whole story underlying the current separation of federal and provincial party systems. The provincial Liberal party did not completely disappear after coalition, but its level of support has been relatively independent of federal successes and failures both before and after. Several variants of socialism had a more significant presence provincially than federally even prior to the formation of the Co-operative Commonwealth Federation.[8] Even today NDP federal and provincial vote shares are only weakly correlated (at .33 from 1949-74).[9]

We do not wish to ignore the impact of federal government activity on provincial politics. From agitation over delayed completion of the Canadian Pacific Railway and a demand for renegotiation of the terms of union in the nineteenth century to conflict over the Columbia River Treaty and off-shore jurisdiction more recently, provincial and federal authorities have had many serious clashes.[10] Yet this may only confirm the significance of economic issues in the province's politics. Arguments that W.A.C. Bennett was able to make political capital in provincial elections by visiting the sins of Liberal or Conservative federal governments on their provincial counterparts[11] ignore the fact that there is no relationship between their shares of the provincial and federal votes. Why would a disgruntled provincial voter punish the federal government by proxy and then ignore its sins against the province in the next federal election?[12] When he called the 1979 provincial election, Premier W.R. Bennett stated that provincial NDP willingness to surrender jurisdiction over the province's oil and natural gas was one of the main reasons governing the timing of the election. Not a single respondent in our survey mentioned this as an issue in either campaign, and support for the NDP increased at both levels.

However the historical record may be interpreted, we would argue that recent electoral developments at the federal level have proceeded independently of those at the provincial level. Conservative successes represent the culmination of revival which has been building since 1968. Liberal losses represent an almost complementary pattern. During the period Pierre Trudeau led the Liberal party its support in the province dropped nearly 20 percentage points (from 41.8 per cent to 22.2 per cent) and its share of the seats from 70 per cent to zero. While Liberal and Conservative leaders glared at each other across the aisle in the House of Commons during the minority Parliament from 1972 to 1974, nearly all their colleagues in the provincial legislature swallowed their differences. They joined Social Credit in a determined, and ultimately successful, bid to oust the provincial NDP from power, a party whose federal members were helping to maintain the Liberals in power in Ottawa.[13]

Federal and provincial elections offer somewhat different sets of choices. Only the Liberals and Conservatives have a realistic chance of forming the government in Ottawa, and despite the fulminations of critics of the modern bureaucratic state and the occasional musings of Pierre Trudeau about the death of free enterprise, the socialist bogey so prominent in provincial politics assumes a lower profile federally. Voters should also have at least as much difficulty as political scientists in assigning positions to the three major federal parties on a left-right continuum, even if the left anchor seems obvious. The decision may have been easier in 1979 given the unusual stridency of Conservative defence of free enterprise and small government, but other issues intervened.

Overlaying the individual/collective responsibility division so prominent in provincial politics are differences with regard to Liberal government language and constitutional policy and attitudes towards Ottawa generally. At least part of the Liberal drop in popularity can be attributed to discontent with the federal government based on an accumulation of separate grievances.[14] For some, alienation has become personified, bound up with attitudes towards Pierre Trudeau, who is seen as aloof, arrogant, occasionally ruthless, and even foreign. Others object to the perceived domination of the national agenda by issues of bilingualism and biculturalism and the demands of Quebec. Such feelings are no doubt enhanced by provincial government rhetoric denouncing federal opposition to various province-building objectives.[15] Even the ill-chosen remark by a Social Credit cabinet minister bemoaning the appearance of the French language on his box of breakfast cereal struck a responsive chord among many members of the public. However, alienation from the federal Liberal government, at least, is independent of choice between the two main provincial parties.[16] More to the point, the three dimensions which appear significant in federal politics—individual/collective responsibility, alienation, and ethnocentrism (our label for attitudes towards bilingualism, biculturalism, and the position of Quebec)—cut across each other at the individual level.[17] An individual with strong collective responsibility sentiments, for example, might be drawn towards the federal NDP, but if repelled by federal language policies, he or she might be attracted by the Conservatives.

The 1979 federal election also presented a different set of strategic circumstances than the provincial contest. All federal constituencies in the province were contested by the Liberals, Conservatives, and the NDP. Nearly half the respondents in our survey found themselves in situations where defections from the third-place party conceivably could determine which of the two front runners emerged victorious. This kind of setting provides an opportunity for voters to engage in "strategic" or "second-choice" voting. Since only the Liberals and Conservatives had a realistic chance of forming the federal government, potential NDP supporters with strong anti-Liberal feelings could perceive a Conservative vote as the best guarantee of Liberal defeat. Voters who supported the NDP provincially but not federally were disproportionately willing to engage in strategic voting and, as we shall see, this may have helped the Conservatives.[18]

It would be a mistake to argue that there are no links between provincial and federal voting patterns. The leadership of the provincial New Democratic Party makes no secret of its federal sympathies. Social Credit leaders, by their words and deeds, telegraphed a preference for the federal party which promised to pay greater attention to provincial aspirations and demands, the Conservatives. Nearly 40 per cent of those eligible to vote in both elections in May 1979 have the same party identification at both levels, and for some of them the federal election presented an opportunity to ratify a preference they are unable or unwilling to express in provincial elections.[19]

Nevertheless, the federal system is not a simple replica of the provincial one. Most federal Conservative voters supported Social Credit in the provincial elections, but so did most Liberals. Even more significantly, federal Liberals and Conservatives as a group are more individualistic than the NDP

TABLE 41

ATTITUDINAL DIVISIONS AMONG FEDERAL VOTERS
BY PROVINCIAL PARTY SUPPORT

		Federal vote				
		Liberal		Conservative		NDP
	Provincial vote:	Social Credit	NDP	Social Credit	NDP	Social Credit[1]	NDP
Attitude scale							
Alienation		2.01	1.79	2.75	2.79	—	2.45
Ethnocentrism		3.19	2.79	3.85	3.89	—	3.03
Collective Responsibility		3.42	4.07	3.24	3.94	—	4.23

1. Table entries are mean scores on the relevant attitudinal dimension exhibited by combinations of federal and provincial voting patterns. Only six respondents reported a Social Credit provincial vote and an NDP federal vote, too few cases on which to calculate a reliable mean score.

(scoring 3.4 on in the individual/collective responsibility scale compared to 4.2 for federal NDP supporters), but each is internally divided on this dimension depending on which provincial party was supported in 1979 (Table 41).[20] The magnitude of differences by provincial vote within these two parties is comparable to Social Credit and NDP differences in the provincial electorate as a whole. Voters who opposed each other on left-right questions in provincial politics are drawn together within each of the Liberal and Conservative parties by similar levels of alienation and ethnocentrism.[21] A more detailed look at the federal voting coalitions also reveals the emergence of time-honoured ethnic and religious divisions between the supporters of the two major federal parties.

THE FEDERAL PARTY COALITIONS

Subjective social class position is linked to choice in federal elections, but class divisions appear less sharp than in provincial elections, even acknowledging the complication introduced by having three serious contenders for the province's federal representation. The NDP provincial majorities among blue collar workers, low income groups, and voters who place themselves in the working class decline to pluralities, and the middle class-working class difference in rates of support for the party decline by just over five percentage points (compare Table 42 to Tables 19 and 21). The drop in working class support (58.0 per cent to 40.3 per cent) was particularly pronounced. Nearly as many in the working class voted Conservative as NDP. Nevertheless, with the exception of education (which did not display a consistent pattern provincially either), the various class indicators divide NDP supporters from Conservative ones. The picture for the federal Liberal party appears more confusing until we realize that the poor performance of the party in 1979 was apparently general. The ability of the Liberals to gather support across class lines has been a major feature of its federal dominance. Critics of the party's elasticity will no doubt appreciate the irony of the pattern's persistence in an electoral rout.

The highest levels of Liberal support in 1979 were found among Roman Catholics and those of French ethnic origin (Table 43). This conforms to the national pattern, but in an overwhelmingly British (in ethnic origin) and Protestant province it was not enough to give the Liberals a firm foothold. Variation by religion in support for the Conservatives and the NDP also conforms to expectations. The Conservatives received strong support from the mainstream Protestant religions, and New Democrats from those with no religious affiliation.[22] With the exception of party preferences among Roman Catholics, these and other religious differences between Conservative and

TABLE 42

SOCIAL CLASS AND FEDERAL VOTE, 1979
(horizontal percentages)

Social class indicator	Federal vote			
	Liberal	Conservative	NDP	
Family Income				
less than $10,000	16.3	37.2	45.0	(95)
10,000-14,999	25.0	41.3	32.5	(68)
15,000-24,999	28.7	43.3	27.0	(145)
25,000-34,999	22.9	50.4	26.0	(109)
35,000 and over	27.3	52.1	19.8	(95)
Education				
Elementary or less	28.1	40.6	28.1	(32)
Some high school	18.2	52.2	28.9	(159)
Some post-secondary	23.6	46.8	28.6	(280)
Some college or university	28.9	40.1	29.8	(242)
Occupation				
managerial/professional	23.2	43.6	31.8	(211)
white collar	24.5	49.1	25.5	(110)
blue collar	15.7	37.8	44.2	(217)
farmer	14.3	64.3	21.4	(14)
Subjective class				
upper middle	18.2	63.6	15.2	(33)
middle	28.4	48.4	22.3	(215)
working	18.8	38.7	40.3	(191)
no class label	25.2	45.6	28.9	(270)
Approximate total[1]	20.9	42.4	35.4	

1. Totals differ given varying amounts of missing data. Row percentages do not add to 100 per cent because Social Credit and "other" federal voters have been omitted.

NDP support are a muted version of Social Credit and NDP differences in provincial elections (compare Table 43 with Table 26). If Roman Catholics are excluded, the rank order of religious groups in terms of Conservative support is precisely the same as the order associated with Social Credit voting provincially.

Religious differences in provincial voting disappeared once class and ideological measures were introduced. The fact that variations in NDP and Conservative federal support are associated with social class differences is one sign that the same may be true for federal voting. However, support for the NDP, the one constant in the federal and provincial contests, declined across all class categories, suggesting that other factors must be at work in federal politics, factors which cut across class lines.

TABLE 43
ETHNICITY, RELIGION AND 1979 FEDERAL VOTE
(horizontal percentages)

	1979 vote			
Religion	*Liberal*	*Conservative*	*NDP*	*Per cent of electorate*
None	18.4	30.6	46.9	21.3
Roman Catholic	41.0	41.0	18.0	14.5
Anglican	17.5	57.9	24.6	16.5
Baptist	13.6	36.4	50.0	3.2
Lutheran	17.9	39.3	42.9	4.1
United Church	24.9	51.3	23.8	27.9
Fundamentalist	18.2	59.1	13.6	3.2
Ethnic Group				
British	19.1	49.8	29.5	61.8
French	42.3	30.8	26.9	3.7
German	25.0	45.0	30.0	5.7
Dutch	40.9	45.5	13.6	3.1
N. Europe	29.5	38.6	29.5	6.3
E. Europe	27.8	42.6	29.6	7.7

Table 44 introduces two possible candidates, alienation from the federal government and central Canada and ethnocentrism, neither of which is strongly related to social class,[23] but each of which is related to federal party support. Conservative and NDP voters are as a group significantly more alienated than Liberal voters, but the difference between them is not statistically significant. Liberals and New Democrats are significantly less ethnocentric than Conservatives, but do not differ between themselves on that dimension. Liberals and Conservatives are each more individualistic than New Democrats, but one group is not significantly more individualistic than the other.

Variations in Conservative support are related to position on all three dimensions: higher scores on ethnocentrism and alienation and lower scores on individual/collective responsibility are associated with higher levels of Conservative voting. There is less variation on the individual/collective responsibility dimension in the case of the Liberals, but they too seem to be more attractive to individualists. However, in contrast to the Conservative case, Liberals are rejected by the highly alienated and ethnocentric. The only clear relationship in the case of NDP support occurs for individual/collective responsibility, although the party's support drops off considerably among the most ethnocentric. Partisan differences associated with these dimensions persist after the introduction of a variety of control variables (Table 45).[24]

Table 45 has been constructed using the same procedures used in earlier chapters where the relative impact of a variety of personal and situational

TABLE 44

ATTITUDINAL DIVISIONS IN THE FEDERAL ELECTORATE
(horizontal percentages)

| Attitudinal dimension[1] | Federal vote | | | |
	Liberal	Conservative	NDP	Total
Individual/collective				
Responsibility: Individual	29.4	57.8	12.8	18.8
	25.4	48.6	26.1	24.8
	21.8	51.2	27.1	29.7
Collective	20.0	30.7	49.0	26.7
Mean score within parties	3.51	3.41	4.19	(572)
Alienation: low alienation	32.2	36.8	29.6	29.3
	26.4	45.7	27.1	24.9
	21.2	44.2	33.6	21.8
high alienation	13.7	57.3	27.4	23.9
Mean score within parties	1.97	2.70	2.44	(512)
Ethnocentrism:				
low ethnocentrism	31.0	31.9	35.3	20.1
	24.1	45.6	27.8	13.7
	25.3	38.6	36.1	14.4
	27.8	48.1	22.2	18.8
	15.0	54.0	31.0	19.6
high ethnocentrism	18.2	62.3	19.5	13.4
Mean score within parties	3.02	3.77	3.09	(570)

1. Scale categories have been collapsed for ease of presentation. However, mean scores are based on the full range of each scale, 0-6 for individual/collective responsibility and ethnocentrism and 0-8 for alienation.

Within each attitudinal category each row of the table has been ordered according to the direction of the scale scores, for example, in the case of individual/collective responsibility, from most individualistic to most collectively oriented. In the most collective category, 20 per cent voted Liberal, 30.7 per cent voted Conservative, and 49.0 per cent voted NDP in 1979.

factors were evaluated for their relative impact on voting. The numbers listed in the three columns of the table measure the effect (size and direction) of the factors listed on the left as explanatory variables on the probability of voting for a given federal party. It is more awkward to represent these effects in a three-party system than in the essentially two-party provincial system. The simplest solution was to compare the characteristics of those who voted for a given party with those who did not, regardless of the alternative they selected. Hence the first column identifies the predictors of the probability of voting Progressive Conservative versus Liberal *or* NDP, column 2 the predictors of a Liberal vote rather than Conservative or NDP, and column 3 predictors of the choice of the NDP over either of the traditional parties.

Most of the explanatory variables should be familiar by now from the use made of them previously. "No religion" dichotomizes the electorate into those with some religious affiliation and those without. "Roman Catholic" divides the electorate in another way, between Roman Catholics and everybody else. The presence of both factors in the table allows us to compare, other things being equal, the voting propensities of the non-religious and Roman Catholics to those of Protestants and adherents of other religions. If no entry appears opposite a given explanatory variable, it means that that characteristic does not have have a significant effect on the vote. Hence, in Table 45 there is, apparently, no specific Roman Catholic effect on the choice between the Conservatives over the Liberals and the NDP. Those with no religion, however, are less likely to vote Conservative than are people with some religious affiliation (of whatever type). For the choice of the Liberals over the other two parties (column 2 of Table 45), only Roman Catholics stand out as distinctively pro-Liberal compared to Protestants, members of other religions, or the non-religious. Finally, in the case of the NDP, the non-religious are more NDP and Roman Catholics less NDP than members of all other religious groups.

Similarly, "middle age" compares those between ages forty and sixty to those under forty or over sixty; "union member" compares union households to households without a union member; professionals and semi-professionals are compared to those in all other occupations (no other occupational distinction proved significant); Liberal and Conservative provincial identifiers are compared to all other voters (including non-identifiers); and those willing to vote strategically under certain circumstances are compared to those who are not.

From the table, it is apparent that the combination of alienation and ethnocentrism is a powerful force behind selection of the federal Conservative party. In fact, nearly 56 per cent of those scoring above the median on both alienation and ethnocentrism scales voted Conservative in 1979. Conversely—no surprise given the results in Chapter 7—a heightened sense of alienation from the federal government and rejection of federal language and cultural policy brings with it increased rejection of the federal Liberal party in British Columbia, as elsewhere in the West.[25] Only 17 per cent of those scoring above the median on both scales voted Liberal.

The importance of attitudes on the individual/collective responsibility dimension to support for the federal NDP already apparent from Table 44 is confirmed by Table 45. But short term forces, which we have tried to capture with the variable measuring willingness to engage in strategic voting, work against the pull of ideology. This variable distinguishes those willing to vote for a party other than their most preferred party in order to prevent victory by a party they strongly dislike from those who would stick with their preferred party in similar circumstantces[26]. The negative sign in the NDP column indicates that the probability of an NDP vote is much less likely among those willing to contemplate this type of behaviour. When coupled with the positive sign on the coefficient for this variable in the Conservative column, signifying a pro-Conservative choice among strategic voters, this result points to the major difficulty encountered by the federal NDP. In national elections, the real contest for power is between the Liberals and Conservatives. For many voters, particularly the highly alienated and those most opposed to federal language and cultural policies, the Liberals were the party to beat. The Conservatives offered the clearest alternative to the Liberals on both these dimensions and a vote for the NDP might easily be seen as a wasted vote in these circumstances.[27]

Liberal support in 1979 was reduced to a central core. Roman Catholics, *provincial* Liberal identifiers (surely the hardiest of party stalwarts), and those whom the federal government failed to alienate had a higher probability of voting Liberal federally than members of other religious groups (and the non-religious), provincial independents or identifiers with other provincial parties, and the highly alienated and ethnocentric. There is a hint that

TABLE 45

DETERMINANTS OF FEDERAL PARTY CHOICE, 1979

	Federal Party[1]		
Explanatory variables	Conservative Effect on vote probability	Liberal Effect on vote probability	NDP Effect on vote probability
No religion	−.16	—	.13
Roman Catholic	—	.17	−.12
Middle age	.12	—	−.12
Working class identifier	—	—	.15
Union member	—	—	.06
Professional occupation	—	—	.11
Liberal or Conservative provincial ID	—	.16	−.16
Willingness to vote strategically	.15	—	−.22
Individual/ collective responsibility	−.05	−.03	.07
Mean alienation ethnocentrism	.07	−.05	—
Metropolitan	.18	—	—
Constant	.22	.43	.20
R^2	.15	.07	.23
F (degrees of freedom)	13.4 (6,462)	8.2 (4,440)	17.1 (9,524)

1. Table entries were obtained using multiple regression analysis, with only the most significant effects (at .05 level) included in the table for each party. The table reports the results of three separate regressions, each one treating the dichotomy represented by the party named at the head of each column versus all other voters as the dependent variable.

increasing collective responsibility scores are also associated with a reduced probability of Liberal voting.

There is little to say about Conservative support beyond what has already been noted. The non-religious are less likely to choose the party over the Liberals or the NDP, and the party did not appeal as strongly to those outside the age group 40 to 60. However, the breadth of its appeal in 1979 (and the narrowness of Liberal appeal) is indicated by its attractiveness to strategic voters, and by the absence of any special significance to identification with the provincial Conservative party.

The core support of the NDP stands out: those who identify themselves as working class, trade union members, and those with no religious affiliation. While the last factor implies less NDP support among those with some religious commitment, the antipathy of Roman Catholics appears to be even more pronounced. The federal NDP is no more attractive to the middle-aged than its provincial counterpart. Another parallel with provincial support, the differential attractiveness of the party to professionals and semi-professionals, is also indicated by the table. Finally, while it may not have helped them very much overall, the NDP's claim to be a party of principle and its emphasis on economic issues in the campaign are reflected in its differential appeal to "sincere" voters,[28] those unwilling to deviate for strategic reasons from their first preference among parties, and to opponents of individualistic policy options.

THE MOVEMENT FROM PROVINCIAL TO FEDERAL PARTY

The task of reconstructing voter decision-making processes is fraught with difficulty, even if we assume that voters can supply reliable information about when they decided how to vote in a given election. Reconstruction of the process and timing of two decisions—choice in the provincial and federal elections of May 1979—is even more difficult. The provincial election was *held* first, but the federal election was *called* first, and an unknown number of voters will have already made up their minds about their federal vote before the possibility of having to make a provincial choice was even raised. The intervention of the provincial election day before the federal election was held may have led some of these voters to reconsider. Other voters will have had standing decisions to support a given party in provincial elections and a different party in federal elections, or the same party in both.[29]

Whatever the sequence of decisions in the minds of voters, behaviour in the two elections provides a sequence which we can analyse for links between provincial and federal voting and for the impact of issue dimensions which were essentially irrelevant in provincial politics.[30] Three such decision sequences involve sufficient numbers of voters to repay consideration: the choice between the Liberals and Conservatives on the part of provincial Social Credit voters; the decision to stick with the NDP or to defect in the case of provincial NDP voters; and, among defectors, the choice between Liberals and Conservatives.[31] Tables 46, 47 and 48, respectively, deal with each of these sequences, using the same techniques employed in constructing Table 45.

We have argued that the different party histories, different issues, and different strategic circumstances in federal elections should affect voters' perceptions of where their interests lie in the two electoral settings. Economic issues were important at both levels in 1979, but the clash between free enterprise and socialism is not the stuff of federal politics. This observation is partly confirmed by the fact that so many provincial NDP voters supported the Conservatives federally. Despite a leavening of free enterprise rhetoric in the Conservative campaign, most notably the promise to dismantle Petro-Canada, the main attraction of the Conservative party was its offer to remedy the neglect of western Canadian interests. More subtly, and despite official party policy, the words and deeds of at least some western Conservative MPs suggested the party was sympathetic to criticisms that concessions to the "French fact" had gone too far.

The overlap of alienation and ethnocentrism among provincial voters precluded their both being used as predictors of the choice between federal Liberals and Conservatives among provincial Social Credit voters (Table 46).[32] Alienation appears to have a slightly stronger impact on that choice, and when it is included in the analysis, ethnocentrism does not make a significant contribution to explanation. Rather than ignore their combined significance, the table has been constructed by using the average of alienation and ethnocentrism scores. The power of these sentiments is undeniable.

TABLE 46

CHOICE BETWEEN FEDERAL CONSERVATIVES AND LIBERALS
AMONG PROVINCIAL SOCIAL CREDIT VOTERS[1]

Dependent variable: probability of voting Conservative versus Liberal		
Explanatory variables	Effect on vote	t
Mean alienation/ethnocentrism score	.076	3.59
Reside in metropolitan region	.287	4.41
Consistent Liberal identifier	−.249	−2.14
Constant	.268	
R² .141		
F(3.216) 12.99		

1. Table entries are regression coefficients. The dependent variable was created by treating the probability described as a dichotomous (1,0) variable. A t-ratio larger than 1.96 signifies a coefficient significant at the .05 level or better.

A difference of 1 point on the combined scale is associated with a difference of 5 percentage points in the probability of choosing the Conservatives over the other two parties. However, other things being equal, the Conservative appeal was much weaker among staunch Liberal supporters (those who consider themselves Liberals both provincially and federally), who in federal politics are able to exercise a choice denied them in provincial politics or perhaps considered unwise given provincial political conditions. The only other factor with a significant effect on federal choice among this group of provincial voters was region. Despite the rural image of the Conservatives in many parts of the West, in British Columbia the party's appeal to provincial Social Credit voters was substantially greater in metropolitan ridings.

TABLE 47

TRANSITION FROM PROVINCIAL NDP VOTE TO FEDERAL NDP VOTE, 1979

Dependent variable: probability of voting NDP both provincially and federally versus voting NDP provincially but Liberal or Conservative federally

Explanatory variables	Effect on vote	t
No religion	.220	3.28
Roman Catholic	−.233	−3.29
Blue collar alienation/ ethnocentrism	−.038	−.239
Fairly strong provincial NDP identifier	.204	2.79
Very strong provincial NDP identifier	.245	3.15
Disliking score for federal Liberal party	.042	3.18
Preference gap for Conservatives over Liberals	−.036	−3.13
Willingness to vote strategically	−.328	−5.50
Constant	.449	
R^2 .313		
F (8,183) 11.87		

See notes to Table 46.

Nowhere is the pull between traditional cleavages and the federal issues of the 1970s better demonstrated than in the transition of provincial NDP voters to the federal arena (Table 47). We have already seen that the federal NDP attracted only 64 per cent of the voters who had supported the provincial party. What accounts for the difference? The federal NDP was better able to retain the support of those with no religion and those with strong or fairly strong ties to the provincial NDP. Highly alienated and ethnocentric blue collar workers were more likely to "defect," that is, vote NDP provincially, but for another party federally.[33] Strong dislike for the federal Liberals helped the NDP, but not if it was coupled with a preference for the Conservatives over the Liberals. The larger the preference gap, the more likely were provincial New Democrats to defect. More flexible provincial New Democrats, whom we have identified by their willingness to engage in strategic voting, are also more likely to have abandoned the NDP for one of the other federal parties in 1979.

TABLE 48

CHOICE BETWEEN FEDERAL LIBERALS AND CONSERVATIVES AMONG
THOSE DEFECTING FROM PROVINCIAL NDP

Dependent variable: probability of voting Conservative versus Liberal		
Explanatory variables	Effect on vote	t
No religion	−.46	−2.43
Roman Catholic	−.677	−4.97
Mean alienation/ethnocentrism score	.092	2.67
Constant	.518	
R^2 .33		
F (3,65) 12.18		

1. See notes to Table 46.

The negative coefficient for the Roman Catholic variable in Table 47 indicates that provincial NDP voters with that religious affiliation are more likely than members of other religious groups to defect in federal elections, a result which becomes easily interpretable when the federal choice among defectors is considered (Table 48)—Roman Catholics are more likely to favour the Liberals. Table 47 showed that provincial NDP voters professing no religious affiliation are less likely to desert the party in federal elections, but among the small group who do, the Liberals seem to be favoured over the Conservatives.[34]

Not surprisingly, the pull of alienation and ethnocentrism on provincial supporters of the NDP was more likely to carry them into the Conservative federal camp than the Liberal one. However, once voters have been pulled away from the NDP, alienation and ethnocentrism affect them all, not just blue collar workers, in the choice between Liberals and Conservatives.

Contrary to expectations, strategic voters, who were more likely to defect from a preference expressed for the NDP in provincial elections (Table 47), were not disproportionately drawn to the federal Conservatives (the strategic voting variable did not make a significant contribution to the equation of Table 48). The most straightforward interpretation suggests that this group of voters—federal Liberals or Conservatives who voted NDP provincially—are more flexible in their *provincial* voting habits. However, a small number (eighteen) of NDP defectors did report having voted strategically in the 1979 federal election. Fifteen of them voted Conservative.

Voting decisions in federal and provincial elections may be linked for some individuals and totally separate for others. Ambiguity in the meaning of a willingness to engage in strategic voting is one example of the difficulties of untangling them. Nevertheless, it seems clear that the emergence of alienation and ethnocentrism, dimensions which have little or no relevance in provincial politics, was crucial in differentiating the federal electoral context from the provincial one.

CONCLUSION

The Tories were British Columbia's omnibus party in 1979. In amassing their largest plurality since 1958, they presented the NDP with stiff competition for the support of the working class and lower income groups. Their worst showing among groups defined according to social class criteria, 37.2 per cent in the lowest income group, was better than the Liberal party's best showing. Even Roman Catholics, the bedrock of Liberal support historically and elsewhere in Canada, voted Conservative in equal numbers.[35]

The federal electoral context offered different choices than the provincial one, a difference which was not just confined to the number of alternatives presented in each case. The philosophical divisions separating the major provincial parties were apparently forgotten by many voters (including nearly 40 per cent of those who voted NDP provincially) who were affected by the conflicts over Liberal centralism and western regionalism, as well as related controversies involving cultural and language policy. The results were startling. The federal Liberal and Conservative electorates in the province contain *within* them groups of voters who are as far apart on the major questions dealing with the social and economic role of the modern state as are the provincial NDP and Social Credit electorates, but who are united in their degree of opposition to or support for policies regarding language, culture, and regionalism. The NDP is stranded on the left, indeed, abandoned, by almost all but its core supporters. The distribution of opinion on the alienation and ethnocentrism dimensions is so favourable to the Conservatives that the NDP can make limited headway federally. They are also vulnerable to strategic voting. Still, the pattern of support for or against the federal NDP gives left versus right a place in federal voting.

Variations in work setting, industrial sector, and neighbourhood socioeconomic composition are important factors for explaining provincial politics. They have no impact in the more complex federal issue space. We saw in Chapter 5 that living in a blue collar neighbourhood contributed to the development of support for collective policy options among blue collar workers. In the federal context individual/collective responsibility attitudes pull blue collar workers in one direction and alienation and ethnocentrism in another, regardless of where they live.

Finally, the 1979 federal election was marked by more volatility. Nearly one in three federal voters going to the polls in both 1974 and 1979 switched votes between the two elections, compared to only one in five in the provincial election. Yet there are signs that this difference may be significantly affected by relatively short-term factors peculiar to the federal setting of the 1970s. The defection rate among Liberal party identifiers was much higher than the rate for Conservatives and New Democrats, and the Conservatives captured nearly 75 per cent of Liberal defectors and over 60 per cent of NDP defectors. The Liberals are still the second largest party among federal party identifiers. Moreover, the federal party electorates still differ from each other in ways (particularly on social class and religious lines) which suggest some continuity with the past.

We have called the issues and attitudes associated with alienation and ethnocentrism relatively short-term factors because they are largely associated with the federal career of one man, Pierre Trudeau.[36] As David Smith notes in his comprehensive account of Liberal decline on the prairies: "The Liberals have passed this way before, a hundred years ago, when they were seen as eastern-oriented, Quebec-obsessed, and small-minded."[37] The Liberals have not always been first in federal politics in British Columbia, especially since the formation of the CCF, but third place is also an unaccustomed position. In the thirteen federal elections between 1935 and 1974 the Liberals finished first or second in popular vote eight times and tied for second in one additional case. Given this history it would be unwise to dismiss their chances of recovery entirely, now that Liberal leadership has changed hands.

Relative Conservative dominance, electoral volatility, and a multidimensional issue space set the federal context apart from the more evenly divided, relatively stable, and bipolar provincial one. However, the two settings are not completely separate. The working class, unionized, non-religious, and left-leaning core of the provincial NDP is the mainstay of the federal party, and those who have a strong or fairly strong identification with the provincial party are also more likely to support the federal one. Even the rout of the federal Liberal party was partially stemmed by the loyalty of its provincial partisans.

The issues which divide federal partisans are not unique to British Columbia. As we saw here and in Chapter 7, even alienation is a phenomenon which potentially links British Columbians to other Canadians. Similarly, despite the idiosyncratic character of the B.C. provincial party system, the forces which shaped it have parallels elsewhere. In the next chapter, we round out the analysis of British Columbia by exploring some of them.

9

The B.C. Voter in Perspective

The focus on British Columbia as a research site has provided an opportunity for intensive exploration of at least two important phenomenona which have occupied the attention of students of Canadian voting for two decades — class voting and divided partisanship. A third phenomenon — western alienation — is of more recent vintage, but it has proved to be of crucial significance to our understanding of the links between B.C. voters and the federal party system. The three phenomena are intertwined in our analysis. Ideological divisions within the provincial electorate, linked in part to social class position, underpin the electoral confrontation between Social Credit and the NDP. Alienation, however, cuts across social class lines and provincial partisan alignments and seems to apply only in federal elections, where it shares a complex issue space with differences between left and right and the politics of culture. As a result, a large number of British Columbians exhibit loyalties to different parties in federal and provincial elections.

The analysis in the preceding chapters hinges on the argument that the behaviour of voters depends on the contexts within which they are embedded. The adoption of leftist policy attitudes on the part of blue collar workers depends in part on whether such workers live in a supportive social environment. The attractiveness of the NDP to some members of the upper status occupational group is linked to employment in the public sector. The development of these divisions and the possibility of expressing them are, in turn, linked to the province's constitutional responsibilities, to transformations in its occupational structure, and to actions of provincial élites anxious to counter the growth of the NDP.[1]

We also argued that federal and provincial elections represent different contexts, that the issues involved in federal politics are different from those raised in provincial politics (or at least add new dimensions), and that the federal and provincial party systems have evolved separately as a result. From a theoretical point of view, there is no reason why this argument should not apply outside B.C. A comprehensive comparison with other provinces is not undertaken here, but the analysis of B.C. will be on firmer ground if we can demonstrate that similar forces operate elsewhere. At the same time, we can assess the implications that our results have for other approaches to these questions.

THE REFERENDUM ON TRUDEAU LIBERALISM

Is British Columbia politically unique? The answer seems obvious when we focus on provincial politics. The highly competitive battle between Social Credit and the NDP appears in no other province, and nowhere else are *both* major federal parties essentially irrelevant in provincial elections. Yet despite assertions that British Columbians are only "half-heartedly attached to their loose and variegated federation,"[2] we saw in Chapter 6 that the province's residents have, in fact, strong positive feelings about Canada. The analysis of federal voting in 1979 presented in the previous chapter demonstrated that the province's voters were participating in the same set of conflicts which engaged other Canadians, and a glance at recent history suggests this is not unusual. British Columbians reacted to the visionary promises of John Diefenbaker in 1958 as strongly as did other Canadians, although disillusionment set in more quickly than in any other province outside Quebec. The Liberal victory led by Pierre Trudeau in 1968, while not as uniform as the Diefenbaker landslide, saw B.C. voters respond generously with sixteen of the province's twenty-three seats going to the Liberal party. The 1979 election was widely perceived as a referendum on the record of Trudeau's previous ten years in office. B.C. joined all the English-Canadian provinces in registering disapproval.

William Irvine has described the 22 May, 1979 federal election as in reality two elections:

> The election in Quebec was about national unity. It was a vote of confidence in Pierre Trudeau's, and the Liberal party's, ability to defend the interests Quebecers feel they have in a country-wide union. . . . The rest of Canada was holding quite a different one. That election was about rising prices and falling dollars. It was won by the Progressive Conservative party, not against Quebec but without Quebec and without a number of other provinces where the Conservative message fell on deaf ears.[3]

Our analysis casts some doubt on this interpretation. Quebecers were more likely than non-Quebecers to mention "national unity" as the major national issue in the pre-election surveys cited by Irvine. But according to results from the 1979 National Election Study, national unity was perceived as "more important than any other problem we face" by majorities in both Quebec and the English-Canadian provinces. In fact, voters in English Canada were somewhat more likely (75 per cent compared to 70 per cent) than Quebecers to agree with the statement. A division between English- and French-speaking voters appears on economic issues as well.[4]

TABLE 49

VOTER RETENTION RATES BY PARTY AND REGION, 1974-79

		Region		
Party	B.C.	English Canada outside B.C.	Quebec	Total
Liberal	47.3	64.4	84.6	70.3
Conservative	88.3	89.7	71.4	88.8
NDP	84.9	75.4	38.1	75.2
Social Credit	—	—	62.9	56.8

1. Table entries represent the percentage of a given party's 1974 voters who supported it in 1979. Only those voting in both elections are included.
Source: Figures for B.C. from 1979 B.C. Election Study. All others from 1979 National Election Study.

Liberal candidates in British Columbia suffered greater losses between 1974 and 1979 than candidates of any other party. Table 49 confirms the generality of this result in English Canada. While Liberal losses were less, on average, in English Canada outside British Columbia than in that province itself, the party was unable to retain as much of its 1974 support as the Conservatives or the New Democrats. In Quebec, the situation was reversed.

What was true of voters in general was true of Liberal identifiers in particular. While most party identifiers voted in accordance with their professed attachment, Liberal identifiers were substantially more likely to desert the party throughout English Canada. Again, British Columbia displays an exaggerated version of the same picture (Table 50).[5]
While economic issues may have been more salient in English Canada than in Quebec, the partisan implications of positions on national unity, language, and the treatment of Quebec were more obvious. The Liberals were blamed by many voters for high levels of inflation and unemployment, but the party certainly did not campaign in favour of them.[6] Voters may have been responding to the government's record in office, but the record contained more than a catalogue of economic mistakes.

The data required for a complete replication of the analysis of alienation and ethnocentrism conducted in the previous chapter do not exist, but several items in the 1979 National Election Study can be combined to yield

TABLE 50

PERCENTAGE VOTING DIFFERENTLY FROM PARTY IDENTIFICATION
BY REGION[1]
(1979 federal election)

	Federal party identification		
Region	Liberal	Conservative	NDP
B.C.	35.9	7.0	13.3
	(184)	(214)	(165)
Other English Canada	16.3	3.9	10.7
	(527)	(536)	(178)
Quebec	4.5	19.1	23.1
	(375)	(47)	(26)

1. Table entries represent the percentage of those with a given federal party identification who voted for a different party in 1979. The total number of identifiers for a given party and region appears in parenthesis.
Source: British Columbia figures from 1979 B.C. Election Study. Other figures from 1979 National Election Study.

approximations of our attitude scales. The first of these, a "Quebec Power Score," appears in Table 51 and represents simply the total number of times "Quebec" was mentioned in response to questions asking which "regions" received more than their fair share of benefits from Confederation, which "provinces" did so, and which provincial governments are more powerful than others. Because of the way these questions were asked in the 1979 national survey, the table is restricted to those (approximately one-quarter of the national sample) who think of Canada as divided into regions and feel that some regions are more favoured or more powerful than others. Given the restriction and the fact that the questions were not designed with a view to measuring ethnocentrism, we wish to do no more than point out that Liberal weakness and Conservative strength throughout English Canada were directly related to feelings that Quebec has too much influence in the federal system. In other words, for some voters support for the Conservatives was associated with a position "against Quebec."

Somewhat more convincing evidence that all Canadians were participating in the same election in 1979 is provided in Table 52. Because "national unity" was a central theme of the Liberal campaign and since making French-speaking Canadians feel at home in Confederation was a major part of the federal government's unity policy, we felt justified in combining the question dealing with the importance of the national unity issue with one advocating federal government support for minority language education to calculate a "unity agenda" score.[7] The minority language protection question did not specify French as the language to be protected, and some respondents may have had linguistic guarantees for English-speaking Quebecers in mind when answering the question. However, given the negative correla-

TABLE 51

QUEBEC POWER SCORE AND 1979 FEDERAL VOTE IN B.C. AND ENGLISH CANADA[1]
(horizontal percentages)

Quebec power score	Vote:	English Canada outside B.C.				
		Liberal	*Conservative*	*NDP*	*Other*	
0		39.5	46.5	14.0	0.0	(43)
1		31.0	48.3	19.0	1.7	(58)
2		37.8	50.0	12.2	0.0	(90)
3		21.6	60.2	17.0	1.1	(88)
		British Columbia				
0		33.3	33.3	33.3	0.0	(3)
1		23.1	61.5	15.4	0.0	(13)
2		17.9	46.4	35.7	0.0	(28)
3		9.5	71.4	19.0	0.0	(21)

1. Each row of the table gives the partisan divisions within each category of the "Quebec Power" scale. For example, of those in English Canada outside B.C. least suspicious of Quebec (scored 0), 39.5 per cent voted Liberal, 46.5 per cent Conservative and 14 per cent NDP.

TABLE 52

UNITY AGENDA SCORE AND 1979 FEDERAL VOTE BY REGION[1]
(horizontal percentages)

Unity Agenda Score	Vote:	British Columbia				
		Liberal	*Conservative*	*NDP*	*Other*	
0		12.1	63.6	24.2	0.0	(33)
1		19.8	46.5	32.7	1.0	(101)
2		32.9	34.2	30.3	2.6	(76)
		English Canada outside B.C.				
0		25.8	55.3	18.2	0.8	(132)
1		32.1	49.5	17.6	0.8	(501)
2		40.1	46.3	13.5	0.1	(684)
		Quebec				
0		33.3	13.9	27.8	25.0	(36)
1		51.8	13.1	9.5	25.5	(137)
2		76.3	13.6	2.5	7.6	(354)

1. Each row of the table gives the partisan divisions within each category of the "National Unity Agenda" scale. For example, of those in British Columbia least supportive of the national unity items (scored 0), 12.1 per cent voted Liberal, 63.6 per cent voted Conservative, and 24.2 per cent voted NDP.

tion (Pearson r = −.16) between the Quebec power score and support for linguistic guarantees, we feel safe in treating the language item as a surrogate for federal bilingualism policies.

Again, support for the focus on national unity and endorsement of government language policy produced Liberal support. Conservative party support
represents the mirror image of that relationship throughout English Canada.
Despite Liberal party appeal along this dimension, the party was able only to
approach parity with the Conservatives in English Canada even among those
who felt that national unity was more important than any other problem *and*
support language guarantees.[8] The election was a "referendum" on Trudeau
Liberalism in significant respects, but as with other referendums in our
history, it revealed regional divisions between supporters of one option
versus the other. It also served to limit debate on ideological questions and,
as argued in the next section, once again restricted the role that social class
differences play in the federal party system.

THE ROLE OF SOCIAL CLASS IN FEDERAL AND PROVINCIAL PARTISANSHIP

The decade of the seventies witnessed the flourishing of province-building.
Provincial governments assumed a major role in economic development
through direct investment, investment in industrial infrastructure, and tax
incentives. The federal government was actively engaged as well, but differences in principle over the appropriateness and extent of government involvement were clouded by jurisdictional questions and conflict over the interregional distribution of burdens and benefits. Increased state activity produced
a mammoth increase in the number of public sector employees, but at
present only about one-quarter fall under federal jurisdiction.[9] Issues of
public service unionization and public service strikes only add to the already
greater significance of labour relations issues in provincial politics.

The size of the state sector has been identified as a critical factor affecting
the ability of governments to deal with the economic problems of the
seventies.[10] Both levels of government are affected, but at the federal level,
problems of economic stagnation are superimposed on a pre-existing backdrop of regional and cultural conflicts. The economic recovery strategies of
the Liberal and Conservative parties have become linked to their positions
on the nature of the federal bargain. Ironically, the NDP, having officially
shed its past as a regional protest party, finds it difficult to communicate its
economic message.[11]

The structures of provincial economies and societies are generally simpler when viewed singly than as part of a complex whole. "Although the
provinces vary greatly in terms of their social complexity, economic modernity,
and structure of interests, no single province has the extraordinary diversity
and, therefore, the potential for cross-cutting cleavages that the nation as a
whole has. Provincial parties can and do adjust their appeals to a narrower

and more homogeneous base of support."[12]

There are several reasons why one would expect conflict between left and right policy views and, by extension, the class cleavage, to be more prominent in provincial elections and more prominent now.[13] By far the largest part of every provincial budget is devoted to health, education, and social welfare services. In 1975, 62.3 per cent of provincial expenditures took place in these areas, an increase from just under 50 per cent in 1950. Moreover, provincial expenditures as a percentage of GNP increased from 5.7 per cent

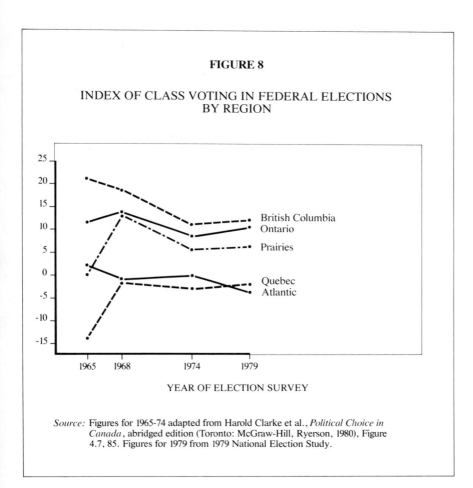

FIGURE 8

INDEX OF CLASS VOTING IN FEDERAL ELECTIONS BY REGION

YEAR OF ELECTION SURVEY

Source: Figures for 1965-74 adapted from Harold Clarke et al., *Political Choice in Canada*, abridged edition (Toronto: McGraw-Hill, Ryerson, 1980), Figure 4.7, 85. Figures for 1979 from 1979 National Election Study.

to 15 per cent over the same period,[14] and interprovincial variation in the budget share devoted to social policy items has decreased.[15] While the federal government makes a major financial contribution to this area its policy role has been sharply reduced. Hence, we would expect controversy over priorities in these areas and the left-right debate to be especially significant in provincial politics.

In the 1979 National Election Study, NDP voters placed themselves on the left of the Liberals and Conservatives in every province, whereas Liberals and Conservatives either did not differ significantly from each other or chose different relative positions on the right depending on the province considered.[16] However, in exploring the implications of the structural argument, we have chosen to focus initially on the nature of support given to the NDP. Since that party has a significant federal and provincial presence only in British Columbia, Saskatchewan, Manitoba, and Ontario, those are the provinces which appear in Table 53. Moreover, it is easier to argue that provincial agendas are dominated by left-right questions west of the Ottawa River than east of it.[17]

The analysis of class and partisanship presented in chapters 5 and 6 underscored the complexity of the relationship between social class and provincial partisanship given contemporary class structures. Despite these changes, British Columbians have consistently exhibited a higher level of class voting[18] in federal elections than voters in other regions (Figure 8).

TABLE 53

NDP SUPPORT AND CLASS VOTING BY LEVEL AND PROVINCE

	Province							
	Ontario		Manitoba		Saskatchewan		B.C.	
Level:	prov.	fed.	prov.	fed.	prov.	fed.	prov.	fed.
NDP vote[1]								
1972	27.1	21.5	42.3	26.6	55.0	35.9	40.1	31.5
1974	28.8	19.1	42.3	23.5	40.1	31.5	38.7	23.0
1979	28.0	21.9	38.6	33.5	47.5	36.3	45.2	35.3
Working class identification with NDP[2] (percentage)	20.3	34.7	36.1	21.3	66.7	27.8	55.4	30.6
Class partisanship index[3]	11.9	15.4	11.1	5.2	26.7	4.2	21.4	11.5

1. Federal vote is for the year indicated. Provincial vote is for the provincial election closest in time to the federal one.
2. The designation "working class" is based on respondent perception of class position after prompting, if necessary.
3. Class partisanship index is calculated by subtracting the percentage of middle class support for the NDP from the percentage of working class support for the NDP.
Source: Provincial and federal voting data based on official sources. Other date from 1979 National Election Study.

Nevertheless, social class position in the form of a working class/non-working class distinction proved to be a better predictor of the vote in B.C. provincial elections than in federal ones. Since its victory in the provincial election of 1972, support for the provincial NDP has always been higher than support for the federal party. The level of class voting in federal elections also dropped while it was increasing provincially. During the same period, support for the NDP has exceeded federal support in every province where the NDP has a significant presence (Table 53).

The most polarized province is thus not alone in expressing greater support for provincial New Democrats over their federal counterparts. Are these other provinces less polarized in federal politics as well?

The remainder of Table 53 provides the relevant evidence linking British Columbia federal partisanship to that in at least two of the three comparison provinces. The percentage of working class voters identifying with the NDP is significantly lower in federal politics in British Columbia, Saskatchewan, and Manitoba. Party identification based on subjective class position also differs by level, and it is less class-based in federal politics in the same three provinces. Ontario appears to represent an anomaly given the theoretical perspective developed here since the "differences" in the impact of class on partisanship are within the range expected given sampling fluctuations and, if anything, point to a greater role for class federally than provincially. Cultural and religious issues do arise at the provincial level and have had at least as long a history as the federal conflicts. Moreover, the province is argued to have significant regional divisions as well. In other words, Ontario may not fit the conditions we have outlined for the relative simplicity of provincial cleavage patterns.[19] Ontario union members, however, are more likely to vote NDP provincially than federally—providing some confirmation for the initial hypothesis.

What about the six provinces in which the NDP is very weak at both levels? Without engaging in a full-blown longitudinal analysis, it is possible to examine federal and provincial contexts in provinces east of the Ottawa River for clues to explain the apparent absence of class politics or system separation. Quebec, the province most similar to British Columbia in the dissimilarity of its federal and provincial party systems, in fact resembles B.C. in other ways. Voters separated between the Parti Québécois and the provincial Liberal party by left-right position co-exist within the ranks of the federal Liberal party.[20] To point this out is not to ignore the cross-class appeal of the PQ on the national question (which also exists in British Columbia regarding other matters) nor the fact that the party has had difficulty living up to its social democratic aspirations.[21] The latter problem, however, has vexed all social democratic parties once in office.

If variation in the relevance of class to political divisions reflects variation in levels of economic development, NDP weakness in the Atlantic region is to be expected.[22] A cultural legacy which treats the NDP as an upper Canadian intruder also cannot be ignored. However, recent analysis of the political economy of the region which looks to the prominence of the "marginal work world" setting as a source of political cynicism and toleration of patronage speaks indirectly to the issues raised in this chapter. "The relatively unskilled, low-paying jobs typical of the marginal work world are usually linked to more capricious authority relations, the absence of opportunities for personal advancement, and job instability."[23] While these factors should work towards increased labour militance and, ultimately, higher levels of class voting, there is a "frequently obvious link between the survival of the marginal work world firm and the political loyalties of its owners and employees."[24] Not only is class conflict thereby attenuated, but a cross-party consensus is also likely to emerge on the economic needs of the province and the appropriate mechanisms for meeting them. The limited financial capacity of provincial governments ensures a strong federal government voice in development plans (and thus an overlap of federal and provincial issue spaces) and constrains provincial authorities in their bargaining with corporations.[25]

We have stressed constitutional, structural, and cultural factors in attempting to account for regional variations in support for the left and in the degree of separation of federal and provincial party systems. To these we might add the effects of the strength of the left itself on the structure of the party system. We tend to describe class voting in terms of working class support for a party of the left, but, as seen in British Columbia, it can also be marked

TABLE 54

DISTRIBUTION OF TYPES OF PARTY IDENTIFIERS BY PROVINCE

	Type of identifier			
Province	Federal only	Provincial only	Consistent	Split	
Newfoundland	3.8	7.5	78.3	10.4	(106)
P.E.I.	2.2	4.3	90.3	3.2	(93)
Nova Scotia	0.6	11.1	82.7	5.6	(162)
New Brunswick	3.5	4.3	84.3	7.8	(115)
Quebec	5.6	16.7	50.6	27.1	(660)
Ontario	7.1	6.6	72.3	4.0	(651)
Manitoba	6.3	5.4	73.0	15.3	(111)
Saskatchewan	6.5	10.9	64.1	18.5	(92)
Alberta	4.5	6.2	73.0	16.3	(178)
British Columbia	9.0	8.5	39.9	42.5	(934)
Total	5.1	10.1	64.6	20.3	

Source: B.C. figures from 1979 B.C. Election Study. All others, including total, from 1979 National Election Study.

by a class-based reaction *against* a strong left. The weakness of the provincial Liberals and Conservatives is directly related to the feeling that only a "coalition" such as Social Credit can counter a strong NDP. A similar phenomenon can be observed in Saskatchewan and Manitoba with Liberal Ross Thatcher (later Conservative Grant Devine) and Conservative Sterling Lyon, respectively, occupying roles similar to those played by W.A.C. Bennett and his son. As shown in Chapter 3, not all Liberal and Conservative voters could fit comfortably within the Social Credit coalition, driving up support for the NDP after Social Credit formed the government in 1975 and thus ensuring that the need for Social Credit would remain.[26] This dialectic may also operate in Saskatchewan and Manitoba. The basis for it has not yet been established elsewhere.

PARTISAN CONSISTENCY AND POLITICAL BEHAVIOUR[27]

In addition to its affects on class voting, the separation of provincial and federal party systems in British Columbia has produced a large number of voters (nearly 43 per cent) with ties to different parties in the two systems (Table 54). As expected, given differences by level in party fortunes, those with dual loyalties are overwhelmingly (69 per cent) provincial Socreds. Most of those whose provincial and federal attachments coincide (65 per cent), labelled "consistent" in the table, are New Democrats although Liberals (16 per cent) and Conservatives (14 per cent) are represented too. Single level identifiers are not so closely linked with a single party. Those with an attachment at the provincial level only are more evenly divided (36 per cent and 46 per cent respectively) between the NDP and Social Credit. The "federal only" identifiers are 53 per cent Liberal, 34 per cent Conservative, and 13.5 per cent NDP. The figures for British Columbia are approached only in Quebec, although in all provinces outside the Atlantic region at least 25 per cent of identifiers have dual loyalties or are independent at one level and identified at the other.

According to the authors of a major study of partisanship in Canada, dual loyalties are linked to volatility—unstable voting preferences. If they are correct, then British Columbians should exhibit very volatile voting habits, yet that would seem to go against the evidence presented in Chapter 8. In 1979, approximately one-third of the respondents in the B.C. Election Study who voted in both the 1974 and 1979 federal elections voted differently; only one-fifth did so in the provincial elections of 1975 and 1979. Moreover, the analysis of post-realignment British Columbia in Chapter 3 revealed the existence of two very stable coalitions of provincial voters, which were later revealed to have strong ideological and socioeconomic underpinnings. Alignments in the federal electorate seem to have been formed on a quite different basis. The large number of dual loyalists appearing in the British Columbia sample combined with the near simultaneous occurrence of the 1979 provincial and federal elections in the province, provide an excellent opportunity to test the validity of the link made between duality and volatility.

The authors of *Political Choice in Canada* base their generalization on an empirical connection between inconsistent partisanship (different party identifications in federal and provincial politics) and reported vote-switching in federal and provincial elections, and on the theoretical argument that the existence of ties to two different parties reduces the psychological hold of party as a guide to behaviour.[28] The test of stable voting habits is a severe one. Respondents were asked, separately for federal and provincial elections, "Have you always voted for the same party . . . or have you voted for different parties?" Unstable identifiers (those who have changed party identification at any time) must almost by definition answer "no" to this question, making it a poor index of differences in the probability of vote-switching between "stable" and "unstable" partisans, regardless of whether they are "consistent" or not.[29]

Nor is it clear why one should expect switching *within* levels to be associated with inconsistent attachments *between* levels, since they agree that "provincial party identification in Canada is not a secondary form of identification, but an attachment *in every sense* equal to federal identification."[30]

TABLE 55

VOTE SWITCHING AMONG CONSISTENT AND SPLIT PARTISANS
BY INTENSITY OF PARTY ATTACHMENT BY REGION[1]

| | *Type of party identification* | | | | | |
| | *Consistent* | | | *Split* | | |
Strength of Federal Party ID:	*Very strong*	*Fairly strong*	*Not very strong*	*Very strong*	*Fairly strong*	*Not very strong*
Atlantic	4.2	18.0	34.6	60.3	78.2	100.0
Quebec	2.5	7.7	14.3	21.4	33.9	42.4
Ontario	11.5	21.5	48.5	8.3	42.6	43.7
Prairies	8.6	28.0	41.8	34.4	29.3	81.3
British Columbia	10.1	28.7	63.2	13.3	15.7	35.0
Total	7.4	19.1	37.4	21.4	35.4	47.1

1. Table entries are the percentage of a given type of partisan (consistent or split) with a given strength of party attachment who voted for different federal parties in the 1974 and 1979 federal elections. For example, 10.1 per cent of consistent identifiers in B.C. (i.e., having the same party identification at both levels), with a strong attachment to their federal party, reported different federal votes in 1974 and 1979.

Source: B.C. figures from 1979 B.C. Election Study. All others, including total from the 1979 National Election Study.

Their expectation seems to be based on the finding that split identifiers are likely to have an attachment to party which is stronger at one level than the other or to have the same intensity of attachment, but weak, at both levels.[31] However, that observation is based on differences in the proportion of strong identifiers making up "consistent" and "split" groups—an aggregate phenomenon. It implies nothing about the behaviour of *individuals* within those groups.

Table 55 is based on a different measure of electoral volatility, a comparison of reported vote in the 1974 and 1979 federal elections.[32] It shows quite clearly that in British Columbia and in every other region the likelihood of switching between elections is inversely related to the strength of party identification for both consistent and split identifiers. Strong partisans are less likely to switch than those with weak party ties. Similar results are obtained when switching between the 1979 and 1980 elections is considered. Although split identifiers seem to be more likely to have switched than consistents regardless of strength of party identification in the Atlantic, Quebec, and prairie regions, the opposite is arguably the case in British Columbia and there is no real difference in Ontario.[33] When provincial voting is analysed in British Columbia, the province with the highest proportion of split identifiers, the results are also clear-cut. Weak partisans are more likely to have voted differently in the 1975 and 1979 provincial elections than strong partisans, regardless of the nature of their ties to federal parties.[34]

There are fewer identifiers who report strong ties to their federal party among split identifiers in British Columbia (and elsewhere in Canada), and the number of split partisans gives them a major impact on aggregate volatility levels. However, the conclusion that dual loyalists (and hence many British Columbia voters) are particularly volatile *because* of their ties to different parties in federal and provincial politics is unwarranted.

We wish to go even further to argue that the large number of dual loyalists in British Columbia and the independence of switching at one level from switching at another reflects a clear separation between federal and provincial party systems in the minds of many voters. Separation is implied by the analysis of federal voting and, in particular, of the choice among federal parties by provincial voters reported in the previous chapter. Nor, apparently, is British Columbia alone. Despite considerable variation among provinces, substantial numbers of voters elsewhere in Canada maintain different loyalties in federal and provincial politics. Data which would allow a comparison of federal and provincial issue spaces across the provinces are not available; however, cross-level differences in the impact of social class on partisanship in several provinces point to similar conclusions about the separation of federal and provincial party systems.

CONCLUSION

It is easy to believe that B.C. politics are *sui generis*. No province other than Quebec operates two such different party systems, and the fact that Quebec is the only exception makes British Columbia's distinctiveness seem more impressive. Two decades of voting studies have turned to the province for evidence that class politics may indeed permeate Canada eventually. Spring arrives sooner and winter later, permitting a life-style which itself is seen as contributing to a distinctive style of politics — hedonistic, impatient with tradition, and volatile.

The separation of federal and provincial party systems in the province has evolved to such an extent that nearly half those who possess a party identification are attached to different parties in federal and provincial politics. We do not wish to downplay this fact. It is testimony to the power of different political contexts in shaping the forces within them. However, there is no evidence that dual loyalists are *torn* between competing loyalties. A strong partisan is one who is likely to support his or her party consistently. It does not seem to matter that the party label differs depending on the context. While B.C. has more dual loyalists, proportionately, than any other province, that fact alone does not alter this conclusion.

But while British Columbia may have carried political dualism to an extreme, it is not the only province in which voters participate in two different political systems. David Smith has argued that one of the reasons for the decline of the Liberal party in the west is that western Liberals perceive the NDP as the main political enemy whereas Liberal governments, backed by a central Canadian caucus, are quite willing to enlist the NDP in their battles with the Tories.[35] Our analysis suggests that the definition of "enemies" is even more dependent on context, and not just that separating the West from the centre. In provincial politics in Manitoba, Saskatchewan, and British Columbia, the clash between left and right perspectives on the management of the economy, labour relations, and the provision of government services is likely to pit the NDP against one or both of the Liberals or Conservatives or, as in British Columbia, a party which includes a partial combination of the two. In fact, although the argument does not depend on it, in recent times only two major provincial competitors remain in these provinces. Federal politics presents different issues and a different alignment of parties. While the Liberals are generally weaker in the West, the "central Canadian" issues still divide Liberals and Conservatives in the West (including Alberta!) as elsewhere in Canada.

The NDP has failed to gain a significant foothold in Canada east of Ontario for a complex of cultural, historical, and, ironically, economic reasons. The relative poverty of the Atlantic provinces is undeniable, but when provincial governments have limited room for manipulation of their own budgets and limited bargaining power with the major corporations whose goodwill is seen as linked to the region's economic survival, the economic experimentation promised by the NDP may be feared even among those classes of society who are supposed to benefit most. Quebec, we would argue, is not in the same economic position as the Atlantic region and does operate two separate political systems, a provincial one where economic philosophies clash and a federal one where economic questions are subordinate to "la survivance."[36]

The failure of a class cleavage to materialize across Canada may partly reflect differences in levels of economic development. But so long as differences in the responsibilities assigned to the two levels of government and regional differences in economic structures persist, the potential for the separation of federal and provincial political systems remains.

10

Conclusion: The Two Worlds of the B.C. Voter

This book began with a series of questions about British Columbia electoral politics stimulated by the dramatic realignment of the 1970s and the increased separation of federal and provincial party systems which it helped to produce. What underlies the growth of the NDP and the revitalization of the Social Credit party? Are voters as polarized between left and right as the dominant provincial parties appear to be? How do B.C. voters respond to the alternatives presented in two different party systems? The answers were sought using a combination of survey data and economic and demographic statistics analysed against a backdrop of history and theory.

We now have a fairly detailed understanding of the federal and provincial political worlds as they exist for the B.C. voter. The conflicts within them sometimes overlap, but, as voting patterns will attest, they are more often driven apart. But British Columbians share one world, the federal world, with other Canadians. The provincial world is the most distinctive, but the clash of economic and social philosophies within it and the structure of party competition it has produced have parallels in other provinces.

In the provincial world, Social Credit and the NDP have carved out sharply contrasting positions regarding the appropriate role for government in economic development, regulation of business and labour, and the degree of state responsibility for the well-being of individuals unable to provide adequately for themselves and their families. These differences were dramatically illustrated during the 1983 election campaign and its aftermath, but they have been present, more or less, since Social Credit and the CCF acquired their stranglehold on the provincial party system in the 1950s.

The 1960s saw the creation of a large public sector in B.C., the natural outgrowth of W.A.C. Bennett's development strategies and the general post-war expansion of state activity. By the 1970s, the size and role of that sector had themselves become issues which helped to define the differences between left and right.

Growth of the state had significant electoral consequences as well. It helped create a new class of public sector employees dependent on the state for its livelihood and confident of its role in creating a better society. Economic development, largely stimulated and directed by the provincial government, extended the province's traditional industrial structure throughout the length and breadth of the province. Development contributed to the spread of the NDP's working class constituency, but it also generated thousands of new middle and working class jobs in finance, real estate, and services at the same time. These changes, we believe, are largely responsible for a major transformation in the structure of the party system and in the links between parties and voters.

The Social Credit party led by W.A.C. Bennett to defeat at the hands of the NDP did not grasp the significance of changes in the geography of party support in the province or the danger of alienating workers in the public sector (now a large component of the labour force), but few did. The NDP victory itself precipitated a further stage in the realignment of the 1970s. Its record in office convinced many Liberals and Conservatives that they could no longer afford the luxury of a separate existence.

Changes in the structure of the party system are obvious. Combined support for the Liberals and Conservatives dropped from an average of 20 per cent to 11 per cent in 1975 and to less than 6 per cent in 1979 and 1983. A revitalized Social Credit party emerged as the victor in the scramble with provincial Liberals and Conservatives for the free enterprise banner and made the NDP a one-term government. The NDP were demoralized by their defeat in 1975, but they emerged from the 1970s as a serious competitor to Social Credit in most areas of the province. The two parties are now separated by only a narrow margin in the electorate as a whole.

The net changes in party standings and the actions of political élites which helped to bring them about were visible as economic and political events unfolded. Less accessible, until now, was a perspective on changes in the attachments of individuals to parties which underlay the shifting alliances of political and economic élites, for which survey data provide indispensable information. Most prominent provincial Liberals and Conservatives made public declarations of support for Social Credit and officially joined the party before the 1975 election, but they did not take all their followers with them. It is clear from this study that Social Credit attracted the largest group of former Conservative supporters and a large number of former Liberals, many, if not most of them, for the same reasons which convinced Conservative and Liberal MLAs to cross the floor of the legislature— Social Credit offered the best chance of defeating the NDP and preventing its return to office. The NDP in contrast, while losing support from many who voted for it in 1972, attracted the largest number of policy-oriented

Liberals and Conservatives and new voters. By the time of the 1979 election, the support bases of the NDP and Social Credit had stabilized. Each party retained the support of 90 per cent of those who had voted for it in 1975. Stability is also the message conveyed by results of the 1983 election. The regional growth in NDP support described in Chapter 3 levelled off, and overall support for the party dropped slightly.

Most observers have identified the boom and bust resource-based economy, the strength of organized labour, the history of bitter labour-management relations, the weakness of tradition, and the single-minded pursuit of economic prosperity by provincial governments as the foundation of a class-based party system. British Columbia voters, in fact, behave in ways which challenge the traditional view or at least qualify it significantly. The modern NDP is not as doctrinaire a socialist party as its predecessor. It has tried to distance itself from organized labour. Its major opponent presides over a large and powerful public sector. As some have suggested, Social Credit populism and fondness for megaprojects give it considerable appeal to blue collar voters. We have measured the extent of populist attitudes in the provincial culture and identified it in both party electorates. Current divisions between the parties have confirmed the significance of left versus right, but in a context where the bulk of the electorate occupies the ideological centre and where social class differences have become more complex. The traditional working class/middle class distinction is no longer sufficient to explain the ideological positions or political choices of voters.

A significant public versus private sector conflict has emerged in British Columbia. The conflict is bound up with differing views about the size of the public sector, the degree to which individuals or the community should assume responsibility for the well-being of individuals and the degree to which the state ought to intervene in the economy for the same reasons. This conflict has driven a wedge between members of both the working class and the middle class. Professionals and semi-professionals, especially those employed in the public sector, are much more likely to support social policy initiatives and government intervention in the economy than others in upper status occupations. Their political preferences are linked to this ideological position, but also directly to self-interest — their livelihoods often depend on an activist state.

Blue collar workers still give the NDP a majority of their votes, but that majority would be larger were it not for the presence of an individualist streak, especially among blue collar workers employed in the resources sector. Self-interest is probably a factor here as well — the Social Credit record and rhetoric stress expansion in that sector. Trade union membership (B.C. remains the most unionized province in Canada), and the anti-labour reputation of Social Credit exercise a restraining influence on those tendencies, but they are significant none the less.

Individuals do not make political choices in a vacuum. Their decisions are shaped by the contexts within which they make them. We have demonstrated the significance of neighbourhood and work-place as important influences on attitudes and political choice. We have also pursued the argument that the constitutional division of powers serves to define different political and economic contexts which help drive the two party systems apart. Debates in provincial politics are shaped by an allocation of powers which gives to the provinces primary responsibility for health, education, social welfare, and management of resources. These areas are of importance in federal politics, but they have usually been overshadowed by constitutional, cultural, and linguistic conflicts. Choices in the two arenas also have different implications for the conduct of government. An NDP victory in provincial politics gives the left real political power. But as Alan Cairns has pointed out, an NDP "victory" in the B.C. portion of the federal party system is mainly of theoretical interest because British Columbia is only part of a national party system in which the NDP is unlikely to obtain power. British Columbia can operate a three-party system in federal politics because the major factor which produced polarization at the provincial level—the strength of the left—is less relevant nationally.[1] However, if minority government reappears in Ottawa and an informal NDP-Liberal alliance is revived or if the federal agenda were to be focused more exclusively on economic and social policy issues, the situation would change. Change could be even more rapid if, as some predict, the NDP replaces the Liberals as the major alternative to the Progressive Conservatives.

The impact of current differences can be seen at the level of voting. The left-right division so prominent in provincial politics does appear at the national level, but it divides supporters of the federal NDP from Liberals and Conservatives as a group. The coalitions of voters at the national level have been formed largely around cultural and linguistic issues combined with disaffection from the government in Ottawa, superimposed on traditional divisions such as those between Protestants and Roman Catholics. The NDP is weaker and the Liberals and Conservatives stronger in federal politics as a result.

This book has identified structural, institutional, and strategic bases for the division between the two worlds of B.C. politics. It has described a population which responds differently to the choices offered in those two worlds and has analysed the bases for those responses. In doing so, it has demonstrated the ability of voters to distinguish between the two worlds. Many of them maintain different party allegiances in federal and provincial politics. The electorates of the parties at each level contain individuals who are partisan opponents at the other level. Intensive analysis of a province containing large numbers of partisans with divided party loyalties has also revealed that voting decisions made at one level, in particular the decision to switch between elections, respond to the separate electoral contexts which the two party systems represent. From this perspective, party attachments which are inconsistent across levels are not a symptom of inherent volatility or instability in the B.C. electorate.

Some of our conclusions regarding other important theoretical and comparative questions are advanced tentatively and must await further study. Nevertheless, the intensive study of one province has helped to clarify the conditions under which ideological differences among voters will be translated into partisan choices, and under which class voting, suitably redefined to take new class groupings into account, may emerge. Moreover, class and ideology can structure political choices in one party system and not another, or at least not to the same extent, even within the same political boundaries.

Can the two worlds continue to co-exist? In part the answer depends on the actions of political élites. W.A.C. Bennett conceived of Social Credit as a device which, free from the entanglements of federal politics, could provide a haven for those fearful of a CCF/NDP victory in provincial politics. The resurrection of Social Credit from the ashes of its 1972 defeat was based on the same kind of reasoning. But as the recent history of federal-provincial relations should remind us, party ties among political leaders are rarely strong enough to prevent disputes between the two levels of government. Conversely, contrasting party ties have rarely prevented the formation of alliances across levels and between provinces. We need only think of the "gang of three" (the federal Liberal government and the Conservative governments of Ontario and New Brunswick) versus the "gang of eight" (a Social Credit government, an NDP government, a Parti Québécois government, and five Conservative governments) in the battle over the Constitution.

Premier Bennett has frequently endorsed the federal Conservative party, but he has no need to merge his party with the provincial Conservatives. There is little incentive to change what has been an exceedingly successful formula. Nor would there be much pay-off in elections given the separation of party systems in the voters' minds. It might, in fact, cost the party some support among those who consider themselves to be Liberals in federal politics. We have already explained why it is unlikely that the provincial Liberals and Conservatives can revive on their own.

It is more interesting to speculate on the possible effects of greater overlap between provincial and federal political agendas. Many observers expected the NDP in the West to be trampled in the rush by voters to defeat the Liberal government in the 1984 federal election. They reckoned without consideration of the basis of Conservative support at the federal level in British Columbia (and arguably in Manitoba and Saskatchewan). Short-term anti-Liberal feelings may have produced the Conservative landslide, but not at the expense of the NDP. If the Conservatives interpret their mandate as an endorsement of small "c" conservative policy views, or right-wingers in the caucus force such policies on the prime minister, the federal salience of the divisions already prominent in provincial politics will increase. Given the division of opinion within the federal Conservative electorate on those issues, a move to the right could cut into support for the party. The federal Liberal party seemed to have sensed the vulnerability of the Conservative electoral coalition on issues related to the role of the state in the social policy field during the 1984 election campaign but were unable to exploit it given their other handicaps. The issue may have even helped the NDP. However, according to our evidence, Liberal decline is linked to disaffection from Ottawa and the legacy of Pierre Trudeau. In that case, it is unlikely to have inflicted permanent harm on the party. History, regionalism, and the division of powers present further obstacles to the rearrangement of the federal political agenda to coincide with the left-right division so prominent in provincial politics.

Throughout this book we have had to deal with the perception that British Columbia is a strange and exotic place. We may have even added to that perception. It is, of course, unique in the sense in which any set of geographical and political boundaries encapsulates a particular complex of physical, economic, and social characteristics and historical memories. Without denying the province's uniqueness in that sense, we have been able to show how British Columbians have responded to the political environment in which they find themselves, an environment which contains features found in other provinces as well—separation of governmental agendas associated with the constitutional division of powers, expansion of the role of government, and a transformation of the economy associated with the expansion of the public sector and changes in the occupational structure of modern capitalism. The pattern of party competition in the provincial world may be unique, but the issues which divide the parties are not. And, notwithstanding their image in the eyes of many commentators and critics, British Columbians are avid participants in the world of federal politics.

Appendix

Attitude scales formed from items in the 1979 B.C. Election Study form an important part of the analysis in this book. The items making up the scales are listed under their titles below. For "agree/disagree" items, the answer corresponding to the direction in which the scale is scored appears in parentheses. Where a scale item is based on a choice between a pair of statements, the choice corresponding to the direction of the scale is indicated. Further details about scale construction are available on request.

POPULISM

1. I don't mind a politician's methods if he manages to get the right things done. (Agree)
2. In the long run, I'll put my trust in the simple, down-to-earth thinking of ordinary people rather than the theories of experts and intellectuals. (Agree)
3. In politics, talk without action is worse than doing nothing at all. (Agree)
4. We would probably solve most of our big national problems if government could actually be brought back to the people at the grass roots. (Agree)
5. What we need is a government that gets the job done without all this red tape. (Agree)
6. In times of trouble, it doesn't really matter so much how you act but whether you act. (Agree)

MORAL RECTITUDE

1. If a politician is a little dishonest about some things, then he's just like everybody else. (Disagree)
2. You can't trust politicians to tell the truth. (Disagree)
3. Politicians have to cut a few corners if they are going to get anywhere. (Disagree)

4. I don't mind if a politician gets a little rake-off so long as he does his job properly in most respects. (Disagree)
5. There is no room in our government for people of loose character. (Agree)
6. No candidate deserves to be elected unless he tells the complete truth. (Agree)

WILLINGNESS TO COMPROMISE

1. The give and take of political compromises is the best way we have to handle the conflicts that arise between groups in our society. (Agree)
2. Compromise and bargaining among politicians is necessary to make democracy work. (Agree)
3. Most of the compromising that goes on in politics turns out to be bad for the public. (Disagree)
4. It is never right for a politician to give up even one of his ideals or principles in order to achieve other important goals. (Disagree)

POLITICAL EFFICACY

1. Sometimes, politics and government seem so complicated that a person like me can't really understand what's going on. (Disagree)
2. The political parties are so big that I doubt I could influence them even if I were active in them. (Disagree)
3. I believe that I can help to change the minds of public officials. (Agree)
4. People like me don't have any say about what the government does. (Disagree)
5. Generally, those elected to parliament soon loose touch with people. (Disagree)
6. So many other people vote in elections that it doesn't matter very much whether I vote or not. (Disagree)
7. I don't think that the government cares much what people like me think. (Disagree)

POLITICAL TRUST

First, I would like to find out how many politicians you think are crooked. For the politicians in Victoria, would you say that most are crooked, some are, not very many, or none are crooked? And how about politicians in

Ottawa? (Not very many, or none)

Thinking about civil servants in Victoria and Ottawa, I would like to find out how wasteful you think they are with the money we pay in taxes. First for Victoria, would you say the civil servants are very wasteful, not very wasteful, or not wasteful at all? And how about civil servants in Ottawa? (Not very wasteful or not wasteful at all)

How many politicians do you feel know what they are doing? First, for the politicians in Victoria, would you say that most know what they are doing, only a few, or hardly any of them know what they are doing? And how about the politicians in Ottawa? (Most know)

And how many civil servants do you feel know what they are doing? First, for the civil servants in Victoria, would you say that most know what they are doing, only a few, or hardly any of them know what they are doing? And how about the civil servants in Ottawa? (Most know)

B.C. ALIENATION

1. Many things the federal government does, provincial governments would do a lot better. (Agree)
2. I don't find people from eastern Canada very attractive. (Agree)
3. The federal government has all but forgotten B.C. (Agree)
4. In B.C., we have more in common with people in Washington than with people of Ontario. *OR* I think of myself as a Canadian first and a British Columbian second. (Chose first statement)
5. B.C. pays more into Confederation than she gets out of it. *OR* On balance, B.C. is much better off in Confederation than out of it. (Chose first statement)
6. Ottawa is so far away, our MPs soon lose touch with the people who elect them. *OR* I sometimes feel that the federal government is more in touch with B.C. opinion than the provincial government is. (Chose first statement)
7. Local questions just don't get the attention they deserve in Ottawa. *OR* Frankly, I'm glad that the federal government resists certain kinds of local pressures. (Chose first statement)

INDIVIDUAL/COLLECTIVE RESPONSIBILITY

(scale scored in collective responsibility direction)
1. After a person has worked until he is 65, it is proper for the community to support him. (Agree)
2. The government ought to make sure that everyone has a decent standard

of living. (Agree)
3. Let's face it, most unemployed people could find a job if they really wanted to. (Disagree)
4. Why should the government spend my tax dollars on sick people; my family always put aside something for a rainy day. (Disagree)
5. Government regulation stifles personal initiative. *OR* Without government regulations, some people will just take advantage of the rest of us. (Chose second statement)
6. If I do my best, it is only right that the government should help me out when I get some bad breaks. *OR* Each individual should accept the consequences of their own actions. (Chose first statement)

ETHNOCENTRISM

1. All around the world, English is the language of commerce and trade, so why fight it here? (Agree)
2. Nobody in B.C. really watches French-language TV; it only restricts our freedom to watch other programs. (Agree)
3. Entirely too much is made of French Canada these days. (Agree)
4. Canada is lucky to be a bilingual country. (Disagree)
5. B.C. has more in common with Quebec than we often think. (Disagree)
6. British Columbia has always been an English-speaking province and it might as well stay that way. (Agree)

Notes

NOTES TO CHAPTER ONE

1. Peter Ward's work, discussed in the next chapter, is an important exception, but covers only the period up to 1939. See his "Class and Race in the Social Structure of British Columbia, 1870-1939," in W. Peter Ward and Robert A. J. McDonald, *British Columbia: Historical Readings* (Vancouver: Douglas and McIntyre, 1981).
2. However, see Jeremy Wilson, "The Impact of Communications Developments on British Columbia Electoral Patterns, 1903-1975," *Canadian Journal of Political Science*, 13 (Sept. 1980), 509-36, which shows that as communication between different parts of the province improved, regional idiosyncrasies in voting patterns were reduced.
3. William L. Marr and Donald G. Paterson, *Canada: An Economic History* (Toronto: Macmillan, 1980), 445.
4. M. Janine Brodie and Jane Jenson, *Crisis, Challenge and Change: Party and Class in Canada* (Toronto: Methuen, 1980), chap. 1.
5. Kenneth McRoberts and Dale Posgate also use a framework which stresses changes in class structures in their analysis of Quebec. See their *Quebec: Social Change and Political Crisis*, revised edition (Toronto: McClelland and Stewart, 1980).
6. R.E. Caves and R.H. Holton, "An Outline of the Economic History of British Columbia, 1881-1951," in J. Friesen and H.K. Ralston (eds.), *Historical Essays on British Columbia* (Toronto: Gage, 1980), chap. 13.
7. See Richard Simeon and David J. Elkins, "Provincial Political Cultures in Canada," in Elkins and Simeon (eds.), *Small Worlds: Provinces and Parties in Canadian Political Life* (Toronto: Methuen, 1980); and chap. 4 in this book.
8. "The Canadian Political Cultures: Toward a Redefinition of the Nature the Canadian Political System," *Canadian Journal of Political Science*, 7 (1974), 438-83.
9. There are significant differences, for example, in the ordering of provinces by level of development and the significance of class cleavages offered by Wilson from that presented by Jane Jenson, "Party Systems," in David J. Bellamy, Jon H. Pammett, and Donald C. Rowat, *The Provincial Political Systems* (Toronto: Methuen, 1976), 118-31.
10. Wilson's explanation, for example, depends on equating support for the provincial Social Credit party with that for the federal Conservatives. See his "The Canadian Political Cultures," 468-69. Our investigation of the relationship between federal and provincial partisanship reported in Chapter 8 undermines that view.
11. Similar hypotheses regarding the greater salience of class issues in provincial politics are advanced by Donald Smiley in his *Canada in Crisis: Federalism in the Eighties*, 3rd edition (Toronto: McGraw-Hill, 1980), 140-41; and Garth Stevenson, "Federalism and the Political Economy of the Canadian State," in Leo Panitch (ed.), *The Canadian State: Political Economy and Political Power* (Toronto: University of Toronto Press, 1977), 90-91.
12. Brodie and Jenson, *Crisis, Challenge and Change*, for example, advance the thesis that Canadian history has offered a number of opportunities for the development of a strong left party based on the working class, opportunities which have been lost because of manipulation of the political agenda by leaders of the bourgeois parties or mistakes by leaders of left parties or trade unions. If this is true, one wonders why the same strategies were not pursued (or failed) at the provincial level in British Columbia (and as

we will argue in Chapter 9, other provinces as well).

13. Ibid., 297-98.

14. See Harold D. Clarke et al., *Political Choice in Canada,* (Toronto: McGraw-Hill, Ryerson, 1979), especially chap. 10.

15. The major sources of national survey data used in this book are the 1979 wave of the Social Change in Canada project directed by Tom Atkinson, Bernard R. Blishen, Michael D. Ornstein, and H. Michael Stevenson at the Institute for Behavioural Research, York University; and the 1974-80 National Election Studies by Harold Clarke, Jane Jenson, Lawrence LeDuc, and Jon Pammett. Data from both studies were made available by the UBC Data Library. Neither the principal investigators nor the Data Library are responsible for the analysis or interpretations in this book.

16. The survey was designed and supervised by David J. Elkins, Donald E. Blake, and Richard Johnston. Field work was done by Canadian Facts Ltd. under the direction of Sherrill Selander. The sample design was a multi-stage, stratified cluster sample. Ten provincial ridings were pre-selected on the basis of political and geographical characteristics to give representation to interior, Vancouver Island, and metropolitan ridings, ranging in competitiveness, with some divided by and others contained within federal constituencies.

Sampling locations within ridings were chosen as follows: census enumeration areas within provincial ridings were chosen with probability of selection based on the EA population age 15 or over according to the 1976 census. Within these clusters dwelling units were chosen using a randomly chosen starting-point and a random interval between dwelling units. Households contacted were inventoried for residents age 16 or over and an individual selected for interview on the basis of a selection pattern which also varied randomly. No substitutes were permitted. Approximately three interviews were completed per cluster. It should be noted that our sample is based on the population age 16 and over and not eligible voters.

A target of 150 interviews per riding was set but could not be met in all cases because the 1980 federal election was called before interviewing was completed. A total of 1,051 usable interviews was obtained. When the sample is weighted according to household size and to compensate for over- or under-sampling certain ridings, the vote and demographic distributions correspond closely to population characteristics. In fact, weighting makes little difference, and the analysis in this book has been conducted using unweighted data.

The use of census enumeration areas as primary sampling units facilitated the linking of individual response data to census data on socio-economic characteristics of the areas in which they lived. Because enumeration areas have small populations, usually from 400 to 600 people, they serve nicely as surrogate neighbourhoods. Using enumeration area maps together with maps of provincial polling divisions (the smallest units for which election results are reported) we were also able to characterize the partisan complexion of respondent neighbourhoods. Further details are available on request.

The data are available from the Data Library at the University of British Columbia and the Inter-University Consortium for Political and Social Research at the University of Michigan.

NOTES TO CHAPTER TWO

1. A useful source on the political histories and dynamics of each of the provinces can be found in Martin Robin (ed.), *Canadian Provincial Politics: The Party Systems of the Ten Provinces* (Scarborough, Ont.: Prentice-Hall, 1978).

2. F.W. Howay, "The Settlement and Progress of British Columbia, 1871-1914," in J. Friesen and H.K. Ralston (eds.), *Historical Essays on British Columbia* (Toronto: Gage, 1980), 25.

3. See Margaret A. Ormsby, *British Columbia: A History* (Toronto: Macmillan, 1958), chap. 10. Ormsby is the best single source on British Columbia politics and history for the period up to World War II.

4. Robert Hamilton Coats and R.E. Gosnell, *Sir James Douglas* (Toronto, 1909), quoted in Allan Smith, "The Writing of British Columbia History," in W. Peter Ward and Robert A.J. McDonald, *British Columbia: Historical Readings* (Vancouver: Douglas and McIntyre, 1981), 21.

5. Howay, "Settlement and Progress of British Columbia," 34.

6. Quoted in Ormsby, *British Columbia*, 336.

7. Martin Robin, *The Rush for Spoils* (Toronto: McClelland and Stewart, 1972), 26.
8. Ormsby, *British Columbia*, 332.
9. Calculated from figures supplied in W. Peter Ward, "Class and Race in the Social Structure of British Columbia, 1870-1939," in Ward and McDonald, *British Columbia*, 581-99.
10. Robin, *Rush for Spoils*, 82-83.
11. A. Ross McCormack, "The Emergence of the Socialist Movement in B.C.," *B.C. Studies*, No. 21 (1974).
12. Ward, "Class and Race," in Ward and McDonald, *British Columbia*, 584-85.
13. Ibid., 588.
14. Robin, *Rush for Spoils*, 125ff.
15. Ibid., 133.
16. See Edith Dobie, "Party History in British Columbia, 1903-1933," in Friesen and Ralton, *Historical Essays*, 70-81.
17. Ibid., 73.
18. Dobie, "Party History," 76-77.
19. Walter Young, "Ideology, Personality and the Origin of the CCF in British Columbia," in Ward and McDonald, *British Columbia*, 558.
20. Robin, *Rush for Spoils*, 260.
21. Ibid., 260-62.
22. Alan C. Cairns, "Socialism, Federalism and the B.C. Party Systems, 1933-1980," presented to the annual meeting of the Learned Societies, Vancouver, 1983, 9-10.
23. Young, "Origin of the CCF in B.C.," 567-70.
24. See Margaret Ormsby, "T. Dufferin Pattullo and the Little New Deal," in Ward and McDonald, *British Columbia*, 533-54.
25. The drop in Liberal popularity in 1941 is usually attributed to Pattullo's performance at the 1940 Dominion-Provincial Conference called to discuss the recommendations of the Rowell-Sirois Commission. Pattullo joined with Aberhart of Alberta and Hepburn of Ontario in refusing to restrict the discussion to what they felt was the centralist thrust of the Commission's proposals. The conference collapsed and Pattullo was widely criticized in the B.C. Press and by the province's business community for selfish partisan behaviour during wartime. See Ormsby, *British Columbia*, 470-71.
26. Cairns, "The B.C. Party Systems," 16.
27. See Donald K. Alper, "From Rule to Ruin: The Conservative Party of British Columbia, 1928-1954" (Ph.D. Diss., University of British Columbia, 1975), especially chap. 5.
28. Cairns, "The B.C. Party Systems," 22-23.

29. The drop in support for the former coalition partners seems to be linked to voter cynicism stimulated by the bitter relations which developed among coalition leaders between 1949 and 1952, combined with the issue of hospital insurance. The hospital insurance plan, a popular move when first introduced in 1947, had begun to incur deficits. The government's response was to raise premiums and introduce co-insurance charges which were very unpopular. See Martin Robin, *Pillars of Profit* (Toronto: McClelland and Stewart, 1973), 115-17.
30. David Elkins, "Politics Makes Strange Bedfellows: The B.C. Party System in the 1952 and 1953 Provincial Elections," *B.C. Studies*, No. 30 (Summer 1976).
31. Robin, *Pillars of Profit*, 128ff.
32. For a detailed account of Bennett's harnessing of Social Credit based largely on interviews with Bennett himself see David J. Mitchell, *WAC: Bennett and the Rise of British Columbia* (Vancouver: Douglas and McIntyre, 1983), chap. 5.
33. Alper, "From Rule to Ruin," 380.
34. Ibid., 393.
35. Provincial and federal CCF/NDP vote shares were correlated at .35 between 1953 and 1979. Shifts between elections were more closely related with a correlation of .69.
36. Cairns, "The B.C. Party Systems," 32-33.
37. A. L. Farley, *Atlas of British Columbia* (Vancouver: University of B.C. Press, 1979), 135.
38. Employers' Council of British Columbia, *British Columbia: Collective Bargaining Environment, 1980*, Table 28, p. 46.
39. Robin, *Pillars of Profit*, 290.
40. A comprehensive account of the NDP period in power is contained in J. Terence Morley, Norman J. Ruff, Neil A. Swainson, R. Jeremy Wilson, and Walter D. Young, *The Reins of Power: Governing British Columbia* (Vancouver: Douglas and McIntyre, 1983).
41. This is the theme developed by Paul Tennant in "The NDP Government of British Columbia: Unaided Politicians in an Unaided Cabinet," *Canadian Public Policy*, 3 (1977), 489-503.
42. These are the initiatives singled out by Philip Resnick in "Social Democracy in Power: The Case of British Columbia," *B.C. Studies*, No. 34 (Summer 1977), 3-20. It is worth noting that even a sympathetic observer like Resnick argues that most of the govern-

ment's moves could not be characterized as "socialist" and that many of them simply represented the implementation in British Columbia of innovations already established in other provinces.

43. The creation of the Insurance Corporation of British Columbia with a monopoly over the issuance of compulsory insurance coverage threatened the livelihood of hundreds of small businessmen who made a living as insurance agents. They were mollified somewhat when the government licensed private agents to issue government insurance. The Land Commission made it much more difficult to convert agricultural land to more profitable uses as residential or industrial land. Real estate speculators were obviously affected, but so too were many farmers on the fringes of the province's major metropolitan areas who contemplated selling their land upon retirement from farming. They would be deprived of substantial profits if sales were restricted to bona fide farmers.

44. A detailed account of the issue and the campaign against the mining royalty legislation is provided by Raymond W. Payne, "Corporate Power, Interest Groups, and the Development of Mining Policy in British Columbia," *B.C. Studies*, No. 54 (Summer 1982), 3-37.

NOTES TO CHAPTER THREE

1. This chapter is based on our "Sources of Change in the B.C. Party System," *B.C. Studies*, No. 50 (Summer 1981), 3-28.

2. For an account of these events see G.L. Kristianson, "The Non-Partisan Approach to B.C. Politics: The Search for a Unity Party, 1972-1975," *B.C. Studies*, No. 33 (Spring 1977), 13-29.

3. For a detailed description of the survey used to analyse individual behaviour see Chap. 1.

4. Throughout this book we follow the standard practice of distinguishing party "identifiers" from those who simply vote for a party without acknowledging a more enduring attachment to it. The distinction will be made clear in the following discussion.

5. The exact question was: "Thinking of provincial politics here in B.C. do you *usually* think of yourself as a Liberal, Progressive Conservative, NDP, Social Credit or what?" It was then followed by a question asking

for an assessment of the strength of that attachment.

6. For an analysis of the aggregate impact of party switching and strategic voting using B.C. data see Richard G.C. Johnston, David J. Elkins, and Donald E. Blake, "Strategic Voting: Individual Reasoning and Collective Consequences," presented at the 1980 annual meeting of the American Political Science Association, Washington, D.C.

7. The strength of attachment on the part of those still loyal to the provincial Liberal and Conservative parties is not noticeably weaker than that of provincial Socreds. New Democrats are much more likely to express very strong attachments to the party.

8. John Wilson and David Hoffman have detected what may be a weaker version of a comparable phenomenon in Ontario—the existence of, in their case, Liberal partisans whose primary orientation is to the federal level of politics and who disproportionately abstain or vote Conservative at the provincial level. See their "The Liberal Party in Contemporary Ontario Politics," *Canadian Journal of Political Science*, 3 (June 1970), 177-204.

9. The higher average age of Social Credit identifiers characterizes all components of the coalitions identified in tables 6 and 7 except perhaps former Liberals, whose average age is 45 compared to 44 for their counterparts in the NDP.

10. See Kristianson, "The Non-Partisan Approach to B.C. Politics."

11. W. Phillips Shively, "The Development of Party Identification among Adults: Exploration of a Functional Model," *American Political Science Review*, 73 (December 1979), 1042.

12. For a discussion of constraints on vote-maximizing behaviour which considers party activists seeking ideological gratification as well as voters, see David Robertson, *A Theory of Party Competition* (London: Wiley, 1977), 40-41.

13. The regional classification of ridings is based on that by Jeremy Wilson, "The Impact of Modernization on British Columbia Electoral Patterns" (Ph.D. diss, University of British Columbia, 1978). Ridings were grouped as follows, with additions from the 1978 redistribution noted in parentheses:

Greater Victoria: Victoria, Saanich and the Islands, Esquimalt, Oak Bay

Island & Central North Coast: Alberni,

Nanaimo, Cowichan-Malahat, Comox, Mackenzie, Prince Rupert (North Island in 1979)

Upper Status Vancouver: West Vancouver-
Howe Sound, North Vancouver-Capilano,
Vancouver-Point Grey

Vancouver-Burnaby: Burnaby Edmonds,
Burnaby North, Burnaby Willingdon, New
Westminster, North Vancouver-Seymour,
Burrard, Centre, East, Little Mountain, South

Vancouver Suburbs & Valley: Chilliwack,
Coquitlam, Delta, Dewdney, Langley, Richmond, Surrey (Central Fraser Valley,
Maillardville-Coquitlam, Coquitlam-Moody
in 1979)

Central Interior: Cariboo, Kamloops,
Yale-Lillooet

Okanagan: North & South Okanagan,
Shuswap, Boundary-Similkameen (Shuswap-
Revelstoke in 1979)

Kootenays: Columbia River, Kootenay,
Nelson-Creston, Revelstoke-Slocan, Ross-
land-Trail

North: Atlin, Fort George, Omineca,
Skeena (Prince George North and South in
1979)

Peace: North and South Peace River.

14. Recalculation of the coefficients in Table 9
adding 1983 data attenuates the NDP slopes
everywhere except Greater Victoria.

15. The standard deviation indicates the geographic concentration of a party's vote in
that the greater the vote share differences
between geographic units, the larger the
standard deviation. Conversely, the more
similar vote shares are to each other, the
smaller will be the standard deviation. The
coefficient of variation is simply the standard deviation divided by the mean of the
distribution. In effect, the coefficient of variation controls for party size and is more
appropriate for comparing geographic con-
centrations where party shares differ.

16. Jeremy Wilson, "The Impact of Communications Developments on British Columbia
Electoral Patterns, 1903-1975," *Canadian
Journal of Political Science*, 13 (Sept. 1980),
509-36, focusing on inter-election swings in
party support since the mid-thirties, demonstrates an even longer-term trend towards
homogenization, although much of the
homogenization he observes took place
within the ten regions rather than between
them. It may be that the increase in the
average between-region variation from Wilson's 1953-63 period to his 1966-75 one reflects
the different trends in each region that we

report in Table 9.

17. Conventional wisdom says that the electoral system is malapportioned and that Social
Credit benefits from the malapportionment.
Social Credit allegedly wins the small, rural
seats. In fact, the electoral system favours
the NDP. Following the 1983 provincial
election, the typical NDP MLA now represents 42,602 residents, while the typical Social
Credit MLA represents 51,635.

18. Our emphases differ from those in Wilson,
"The Impact of Communications Developments," although some of our findings complement his. To the extent that we emphasize the role of union membership in linking
individuals in different parts of the province,
we complement his concern with communication patterns. But we want to also to suggest that industrialization and unionization
have promoted substantive policy conflict
and that this conflict has become more similar across locales.

19. Some of the change in Table 11 is an artifact
of 1967-77 census region boundary changes.
Most important is the transfer of Trail from
the West Kootenay region to the Okanagan
region; the latter is thus made to seem one
of the very highest growth regions. Other
changes had equivocal effects or were compensated for by yet other boundary changes.
The northern Columbia River area was trans-
ferred from East Kootenay to West Kootenay
(the latter region is now called Central
Kootenay; we have retained the 1967 nomen-
clature as more consistent with ordinary
usage). The Shuswap Lake area was moved
from Thompson-Lillooet to West Kootenay.
Squamish moved from the Lower Mainland
to Thompson-Lillooet. Powell River moved
from Skeena-Stikine to the Lower Mainland (in fact, Powell River and Ocean Falls
together made up the Central Mainland Coast
region, but employment and productivity
figures for the region were merged with the
Skeena figures; the census reorganization
abolished the region and assigned Ocean
Falls and Powell River to the adjacent coastal
regions). Finally, Williams Lake was moved
from Thompson-Lillooet to Central British
Columbia.

20. A.L. Farley, *Atlas of British Columbia:
People, Environment and Resource Use*
(Vancouver: University of British Colum-
bia Press, 1979), map 30 and pp. 31, 65, 67.

21. Ibid., maps 32 and 33, pp. 69, 71.

22. Ibid., maps 34 and 35, pp. 73, 75.

23. See above, Table 7.
24. Public employment data are notoriously difficult to gather for British Columbia. The government of the province refuses to divulge the employment data on which Statistics Canada bases its *Provincial Government Employment* series (Catalogue 72-007). Revenue Canada *Taxation Statistics* must serve instead. Tax return series for the 1946-75 period are available in David K. Foot (ed.), *Public Employment in Canada: Statistical Series* (Toronto: Butterworth, 1979), vol. 4 in the IRPP Series on Public Sector Employment in Canada. Figures in the text are from 20-21 and 26-27. For thoughts on the electoral role of public employees see Richard Johnston, "Bureaucrats and Elections," in Meyer W. Bucovetsky (ed.), *Studies in Public Employment and Compensation* (Toronto: Butterworth, 1979), vol. 2 in the IRPP Series on Public Sector Employment in Canada, 262-77.

NOTES TO CHAPTER FOUR

1. This chapter has been improved by the criticisms and advice of Donald Blake, Richard Johnston, Jean Laponce, and Campbell Sharman. I also wish to thank Jim Bruton and Steve Tomblin for research assistance.
2. See, for example, W. Peter Ward, *White Canada Forever* (Montreal: McGill-Queen's University Press, 1978) and Thomas R. Berger, *Fragile Freedoms: Human Rights and Dissent in Canada* (Toronto: Clarke, Irwin, 1981).
3. Daniel J. Elazar, *American Federalism: A View from the States*, 2nd edition (New York: Thomas Y. Crowell, 1972), 85.
4. The 1979 B.C. Survey asked people about the political issues of concern to them. Many of the people who mentioned "fisheries" as an issue explained that one of the big problems facing fishermen was the difficulty of collecting unemployment insurance during the off-season.
5. For more details about the development of transportation in the province, see R. Cole Harris, "Moving Amid the Mountains, 1870-1930," *B.C. Studies*, No. 58 (Summer 1983), 3-39.
6. For comprehensive information on B.C. geography and the changing patterns of communication and isolation as they affect electoral politics, see R. Jeremy Wilson,

"The Impact of Modernization on British Columbia Electoral Patterns: Communications Development and the Uniformity of Swing, 1903-1975" (Ph.D., University of B.C., 1978); "The Impact of Communications Development on British Columbia Electoral Patterns, 1903-1975," *Canadian Journal of Political Science*, 13 (Sept. 1980), 509-35; and "Geography, Politics, and Culture: Electoral Insularity in British Columbia," *Canadian Journal of Political Science*, 13 (Dec. 1980), 751-74.
7. W. Peter Ward, "Class and Race in the Social Structure of British Columbia, 1870-1939," *B.C. Studies*, No. 45 (Spring 1980), 17-35.
8. The 1981 Canadian census found that 2.4 per cent of the B.C. population claimed "native peoples" as their sole ethnic origin and another 0.7 per cent claimed a joint origin of native plus some other designation. The comparable figures for Canada were 1.7 per cent and 0.3 per cent, respectively. These and other figures below from the 1981 census were taken from a 24-page brochure of "advance information" published by Statistics Canada (no date).
9. See the informative article by Carol Volkart, "English is foreign to almost half city pupils, trustee says," the *Sun*, 11 May 1983.
10. D.J. Elkins and R.E.B. Simeon, "A Cause in Search of Its Effect, or What Does Political Culture Explain?", *Comparative Politics*, 11 (Jan. 1979), 127-45, contains a much more extensive discussion of my views on the nature of political culture.
11. For a similar analysis of American political culture, see Daniel Elazar, *Cities of the Prairie* (New York: Basic Books, 1970), especially Chap. 6, "Political Culture and Politics in State and Community."
12. Marjorie Nichols, Victoria columnist for the *Sun*, has repeatedly noted similarities between the parties, although she does not use the term "political culture." See, for example, "Roll Back a Decade or So," the *Sun*, 27 July 1983, p. A4.
13. Other commentators on B.C. politics emphasize the combative, high stakes atmosphere of provincial politics. See, for example, Martin Robin, "British Columbia: The Politics of Class Conflict," in Martin Robin (ed.), *Canadian Provincial Politics* (Scarborough: Prentice-Hall, 1972); Edwin R. Black, "British Columbia: The Politics of Exploitation," in Hugh G. Thorburn (ed.), *Party Politics in*

Canada, 4th edition (Scarborough: Prentice-Hall, 1979); and J. Terence Morley, "British Columbia's Political Culture: Healing a Compound Fracture," paper delivered at symposium on "Reflections on a Decade: B.C. Politics in the 1970s," University of British Columbia, June 1983.

14. In fact, Philip Resnick argues that these initiatives were not particularly "socialistic" either. See his "Social Democracy in Power: The Case of British Columbia," *B.C. Studies*, No. 34 (Summer 1977), 3-20.

15. Black, "Politics of Exploitation."

16. Herschel Hardin, *A Nation Unaware: The Canadian Economic Culture* (Vancouver: J.J. Douglas, 1974).

17. Elkins and Simeon, *Small Worlds*, Chap. 2, "Provincial Political Cultures," 37-40, 53-55.

18. Ibid., 40-43, 55-58.

19. For details, see David J. Elkins, Donald Blake, and Richard Johnston, "Who Trusts Whom to Do What?", paper delivered at the Canadian Political Science Association meetings, Montreal, June 1980.

20. *Small Worlds*, 44.

21. Ibid., 42, 44, 58-62, also used this same procedure. Interested readers may compare the B.C. results to those in other provinces.

22. Quoted by Allan Fotheringham, "Bennett the Second: Horatio Alger with a Head Start," *Weekend Magazine*, vol. 26, no. 8 (21 Feb. 1976), 4.

23. One of the best sources for understanding the outlook and mood of the Populists is Lawrence Goodwyn, *The Populist Moment: A Short History of the Agrarian Revolt in America* (New York: Oxford University Press, 1978). Although not specifically on populism, T.J. Jackson Lears, *No Place of Grace: Antimodernism and the Transformation of American Culture, 1880-1920* (New York: Pantheon Books, 1981) is a brilliant evocation of turn-of-the-century American social thought. For a very personalized account of populist politics in one of its original core areas, central Texas, see Robert Caro, *The Years of Lyndon Johnson: The Path to Power* (New York: Alfred A. Knopf, 1983), especially chaps. 2, 14, 18, and 29.

24. The best, concise discussion of populism on the Prairies is John Richards and Larry Pratt, *Prairie Capitalism* (Toronto: McClelland and Stewart, 1979), especially chap. 2.

25. Black, "Politics of Exploitation," and Robert Sarti, "Direct Action Speaks Louder than Words!" The *Sun*, 28 Feb. 1983, p. A5.

26. Richards and Pratt, *Prairie Capitalism*, 20-23; and John Richards, "Populism and the West," in Larry Pratt and Garth Stevenson (eds.), *Western Separatism* (Edmonton: Hurtig, 1981), especially 74-76.

27. Robert Axelrod, "The Structure of Public Opinion on Policy Issues," *Public Opinion Quarterly*, 31 (Spring 1967), 51-60.

28. The Social Credit government departed from these practices in a major way when it centralized power over the community college system and closed down the David Thompson University Centre in Nelson, a small city in the Kootenays. The community's response to the latter fits nicely within the perspective developed here—residents of Nelson moved in to occupy the buildings to prevent the college's assets from being dispersed.

29. Some of the items in the Populism Scale were developed by Herbert McClosky.

30. The two scales were originally developed in the United States and Britain by Jack Citrin and David J. Elkins. See their *Political Disaffection among British University Students: Concepts, Measurement, and Causes* (Berkeley: Institute of International Studies, University of California, Research Series, Monograph No. 23, 1975).

31. This is also the conclusion of Black, "Politics of Exploitation."

32. One is reminded that the original collective manifestations of Canadian populism on the Prairies, the grain growers co-operatives, were private organizations. Only later were they to serve as models for Crown corporations and as a training and recruiting ground for the CCF.

33. For details, and for the flavour of debate and personal accusations, see the *Sun* or the *Province* during the period following 19 Sept. 1983. The details of the "restraint" package itself were outlined in these two newspapers throughout July and August 1983.

34. If one used the provincial vote in 1979 rather than party identification, almost identical results obtain, but the number of cases for Liberals and Conservatives would be smaller.

35. Richards and Pratt, *Prairie Capitalism*; and Richards, "Populism and the West."

36. Daniel J. Elazar, *American Federalism: A View from the States*, Chap. 4, "The States and the Political Setting," quotation on 90-91.

37. Ibid., 94-102.

NOTES TO CHAPTER FIVE

1. Martin Robin, "The Politics of Class Conflict," in Robin (ed.), *Canadian Provincial Politics*, 2nd edition (Scarborough, Ont.: Prentice-Hall, 1972, 29-30.
2. "British Columbia," in David J. Bellamy, Jon H. Pammett, and Donald C. Rowat (eds.), *The Provincial Political Systems* (Toronto: Methuen, 1976), 69.
3. "The Politics of Class Conflict," 40.
4. Galbraith ("British Columbia") asserts without evidence (p. 70) that "supporters of one belief view the adherents of another persuasion as representing an alien, evil, incomprehensible force. People can and do live entire lives within one or the other universe of political discourse."
5. Martin Robin, *The Rush for Spoils: The Company Province 1871-1933* (Toronto: McClelland and Stewart, 1972), 28-29.
6. These figures are based on our survey results for members of the B.C. Labour force over age 16, including part-time workers, and using the industry groupings defined by Statistics Canada.
7. "The Politics of Class Conflict," 35.
8. *Pillars of Profit: The Company Province 1934-1972*, 187.
9. Ibid., 195.
10. "British Columbia: The Politics of Exploitation," in Hugh G. Thorburn (ed.), *Party Politics in Canada*, 4th edition (Scarborough, Ont.: Prentice-Hall, 1979), 293-94.
11. "Social Credit and the British Columbia Electorate," *B.C. Studies*, No. 12 (Winter 1971-72), 34-45.
12. See Donald E. Blake, "Another Look at Social Credit and the British Columbia Electorate," *B.C. Studies*, No. 12 (Winter 1971-72), 53-62.
13. "Class and Race in the Social Structure of British Columbia, 1870-1939," *B.C. Studies*, No. 45 (Spring 1980), 17-35.
14. Ibid., 25-26.
15. Scholars following upon the heels of those responsible for any "accepted view" are inevitably drawn to focus on qualifications and exceptions to the rule. The focus on class may itself have been partly a result of this intellectual tendency. Allan Smith has argued that with few exceptions until the 1960s, "British Columbia historians...maintained a peculiar blindspot when it came to social and economic conflict..." See his "The Writing of British Columbia History," *B.C. Stud-*

ies, No. 45 (Spring 1980), 98.

Much of that literature as it pertains to analysis of voting behaviour will be critically examined here, however, its contributions to the explanatory framework used must be recognized. Until the B.C. Election Study was conducted, data appropriate for testing many of the arguments in the literature were not available.

16. See Patricia Marchak, "Class, Regional and Institutional Sources of Social Conflict in B.C.," *B.C. Studies*, No. 27 (Autumn 1975), 30-49; and, Daniel J. Koenig and Trevor B. Proverbs, "Class, Regional and Institutional Sources of Party Support within British Columbia," *B.C. Studies*, No. 29 (Spring 1976), 19-28.

   A detailed analysis of changes in the occupational structure of British Columbia can be found in Rennie Warburton and David Coburn, "The Rise of Non-Manual Work in British Columbia," *B.C. Studies*, No. 59 (Fall 1983), 5-27.

17. The classic study is Robert Alford's *Party and Society: The Anglo-American Democracies* (Chicago: Rand McNally, 1963). For a more recent study using Alford's class voting index as well as socioeconomic status indicators, see Harold Clarke, Jane Jenson, Lawrence LeDuc, and Jon Pammett, *Political Choice in Canada* (Toronto: McGraw-Hill, 1979).

18. For further analysis of these distinctions and a comparison of the explanatory power of alternative measures in accounting for voter positions on a variety of ideological measures, see Michael D. Ornstein, H. Michael Stevenson, and A. Paul Williams, "Region, Class and Political Culture in Canada," *Canadian Journal of Political Science*, 13 (June 1980), 227-71. In this article the authors use Marxist class categories developed by Erik Olin Wright. William Johnston and Michael D. Ornstein have pursued a parallel analysis, yielding similar results, using another typology developed by G. Carchedi. See their "Class, Work and Politics," *Canadian Review of Sociology and Anthropology*, 19 (1982), 196-214.

19. "Class Structuration and Class Consciousness," in Anthony Giddens and David Held (eds.), *Classes, Power and Conflict* (London: Macmillan, 1982), 162.

20. The exact questions were: "People often think of themselves as belonging to one social class or another. Most people say

they belong to the upper-middle class, the middle class, or the working class. Do you *ever* think of yourself as belonging to one of these social classes? (Which one?)" (If class position selected) "What does class mean to you?" (If no definition forthcoming) "For example it might mean: what you do for a living, whether you own property or the style of life you lead." "Whatever class means, is your class really important in how you think of yourself?"

Those who did not select a class in response to the first question were asked whether some other associational or nominal group membership was important to their self-definition. Those who assigned themselves to a class group were also asked whether one of these other group memberships was more important than class. Forty per cent of those who said class was important to them agreed that some other group was *more* important than class. The relevant question listed religious group, ethnic group, party supporter, and city or country person as possible alternatives. "City or country person" was the most popular choice followed by "religious group," among 45 per cent and 29 per cent, respectively, of those who selected some group as more important than class.

21. The effect of encouraging those who do not initially choose a class label to select one has the effect of reducing the size of the middle class and increasing the size of the working class in the 1979 National Election study. If only those who ever consider themselves as members of a social class are considered, the middle class-working class ratio is 58 per cent to 26 per cent. When those who are encouraged to choose do so, the ratio is reduced to 49 per cent to 35 per cent. Forcing people to choose a class label and then doing analysis without taking that into account would also seem to undermine the theoretical justification for using subjective class in the first place.

The only Canadian study we are aware of which considers the implications of resistance to self-placement is by Daniel J. Koenig et al., "The Year that British Columbia Went NDP: NDP Support Pre- and Post-1972," *B.C. Studies*, No. 24 (Winter 1974-75), 65-86. The authors report that those who did not select a class label in a mailed questionnaire were disproportionately NDP voters. As shown below, our own study does not

show such a link.

22. Analysis of the relationship between subjective social class and provincial party identification based on the 1965 National Election study offers further support for the argument. See Blake, "Another Look at Social Credit," Table IV, 58.

23. The class measures are correlated at a modest level (Pearson r):

	Education	Family Income	Subjective Class
Occupational status	.13	.18	.08
Education		.32	.36
Family income			.35

Correlations involving subjective class (scored from working class = 1 to upper middle class = 3) are based on the subset of the sample who accept a class label. Education is measured in years and family income on a 10-point scale. Occupational status is measured using the Blishen score assigned on the basis of his/her occupation or, if not in the labour force, on the basis of the occupation of spouse, former spouse, parent, or close family member. Blishen scores rank occupations according to the income and educational levels associated with them. See B. Blishen and H. McRoberts, "A Revised Socioeconomic Index for Occupations in Canada," *Canadian Review of Sociology and Anthropology*, 13 (Feb. 1976), 71-79.

24. The highest educational group exhibits one curious property—a relatively high level of attachment to the provincial Liberal party and a relative unwillingness to *identify* with (as opposed to vote for) Social Credit. The highest income group also contains an above average number with a residual affection for the provincial Liberals. While the numbers are too small to bring joy to the provincial Liberal leadership, they do suggest that the Social Credit party has not completed its conquest of the upper class.

25. The classification in Table 21 is similar to but not identical to those used in calculating the correlations reported in note 23. The 10-point family income scale has been collapsed (approximately) into quintiles to facilitate presentation in tabular form; educational divisions are based on separate questions about level of school attended; and occupational divisions are based on an ordinal ranking of occupations suggested by P. Pineo, J. Porter, and H. McRoberts, which is itself based on Blishen scores. See "The

1971 Census and the Socioeconomic Classification of Occupations," *Canadian Review
of Sociology and Anthropology*, 14 (Feb.
1977), 91-102.

The "managerial/professional," "other
white collar," and "blue collar" groupings
were produced by collapsing Pineo/Porter
categories. Managerial/professional includes
self-employed professional, employed professionals, semi-professionals, high-level
managers, middle managers, technical
occupations, and supervisory occupations.
Other white collar includes skilled and semi-
skilled clerical, sales, and service occupations. The blue collar grouping includes
foremen, skilled crafts and trades, semi-skilled
crafts and trades, unskilled clerical, sales
and service, unskilled labourers, and farm
labourers. Williams and Ornstein ("Class
and Work") treat foremen as akin to supervisors because of their management responsibilities. Although they have been treated
as blue collar workers here, where relevant,
tests were conducted to see whether they
differed in significant ways from other blue
collar workers.

26. The implications of the populist division
within the NDP electorate given appeal of
the post-1983 Social Credit restraint policy
are explored in Donald E. Blake, "The Electoral Significance of Public-Sector Bashing,"
B.C. Studies, No. 62 (Summer 1984), 29-43.
There the existence of a division between
public sector and private sector blue collar
workers is revealed, with private sector
workers, especially those in unionized occupations, exhibiting more populist attitudes
including suspicion of bureaucrats.

27. The difference is statistically significant at
the .01 level. Mean scores differ in the same
way when party identification is considered.
Moreover, those who still identify with the
provincial Liberals or Conservatives have
identical mean scores but midway between
the NDP and Social Credit extreme.

28. B.C. populism is discussed at length in Chapter 3. For exact question wording see Appendix.

29. The similarity between parties on the populist dimension does not seem to have been
affected by the realignment which occurred
over the elections of 1972-75, despite the
fact that many Liberals and Conservatives,
whose parties are not known for populist
appeals, migrated to Social Credit and the
NDP. Populism scores for those who formed

an attachment to either party before 1972
are virtually identical to scores among newer
adherents.

30. The abortion issue represents a partial exception to this generalization. Opponents of
abortion are more prominent within the ranks
of Social Credit, and it is an issue on which
religious groups have taken strong stands.
However, neither party has made abortion
a campaign issue.

31. Dennis Forcese, in *The Canadian Class Structure*, 2nd edition (Toronto: McGraw-Hill
Ryerson, 1980), cites several studies which
demonstrate that religious groupings are associated with Canada's stratification pattern.
He also argues (p. 130) that "the ideology of
the several religions will reinforce existing
class attitudes, behaviour, and structure," a
possibility which has been virtually ignored
by political scientists.

32. The estimates in Table 27 and Figure 3 were
produced by probit analysis, which treats a
given dependent variable (Social Credit versus NDP in this case) as a linear combination of the explanatory variables. The use
of probit (or some other maximum likelihood technique) is preferable on mathemati-
cal grounds when the dependent variable
takes on a restricted range of values. In our
case, the dependent variable has only two
possible values since a voter either voted
for Social Credit or he did not. For an excellent discussion of probit analysis relatively
free from complex technical language, see
Morris P. Fiorina, *Retrospective Voting in
American National Elections* (New Haven:
Yale University Press, 1981).

Ordinary least squares regression analysis is used in subsequent chapters, where
the calculation of unbiased estimates is not
essential to the argument. The results of
regression analysis are also somewhat easier to communicate in simple language.

33. Analysis using party identification as the
dependent variable or including all voters
does not change the impression conveyed
by Table 27 and Figure 3.

34. "Middle age" and "union membership" are
used to create dichotomies. Each should be
interpreted as the effect of membership
in the group specified compared to non-
membership. For example, the significant
negative coefficient for "union membership"
shows that voters in union households have
a lower probability of voting Social Credit,
other things being equal, than voters in non-

union households.

35. The estimation procedure requires three steps: evaluation of the equation by multiplying each coefficient by the actual value of the independent variable for a given individual, summing the result, and consulting the table of probabilities associated with the normal distribution. The calculated sum gives a point on the x-axis corresponding to the estimated probability.

The .76 probability was arrived at by assuming a value of "3" for family income, "0" for union membership, "1" to indicate a professional occupation, and "3" for individual/collective responsibility. When multiplied by the appropriate coefficients and summed together with the constant, the equation yields a figure of .72 corresponding to a probability of .76.

NOTES TO CHAPTER SIX

1. Ornstein et al. place more emphasis on the *strength* of the relationship between ideological position and a variety of social class measures in a study using national survey data, but they were mainly interested in demonstrating the importance of social class differences compared to regional differences. However, this study and theirs both demonstrate the significance of distinctions within conventional occupational status groupings.

Although they use different measures of ideology than those used here, there is some overlap. Moreover, they found only weak links between ideology and federal partisanship, a position which is supported in chapters 8 and 9 of this book when the federal political world is examined. See Michael D. Ornstein, H. Michael Stevenson and A. Paul Williams, "Region, Class and Political Culture in Canada," *Canadian Journal of Political Science*, 13 (June 1980), 227-71.

2. See Stuart Jamieson, "Regional Factors in Industrial Conflict: The Case of British Columbia," in J. Friesen and H. K. Ralston (eds.), *Historical Essays on British Columbia* (Toronto: Gage, 1980), 228-42.

3. Vancouver *Sun*, 24 Sept. 1983. Sample size was 870, selected using systematic sampling of telephone listings.

4. For a thorough critique of that position see A.R. Dobell, "What's the B.C. Spirit? Recent Experience in the Management of Restraint," University of Victoria, Sept. 1983.

5. V. Keddie, "Class Identification and Party Preference among Manual Workers," *Canadian Review of Sociology and Anthropology*, 17 (1980), 24-36. Keddie compares 4 communities (Sudbury, Lindsay, Hamilton, and Ottawa, Ontario) which differ in scale, type and heterogeneity of industrial settings. Also see David Lockwood, "Sources of Variation in Working Class Images of Society," *Sociological Review*, 14 (1979), 249-67.

A useful review of the literature on this topic is contained in Alex Himelfarb, *The Social Characteristics of One-Industry Towns*, a background study prepared for the Royal Commission on Corporate Concentration (Ottawa: Supply and Services, 1977).

6. See among others, Martin Robin, "The Politics of Class Conflict," in Martin Robin (ed.), *Canadian Provincial Politics* (Scarborough, Ont.: Prentice-Hall, 1972); J.H. Bradbury, "Class Structures and Class Conflicts in 'Instant' Resource Towns in British Columbia— 1965-1972," *B.C. Studies*, No. 37 (Spring 1978), 3-18; John C. Leggett, "The Persistence of Working Class Consciousness in Vancouver," in J.A. Fry (ed.), *Economy, Class and Social Reality* (Toronto: Butterworth, 1979); and William Johnston and Michael D. Ornstein, "Class, Work, and Politics," *Canadian Review of Sociology and Anthropology*, 19 (1982), 196-214.

7. Carol Nackenoff, "O'Connor's Sectoral Model of the United States Economy: Examining Some Political Consequences," *British Journal of Political Science*, 12 (Apr. 1982), 221-39.

8. Patrick Dunleavy, "The Political Implications of Sectoral Cleavages and the Growth of State Employment: Part 2, Cleavage Structures and Political Alignment," *Political Studies*, 28 (Dec. 1980), 527-49.

9. James E. Alt and Janet Turner, "The Case of the Silk-Stocking Socialists and the Calculating Children of the Middle Class," *British Journal of Political Science*, 12 (Apr. 1982), 239-48.

10. Johnston and Ornstein, "Class, Work, and Politics."

11. The large "service" category identified by the census was broken up. Services to business and industry were reclassified according to the sector to which services were rendered. Personal services and services which could not be reclassified in this fashion or which did not fit into the category of

"educational, medical and related services" were added to the miscellaneous category.

A separate "resource" category combining the primary category with occupations in the manufacturing sector directly related to the primary sector (pulp and paper mills, sawmills, plywood mills, and mineral processing) was also created.

Daniel J. Koenig and Trevor B. Proverbs use a similar but less comprehensive classification distinguishing among legal authority, commerce, manufacturing, education, and extractive. See their "Class, Regional and Institutional Sources of Party Support within British Columbia," *B.C. Studies*, No. 29 (Spring 1976), 19-28.

12. Patricia Marchak was one of the first students of B.C. politics to argue that variations in the province's industrial structure produce political differences within class groups. To the social class and regional (metropolitan versus hinterland) divisions normally used in analysing social and political conflict in the province, she adds an "institutional" division consisting of six categories: (1) industrial and financial corporations in an oligopolistic market; (2) government and the public sector; (3) trade unions; (4) small business in competitive markets, independent professional practices, and non-corporate farms; (5) non-government and non-commercial institutions such as churches; (6) the family. See her "Class, Regional and Institutional Sources of Social Conflict in B.C.," *B.C. Studies*, No. 27 (Autumn 1975), 30-49.

13. See, however, Terence H. White, *Organizational Size as a Factor Influencing Labour Relations*, and John W. Gartrell, *Organization Size and Alienation*, background reports prepared for the Royal Commission on Corporate Concentration (Ottawa: Supply and Services, 1977).

Gartrell shows that mean levels of worker alienation increase according to the following ordering of employment types: self, government, government-funded, small private, and large private. White finds size to be of minor significance to job satisfaction compared to opportunities for mobility, supervision style, opportunities to use skills on the job, and autonomy on the job.

14. See Chapter 5, note 25 for a detailed description of the measures of occupational class used here.

15. A separate analysis revealed no difference in level of NDP support between members of Canadian and international unions.

16. See, however, Alt and Turner, "Silk-Stocking Socialists." Johnston and Ornstein, "Class, Work, and Politics," report (p. 258) that members of upper status occupational groups are more likely to restrict their liberalism to civil liberties type issues rather than to endorsements of equality of opportunity.

17. Marchak, "Class, Regional and Institutional Sources of Social Conflict," 47.

18. Ibid., 41.

19. Data on educational levels by enumeration area from the 1976 census were used to classify the neighbourhoods of the survey respondents. An income-based measure might seem preferable, or at least desirable for comparative purposes, but it was not available in the census data. Moreover, given the high wages commanded by some blue collar occupations in B.C., it is not obvious that a measure based on income would be superior.

20. See, for example, Kevin R. Cox, "The Spatial Structuring of Information Flow and Partisan Attitudes," and David R. Segal and Marshall W. Meyer, "The Social Context of Political Partisanship," both in Mattei Dogan and Stein Rokkan (eds.), *Social Ecology* (Cambridge, MA: MIT Press, 1974).

21. R. Robert Huckfeldt, "Variable Responses to Neighbourhood Social Contexts: Assimilation, Conflict, and Tipping Points," *Political Behavior*, 2 (1980), 235-36.

22. "Class, Regional and Institutional Sources of Social Conflict," 35-40.

23. R. Murphy and R. Morris, "Occupational Status, Subjective Class Identification and Political Affiliation," *American Sociological Review*, 26 (1961), 390ff.

24. "The Persistence of Working Class Consciousness," 246-47; see also Lockwood, "Working Class Images of Society."

25. Johnston and Ornstein, "Class, Work, and Politics," 207.

26. Each table was produced by treating the individual/collective responsibility score as the dependent variable in a regression containing the contextual variables identified earlier as well as measures of individual socioeconomic characteristics which could plausibly be connected to attitudinal differences. Those making a significant contribution to explanation were then included in a regression using vote as the dependent variable. The individual/collective respon-

sibility score was also included in that regression. With these variables fixed, all the other contextual and individual level variables were tested for their effects on vote, and the statistically significant ones retained. We also tested for differences in attitudes and vote between skilled and unskilled blue collar workers and between professionals and the rest of the upper status occupational grouping (owners, high and medium level managers, supervisors, and technicians).

27. The candidate variables at the individual level were type of training (skilled versus unskilled for blue collar workers; professional and semi-professional versus the rest in the upper status group), family income, and years of education. The last two were selected on the grounds that inter-industry differences in levels of remuneration and levels of education of the work-force could account for the observed differences in attitudes and partisanship. Family income was used rather than personal income for comparability with the analysis in Chapter 5. In fact, the results do not differ when personal income is used. While there are undoubtedly other sources of variation in attitudes towards individual versus collective responsibility and partisanship, the concern to test for the possible spuriousness of the observed contextual effects dictated our choice.

28. The sector variables are all dummy variables which serve to distinguish statistically between group averages on the ideological dimension or average levels of party support between groups. A significant coefficient for a dummy variable is an indication that the differences between groups divided by that variable is not due to chance and is independent of other characteristics of individuals in those groups which are also important. The sign of the coefficient gives the direction of difference.

29. The analysis is restricted to labour force members, and when NDP vote is used as the dependent variable it is scored "1" for an NDP vote in 1979 and "0" for a vote for any other party. The results are not much different when only NDP or Social Credit voters are considered, or when the analysis includes respondents who are not members of the labour force.

30. The beta coefficients measure the effect on the dependent variable of a difference of one standard deviation on a given indepen-

dent variable.

31. Mean collective responsibility scores ranged from 2.9 in "construction" to 4.0 in "public administration" in the case of managerial and professional workers, and from 3.2 in "educational/medical services" to 4.4 in "transportation / communication / utilities" for white collar workers. Private versus public sector differences were 3.6 versus 3.9 for the managerial/professional group. White collar workers did not differ significantly on this dimension.

32. As was the case with blue collar workers, results do not differ appreciably when respondents from managerial/professional families who are not members of the labour force are added or when the analysis excludes those who voted other than NDP or Social Credit.

33. Nearly 50 per cent of blue collar New Democrats agree that "most unemployed people could find a job if they really wanted to," compared to 40 per cent of the managerial/ professional workers who vote for the party. On the question of environmental protection versus job creation (not used in creating the individual/collective responsibility scale), 26 per cent of blue collar NDP voters chose the statement "People who constantly argue for a clean environment just don't understand that this means less investment and fewer jobs" over the statement "If having cleaner air means less money for me, then that's the way it has to be" when forced to choose between the two. Only 10 per cent of managerial/professional NDP voters chose the first statement.

NOTES TO CHAPTER SEVEN

1. I wish to thank Donald Blake, Alan Cairns, Richard Johnston, Jean Laponce, and John Wood for helpful comments, and Steve Tomblin for data processing. I owe an extra debt to Karen Layng for invaluable assistance with coding, scale construction, and data analysis.

2. "Western" also implies that these feelings are *unique* to the West. Of course, some political grievances, such as the status of the Crowsnest freight rates, may be confined to parts of the West; but many of the patterns of feelings reported below would be found in the Maritimes and elsewhere.

3. Other conceptions of alienation do not inevi-

tably lead to this conclusion. Anomy, normlessness, and psychological pathologies often form key elements of some scholars' conceptions of alienation, and such conceptions may reveal patterns of estrangement without a collateral sense of attachment to other objects or units of analysis.

4. David J. Elkins, "The Sense of Place," chap. 1 of D.J. Elkins and Richard Simeon, *Small Worlds: Provinces and Parties in Canadian Political Life* (Toronto: Methuen, 1980), especially 21-24.

5. "The necessary—it may not be sufficient—social condition making such freedom possible is the presence of a variety of loyalties in the social order. . . . Where the individual holds membership in many groups, each erects a barrier against the imperialisms of the others. Although one still devotes himself to the particular cause, he does so in accordance with his own will, and his devotion is qualified by the existence of other, often competing, objects of loyalty. He attains freedom and self-development in the service of numerous objects of loyalty." John H. Schaar, *Loyalty in America* (Berkeley: University of California Press, 1957), 26, 28.

6. Roger Gibbins, *Prairie Politics and Society: Regionalism in Decline* (Toronto: Butterworth, 1980); Gibbins, "Western Alienation and the Alberta Political Culture" and Robert R. Gilsdorf, "Western Alienation, Political Alienation, and the Federal System: Subjective Perceptions," both in Carlo Caldarola (ed.), *Society and Politics in Alberta* (Toronto: Methuen, 1979).

7. See Gibbins, "Western Alienation and the Alberta Political Culture," 147, for the proportions of Albertans who express similar feelings.

8. Discussions of the "overload" thesis reach a similar conclusion from a different perspective. See, for example, Richard Simeon, "The 'Overload Thesis' and Canadian Government" and John Meisel, "Citizen Demands and Government Response," both in *Canadian Public Policy*, 2 (Autumn 1976), 541-52 and 564-76; Samuel H. Beer, "Political Overload and Federalism," *Polity*, 10 (Fall 1977), 5-17; and references cited by these authors.

9. Respondents were asked to think of all the things they liked about a particular object (such as Canada) and then éxpress the degree of liking on a scale from zero to ten, where zero indicates no feelings at all and ten

indicates extreme liking. Then they were asked to think of all the things they dislike, and to rate the degree of disliking on a scale of zero to ten, where zero again indicates absence of feeling and ten indicates extreme disliking. The ratings are quite independent; people do not necessarily dislike the things that they fail to like; similarly, they may like a lot and dislike a lot the same object.

10. It may be that some respondents are better informed, more articulate, or more involved in political controversies and therefore offer more critical or negative assessments of all sorts of political objects. In doing so, they appear more alienated; yet they are also, by reason of their interest and involvement, more allegiant. We will see some evidence for this in the next section.

11. See the references in note 6.

12. One must be cautious in interpreting these feelings of liking and disliking. For some respondents, liking Canada more than B.C. may mean that they are "Canadians first and British Columbians second"; and conversely, liking B.C. more than Canada may reflect a feeling of being a British Columbian first and a Canadian second (or third, or whatever). An area of uncertainty, however, remains: what exactly does it mean to be X first and Y second? Under what conditions would such a person unequivocally choose to be only an X and sever the ties with Y? Until that question is answered, one cannot say for certain whether these feelings of provincial, regional, or local attachment pose an *alternative* to Canadian loyalty or patriotism or if they are instead a vehicle for expressing the *nature* of one's Canadian identity or loyalty. For further speculations along these lines, see Elkins and Simeon, *Small Worlds*, Introduction, chap. 1, and Conclusion.

13. Karl Deutsch has argued ("Social Mobilization and Political Development," *American Political Science Review*, 55 [Sept. 1961] , 493-514) that people are mobilized as a result of breaking prior bonds and acquiring new loyalties and identifications. Since David Elkins has criticized this view in detail elsewhere ("Social Mobilization and Political Development in South India," *Pacific Affairs*, 47 [Fall 1974] , 326-43), here we emphasize only that old attachments are rarely broken; instead, change occurs by adding new loyalties to old, creating complex, multiple, and competing identities. For example, in order

to marry and have one's own family, one need not sever all ties to one's parents or friends.

14. Many respondents mentioned more than one government or group as responsible. Some wanted federal and provincial sharing of responsibility, for example, and they were counted under each of these headings. Hence, these results are not contaminated by the omission of respondents who wanted sharing, balanced, or joint jurisdiction.

15. For details, see David J. Elkins, Donald E. Blake, and Richard Johnston, "Who Trusts Whom to Do What?" paper delivered to the CPSA meetings, Montreal, June 1980.

16. These three measures were combined into an Index of Provincial Orientation which is reported in Table 36. For details of how this Index was built and some related findings, see Donald E. Blake, "The Consistency of Inconsistency: Party Identification in Federal and Provincial Politics," *Canadian Journal of Political Science*, 15 (Dec. 1982), 691-710.

17. Gibbins, "Western Alienation," 153, finds the same pattern in Alberta.

18. Gibbins, "Western Alienation," 153, found that the Independents were less alienated than the supporters of the Conservatives or the NDP, but more alienated than Liberals in Alberta.

19. Thanks are due to Richard Gwyn, *The Northern Magus* (Toronto: McClelland & Stewart, 1980) for developing in some detail the metaphor of the magus, as derived from John Fowles's novel of that name.

20. Although it summarizes data only on disliking of leaders and parties, Table 38 reveals the same patterns as we would see if liking scores were also presented. The same patterns arise also when one measures partisanship by vote in 1979 or 1980 rather than by party identification.

21. Gibbins, "Western Alienation," 154, Table 6.

22. Larry Pratt and Garth Stevenson (eds.), *Western Separatism: The Myths, Realities and Dangers* (Edmonton: Hurtig, 1981), especially the chapters by Denise Harrington, John Richards (on "left" and "right" populism), Richard Cleroux (on the conservative and "right-wing" early separatists in Quebec and Alberta), and Garth Stevenson.

23. Indeed, the arguments of John Richards in *Western Separatism* and of Richards and Larry Pratt in *Prairie Capitalism* (Toronto:

McClelland & Stewart, 1979) suggest both similarities and important differences between proponents of province-building, "alienation," and "separatism" in Alberta and Saskatchewan. Gibbins, *Prairie Politics and Society*, has argued forcefully and cogently for the diversity of the three prairie economies and polities in areas encompassing but going beyond "western alienation." Really thorough and comparable data on Saskatchewan and Manitoba especially are, unfortunately, still lacking; but initial conclusions about "the West" as a region seem doomed to fall before the ever-increasing accumulation of evidence about diversity within this region of Canada.

24. The significance of a chi-square test was .89, and of an F-test was .15; Cramer's V had a value of .04 for the relationship between the two scales, which is not significant.

25. The significance level of a chi-square test was .0001, and of an F-test was also .0001; Cramer's V had a value of .14, which is significant beyond the .05 level.

26. Kenneth H. Norrie, "Some Comments on Prairie Economic Alienation," in Carlo Caldarola (ed.), *Society and Politics in Alberta* (Toronto: Methuen, 1979), 131-42, challenges the factual basis of many of these perceptions without denying that they are believed and have strong effects in motivating political behaviour. See also Norrie and Michael Percy, "The Economics of a Separate West," in Pratt and Stevenson (eds.), *Western Separatism*; and Howard Darling, *The Politics of Freight Rates* (Toronto: McClelland and Stewart, 1980).

27. A separate measure of opposition to federal cultural and language policies and the treatment of Quebec is developed in the next chapter in the form of an "ethnocentrism" scale. The correlation between ethnocentrism and alienation is .32 (Pearson r). Alienation and ethnocentrism prove to be powerful predictors of federal voting choices in B.C.

28. Paul Sniderman, *A Question of Loyalty* (Berkeley: University of California Press, 1981) argues cogently that political disaffection in the United States in recent years is at least in part a hopeful sign of realism after two decades of racial tensions, the Vietnam War, Watergate, and political scandals. The same may be said of alienation in Canada as a response to political events.

29. There are a few statistically significant

variations, but none qualify this conclusion. For example, self-employed respondents were more alienated than those who work for someone else, and the divorced express slightly more alienation than married respondents. More comprehensive measures of personal isolation (including living alone, being a recent arrival in B.C. or in one's neighbourhood, and not belonging to voluntary organizations) reveal no relationship to alienation. There are, in short, few purely personal roots of B.C. alienation. Those which can be located seem less "personal" in an idiosyncratic sense than simply specifications of *how* political variables come to operate on individuals in all parts of B.C. to engender feelings of alienation or not, as the case may be. This still leaves a few people who display alienation because of personal isolation, inadequate social support, lack of education or information, or age cohort specific experiences. But for many British Columbians, aspects of the political realm itself serve as the major and predominant source of alienation, just as for many (especially Liberal party supporters), they serve as bulwarks against the alienation one might expect from their social and personal circumstances.

30. Schaar, *Loyalty in America*, 28.

NOTES TO CHAPTER EIGHT

1. R. M. Burns, "British Columbia and the Canadian Confederation," in R. M. Burns (ed.), *One Country or Two?* (Montreal: McGill-Queen's, 1971), 268.
2. "Apparently" is used here because as is clear from Chapter 3, British Columbians continue to exhibit high levels of political efficacy.
3. The federal and provincial electorates are not the same. In 1979, provincial electoral law enfranchised British subjects who are not Canadian citizens. Federal law enfranchised 18-year-olds whereas the provincial minimum age is 19. Comparisons are complicated further by the fact that in 1979 the provincial voters list contained an unknown number of names of voters who were deceased or who had left the province and, because provincial authorities did not conduct the kind of ruthless enumeration of eligible voters characteristic of their federal counterparts, a number of otherwise eligible provincial voters did not appear on the provincial list. While the actual number is impossible to estimate, the fact that 46,515 ballots were cast (and not counted) by residents of the province claiming to be eligible reflects the problem and complicates estimates of turn-out. If this number is added to the official count of registered voters voting, the provincial turn-out rate (69 per cent) would increase to nearly 72 per cent, much closer to the federal turn-out rate of 74.7 per cent. Looked at another way, official figures produced by each level of government suggest that the provincial eligible electorate is approximately 4 per cent larger than the federal one despite the federal enfranchisement of 18-year-olds. Applying the federal turn-out rate to the actual number of provincial voters would imply a provincial electorate about 4 per cent smaller than the federal one, a difference in the same direction as that revealed by our survey. Provincial vote tabulators may also be tougher than federal ones since the provincial rate of spoiled ballots is more than 8 times the federal rate.

The analysis in this chapter has been restricted to those eligible to vote in both provincial and federal elections in 1979 because of the importance of comparisons across levels.

4. Richard Johnston, "Federal and Provincial Voting: Contemporary Patterns and Historical Evolution," in David J. Elkins and Richard Simeon, *Small Worlds: Provinces and Parties in Canadian Political Life* (Toronto: Methuen, 1980), Table 9, p. 157.
5. Ibid., Table 8 and pp. 156-57.
6. See Chapter 2, and Donald Alper, "The Effects of Coalition Government on Party Structure: The Case of the Conservative Party in B.C.," *B.C. Studies*, No. 33 (Spring 1977), 40-49.
7. See Edwin R. Black, "Federal Strains within a Canadian Party," in Hugh R. Thorburn (ed.), *Party Politics in Canada*, 4th edition (Scarborough, Ont.: Prentice-Hall, 1979), chap. 8.
8. While Peter Ward argues that the extent of support for socialism in B.C. before the Great Depression has been exaggerated, he provides figures which demonstrate that its strength was greater in provincial politics in terms of votes and seats. See his "Class and Race in the Social Structure of British Columbia 1870-1939," *B.C. Studies*, No. 45 (Spring 1980), 22-24. Also see Chapter 2 in this

book.

9. Johnston, "Federal and Provincial Voting," Table 9, p. 157.

10. For an account of recent patterns of federal-provincial conflict involving British Columbia see J. Terence Morley, Norman J. Ruff, Neil A. Swainson, R. Jeremy Wilson, and Walter D. Young, *The Reins of Power: Governing British Columbia* (Vancouver: Douglas and McIntyre, 1983), chap. 9.

11. See for example Martin Robin, *Canadian Provincial Politics*, 2nd edition (Scarborough, Ont.: Prentice-Hall, 1978), 40: "By doing battle with the federal authorities, the Socreds and their predecessors prey on and activate regional sentiments and deflect internally divisive sentiments on to an external enemy."

12. Not all episodes of federal/provincial conflict cast the provincial government as popular champion. Historians attribute the decline and fall of Liberal Premier Duff Pattullo in 1941 to his vocal opposition to the recommendations of the Rowell-Sirois Commission favoured by the federal Liberal government. See Margaret Ormsby, *British Columbia: A History* (Toronto: Macmillan, 1958), 470-77.

The point regarding punishment by proxy may not be easily generalizable beyond the post-war British Columbia setting. One could argue that the success of the Parti Québécois in the provincial elections of the 1970s was based on its ability to tar the provincial Liberal party with the brush of Trudeau's opposition to Quebec's autonomy demands. We are indebted to Philip Resnick for this observation. However, we also note that the recent revival of the provincial Liberal party in Quebec occurred despite the total exclusion of the government of Quebec from the constitutional accords of 1982.

13. The correlations between liking scores for federal and provincial parties are high but not remarkably so except in the case of the NDP. The relevant correlations (Pearson r) are .60 for the Liberals, .53 for the Conservatives, and .83 for the NDP.

14. See Chapter 7.

15. For an assessment of the role of élite manipulation in anti-Ottawa sentiments see Alan Cairns, "The Governments and Societies of Canadian Federalism," *Canadian Journal of Political Science*, 10 (Dec. 1977), 695-726.

16. The difference between the NDP mean of 2.43 and the Social Credit mean of 2.53 on the alienation scale is not statistically significant. However, Social Credit provincial voters are significantly more ethnocentric (mean score 3.66) than NDP voters (mean score 3.19).

17. Alienation and individual/collective responsibility have been discussed earlier. Individual/collective responsibility figures prominently in the analysis of chapters 5 and 6. Ethnocentrism is our label for an attitudinal scale focusing on support or opposition to bilingualism, biculturalism, and special status for Quebec. For a list of scale items see Appendix. In the overlapping federal and provincial electorates considered here alienation and ethnocentrism are correlated (Pearson r) at -.05 and -.12, respectively, with individual/collective responsibility and .32 with each other.

18. For a discussion of these circumstances and an analysis of the impact of strategic voting in the 1979 federal election in B.C. See Richard Johnston, David J. Elkins, and Donald E. Blake, "Strategic Voting: Individual Reasoning and Collective Consequences," a paper presented to the annual meeting of the American Political Science Association, Washington, D.C., 1980.

19. For an analysis of the factors associated with the adoption of a provincial party identification (or an independent stance) different from federal party identification see Donald E. Blake, "The Consistency of Inconsistency: Party Identification in Federal and Provincial Politics," *Canadian Journal of Political Science*, 15 (Dec. 1982), 691-710.

20. The ideological differences within the major provincial parties associated with federal voting are, in contrast, minor. Provincial NDP voters average 3.9, 4.1, and 4.2 on the individual/collective responsibility scale depending on whether they voted Conservative, Liberal, or NDP, respectively, at the federal level. Federal Liberal/provincial Social Credit and federal Conservative/provincial Social Credit voters score 3.4 and 3.2, respectively.

21. The differences in means between Social Credit and NDP voters within the Liberal and Conservative columns of Table 41 are statistically significant only in the case of individualism/collectivism.

22. Harold D. Clarke et al., *Political Choice in Canada* (Toronto: McGraw-Hill Ryerson, 1979), chap. 4, contains a summary of socio-economic divisions affecting federal party

support in Canada as a whole.

23. The ethnocentrism mean for the self-identified working class (3.8) is significantly higher than that for the self-identified middle class (2.9). However, when the electorate is classified by family income (which includes more respondents) only the lowest income group (less than $10,000 per annum) stands out as distinctively ethnocentric.

24. All the individual and contextual variables considered in chapters 5 and 6 were considered as control variables in addition to variables developed to take into account special circumstances in the federal setting: willingness to engage in strategic voting, and links across levels via party identification.

25. See for example, Roger Gibbins, *Prairie Politics and Society: Regionalism in Decline* (Toronto: Butterworth, 1980), chap. 5. Gibbins' analysis of alienation does not deal extensively with the ethnocentrism dimension.

26. Those who answered yes to either of the following questions were considered potential strategic voters: "Sometimes the party a person likes best has little chance of winning. Suppose in your riding the party you liked best had very little chance of winning, but the party you like *least* had a good chance of winning. In this situation, would you consider voting for a party other than your favourite in order to keep the party you did not like from winning?" "Let's think now about the province as a whole and not just your riding. Suppose there was an election in which the party you most preferred had little chance of forming the government. In this situation, would you consider voting for a party other than your favourite in order to keep the party you did not like from forming the government?"

27. Respondents were also asked to provide information about strategic behaviour. Although many perceived no strategic opportunity in 1979, the numbers who did and who claimed to have voted in accordance with answers given in the hypothetical situations was enough (extrapolating from the sample figures to the population) to affect the outcome in some circumstances. See Johnston et al., "Strategic Voting," 7-9.

28. The term "sincere" voting in this context means simply voting for one's most preferred party. No normative judgement on the motives of voters is intended.

29. The decision to analyse the movement from

provincial to federal politics was dictated, in part, by the chronology of events, but mainly by the desire to provide a thorough understanding of the provincial political world before moving beyond it. Some analysis of movement in the other direction, from federal to provincial, has been undertaken using the 1979 B.C. Election Study. See Blake, "The Consistency of Inconsistency." In his intensive study of Vancouver Burrard in the 1960s, Jean Laponce explored federal to provincial migrations as well; however, he reports (p. 176) that his analysis was hampered by the absence of data on the kinds of attitudinal characteristics measured in this study. See his *People vs. Politics* (Toronto: University of Toronto Press, 1969).

30. It is possible that the provincial Liberals are doomed until feelings of alienation in the province ease. However, the situation they now find themselves in was not of the federal party's making. For a counter-argument in the case of Alberta see Terrence J. Levesque and Kenneth H. Norrie, "Overwhelming Majorities in the Legislature of Alberta," *Canadian Journal of Political Science*, 12 (Sept. 1979), 451-70.

31. A small number of provincial voters did not vote in the federal election even though eligible to do so. Equally small numbers were involved in transfers between provincial and federal parties other than those addressed here (see Table 34).

32. The candidate explanatory variables were the same as those used in Table 46 with the addition of affect measures involving the Liberals and Conservatives in the case of defectors from the NDP (Table 48). Affect was measured by asking respondents to indicate how much they "liked" a given party on a scale of 0 to 10. This measure is also used in Chapter 7.

The strategy of averaging alienation and ethocentrism scores was chosen rather than using their product because their mean had a higher correlation with each of the components—.78 with alienation and .83 with ethnocentrism.

33. The alienation/ethnocentrism term in Table 47 was constructed by multiplying the average of the two scores by the dummy variable distinguishing blue collar workers from all others. Alienation/ethnocentrism has an impact on NDP defection only in this form.

34. Strictly speaking the two coefficients involving religion in Table 48 represent differ-

ences in the probability of Liberal or Conservative voting between those in the grouping represented by a given variable (Roman Catholic and no religion) and all those with any other religious attachment.

35. According to the 1979 National Election Study, 58 per cent of Roman Catholics voted Liberal in Canada as a whole. Only 29 per cent voted Conservative.

36. Also see Chapter 7 for an analysis of the links between alienation and dislike for Trudeau among Liberal identifiers.

37. *The Regional Decline of a National Party: Liberals on the Prairies* (Toronto: University of Toronto Press, 1980), 150.

NOTES TO CHAPTER NINE

1. Michael D. Ornstein, H. Michael Stevenson, and A. Paul Williams, whose work is used in chapters 5 and 6, detect important ideological divisions in the federal electorate, but party alignments which do not reflect them very strongly. See their "Region, Class and Political Culture in Canada," *Canadian Journal of Political Science*, 13 (1980), 227-71. M. Janine Brodie and Jane Jenson, *Crisis, Challenge and Change: Party and Class in Canada* (Toronto: Methuen, 1980) argue that the weakness of class ties to party in federal politics can be traced to manipulation of the national agenda by the leaders of the traditional parties and the failure of the NDP and its predecessors to grasp historical opportunities presented by economic crises. We argue in this chapter that institutional impediments to class voting must also be taken into account, since ideology is a crucial determinant of political choice in the B.C. provincial party system but less important in the federal one.

2. Martin Robin, "British Columbia: The Company Province," in Martin Robin (ed.), *Canadian Provincial Politics*, 2nd edition (Scarborough, Ont.: Prentice-Hall, 1978), 28.

3. William P. Irvine, "The Canadian Voter," in Howard Penniman (ed.), *Canada at the Polls, 1979 and 1980* (Washington: American Enterprise Institute, 1981), 83.

4. Ibid., 71-72.

5. The regional groupings conceal the fact that the Liberals actually did better among their own identifiers than did the other parties in Manitoba, New Brunswick, and Prince Edward Island. The presence of large French-Canadian minorities may account for these exceptions in Manitoba and New Brunswick. The argument developed in this chapter would certainly lead to that conclusion.

6. There is also some evidence that fluctuation in Liberal popularity is relatively immune to economic perturbations, and that the party might even be favoured during times of increasing unemployment. See Lynda Erickson and Kristen R. Monroe, "The Economy and Public Support for the Canadian Government and Political Parties, 1954-1978," CPSA, Halifax, 1981.

7. The question about language protection was contained within a battery of questions dealing with appropriate areas of federal government activity. The actual statement read: "The federal government should ensure that people have the right to have their children taught in the language of their choice, even in areas in which they are a minority."

   The fact that linguistic educational rights are apparently not viewed in the same light as civil rights is indicated by the low correlation (Pearson r = .06) between this item and a neighbouring question dealing with the protection of civil rights.

8. Analysis using a "support for bilingualism" scale developed from the 1979 wave of the Social Change in Canada Study confirms these results. Because that study was not explicitly related to an election context, and given the amount of statistical material already presented, it seemed preferable not to include the results in the text.

9. Calculated from figures supplied in Dan Butler and Bruce D. Macnaughton, "Public Sector Growth in Canada: Issues, Explanations and Implications," in Michael S. Whittington and Glen Williams (eds.), *Canadian Politics in the 1980s* (Toronto: Methuen, 1981), Table 5.4, 94.

10. See Brodie and Jenson, *Crisis, Challenge and Change*, 274.

11. Ibid., 297.

12. Marsha A. Chandler and William M. Chandler, *Public Policy and Provincial Politics* (Toronto: McGraw-Hill, Ryerson 1979), 41.

13. For other arguments supporting a structural hypothesis see Donald Smiley, *Canada in Crisis: Federalism in the Eighties*, 3rd edition (Toronto: McGraw-Hill, 1980), 140-41; and Garth Stevenson, "Federalism and the Political Economy of the Canadian

State," in Leo Panitch (ed.), *The Canadian State: Political Economy and Political Power* (Toronto: University of Toronto Press, 1977), 90-91.

14. Chandler and Chandler, *Public Policy*, 178-79.

15. See Richard Simeon with Robert Miller, "Regional Variations in Public Policy," in David J. Elkins and Richard Simeon, *Small Worlds: Provinces and Parties in Canadian Political Life* (Toronto: Methuen, 1980).

16. Respondents were asked to place themselves on a 7-point scale from left to right. The means by 1979 federal vote and region are:

Region	Federal Vote		
	Liberal	**Conservative**	**NDP**
Atlantic	4.50	4.37	3.92
Quebec	4.69	4.37	3.68
Ontario	4.34	4.72	3.78
Prairies	4.27	4.62	3.81
B.C.	4.82	4.74	3.72
Total	4.51	4.64	3.77

17. An application of the separate systems argument to Quebec and the Atlantic region will be introduced later. For an imaginative treatment of Alberta politics which argues that (essentially) left-right questions fluctuate in salience in provincial elections depending on the state of relations with the federal government see Terrence J. Levesque and Kenneth H. Norrie, "Overwhelming Majorities in the Legislature of Alberta," *Canadian Journal of Political Science*, 12 (Sept. 1979), 451-70.

18. The class voting index is based on the technique made popular by Robert Alford, *Party and Society: The Anglo-American Democracies* (Chicago: Rand McNally, 1963), and is simply the percentage of working class support for the party of the left minus the percentage of non-working class support. The index is insensitive to the size of the left party. As used here, and contrary to Alford, who combines the NDP and Liberals as parties of the left, the index is based on support for the NDP.

19. However, the account of Ontario politics provided by John Wilson and David Hoffman points out differences in provincial and federal cleavage patterns, and suggests that the provincial Liberals, with a relatively class-less image, are being increasingly squeezed between the more class-distinctive Conservatives and New Democrats. See their

"Ontario: A Three-Party System in Transition," in Martin Robin (ed.), *Canadian Provincial Politics* (Scarborough, Ont.: Prentice-Hall, 1972).

While they do not directly address socioeconomic divisions in federal elections, John Courtney and David Smith, "Saskatchewan: Parties in a Politically Competitive Province," in Martin Robin, *Canadian Provincial Politics*, describe provincial divisions as a "liberal-conservative dichotomy" (p. 304), and note that "to attempt to explain the provincial party system and provincial voting patterns by referring to federal party politics would be futile" (p. 303).

Thomas Peterson, "Manitoba: Ethnic and Class Politics," in the same volume, ignores federal voting behaviour in the province, but outlines a "sequence from ethnic to class politics" (p. 108) in provincial elections.

Recent controversy over proposals to entrench French language rights in the Constitution suggest that ethnic conflict is not dead in Manitoba. It remains to be seen whether this conflict will surface in the next provincial election, thus undermining our conclusions.

20. Federal Liberal identifiers in Quebec differ significantly on the left-right dimension presented to respondents in the 1979 National Election Study depending on whether they identify with the provincial Liberals or the Parti Québécois (means of 4.75 and 4.30, respectively). The parallel with B.C. is not perfect, however, since the most left-wing Péquistes who have a federal party tie identify with the NDP (mean 3.1).

21. See Kenneth McRoberts and Dale Posgate, *Quebec: Social Change and Political Crisis*, revised edition (Toronto: McClelland & Stewart, 1981), chap. 9, which argues that the party failed to live up to all its promises, but nevertheless supports its claim to being more sympathetic to the working class than the Liberals.

22. The most systematic attempt is to be found in John Wilson, "The Canadian Political Cultures: Towards a Redefinition of the Nature of the Canadian Political System," *Canadian Journal of Political Science*, 7 (Sept. 1974), 438-83.

Jane Jenson, "Party Systems," in David J. Bellamy, Jon H. Pammett, and Donald C. Rowat, *The Provincial Political Systems: Comparative Essays* (Toronto: Methuen, 1976) also utilizes a developmental framework.

23. Richard Apostle and Paul Pross, "Marginality and Political Culture: A New Approach to Political Culture in Atlantic Canada," a paper presented to the 1981 meeting of the Canadian Political Science Association, Halifax, 26. Apostle and Pross direct their attention towards Atlantic political culture and, in particular, to correlates of trust, efficacy and involvement rather than to voting patterns provincially or federally.

24. Ibid., 27.

25. The rewriting of provincial labour legislation in Nova Scotia at the behest of the Michelin Tire Company to make it difficult for the company's work-force to be organized by the union movement probably has parallels elsewhere, but seems particularly apropos.

26. I am indebted to Alan Cairns for this suggestion. See his "Socialism, Federalism and the Party Systems, 1933-1980," a paper presented to the meeting of the Learned Societies, Vancouver, 1983, for his analysis of the separation of party systems in B.C.

27. Parts of this section are taken from Donald E. Blake, "The Consistency of Inconsistency: Party Identification in Federal and Provincial Politics," *Canadian Journal of Political Science*, 15 (Dec. 1982). That article also contains an analysis of the correlates of split- and single-level partisanship.

Here, as in previous chapters, party identification was measured using responses to the standard question: "Thinking of federal politics, do you usually think of yourself as a Liberal, Progressive Conservative, NDP, Social Credit or what?" "Leaners," those who consider themselves "close" to one party but did not choose a party in response to the first question were not treated as identifiers in this analysis.

28. Harold D. Clarke, Jane Jenson, Lawrence LeDuc, and Jon Pammett, *Political Choice in Canada*, abridged edition (Toronto: McGraw-Hill, Ryerson, 1980), 107.

29. Additional data from the 1974 National Election Study also undermine the utility of this variable as a measure of stable voting habits. Among those who voted in both 1972 and 1974 and claim to have always voted the same way, 15.6 per cent actually report different votes when questioned about the two elections.

30. *Political Choice in Canada*, 99, emphasis added.

31. Ibid.

32. Analysis of the 1974-79 panel component in the 1979 National Election Study reveals a fairly large number of voters (22 per cent of those who reported 1974 votes in 1974 and, again, in 1979) who gave different reports of vote in 1974. The discrepancy also varies by party.

Table 55 is based on vote recall (i.e., 1974 vote as recalled in 1979) for all respondents in the National Study and in the B.C. Election Study. The results do not differ appreciably when only the 1974-79 panel is analysed using report of 1974 vote as given in the 1974 interview.

33. Estimates of the number of split partisans and their switching behaviour in the Atlantic region must be considered tentative given small Ns. In Quebec, most dual loyalists are provincial Péquistes and one would want to examine their behaviour in 1974 and 1979 very carefully before concluding that dual loyalists in that province are inherently unstable.

34. Blake, "The Consistency of Inconsistency," Table 6.

35. See his *The Regional Decline of a National Party: Liberals on the Prairies* (Toronto: University of Toronto Press, 1980).

36. The parallel between British Columbia and Quebec is not perfect, because competing constitutional positions are a major factor in Quebec provincial politics. Nevertheless, conflicts over social and economic policy issues are more prominent in provincial campaigns than federal ones in both provinces.

NOTES TO CHAPTER TEN

1. See his "Socialism, Federalism and the Party Systems, 1933-1980," a paper presented to the meeting of the Learned Societies, Vancouver, 1983.

Index